COLLECTED PIECES
BY
Ned Rorem

*O*ther
*E*ntertainment

SIMON & SCHUSTER

SIMON & SCHUSTER
Rockefeller Center
1230 Avenue of the Americas
New York, NY 10020

10   9   8   7   6   5   4   3   2   1

Library of Congress Cataloging-in-Publication Data

Rorem, Ned, 1923–
    Other entertainment : collected pieces / by Ned Rorem.
      p.   cm.
    Includes index.
    1. Music — 20th century — History and criticism.   2. Musicians —
Biography.   3. Literature, Modern — 20th century — History and criticism.   I. Title.
ML60.R7843   1996
700'.9'04 — dc20   96-18213   CIP   MN
ISBN 0-684-82249-0

Continued on page 336

I am a composer who also writes, not a writer who also composes. Some years ago the Internal Revenue Service, at a loss for how to classify me, simply checked me into the category "Other Entertainment."

—NR

Contents

Introduction

> The sun is the only creator without ambivalence about the daily recurrence of his daily project. The human author, addressing his reader, has considerably more mixed feelings about literary recurrence, since his new book depends on so many old themes . . .
>
> HELEN VENDLER, from a review of
> James Merrill's *To the Reader*

> If certain scenes and situations
>   ("work,"
> As the jacket has it, "of a blazingly
> Original voice") make you look
>   up from your page
> —But this is life, is truth, is
>   me!—*too many*
> Smack of self-plagiarism. Terror and tryst,
> Vow and verbena, done before to death,
> In earlier chapters, under different names . . .
> You'd like to think a structure will emerge . . .
>
> JAMES MERRILL, from *To the Reader*

I was forty before becoming a professional writer. True, there had been sad little stories in the high school monthly, occasionally poems for which I had no gift. (Is that why I've set some 200 other poets to music?)

Then in 1959, age thirty-five, I accepted a three-term professorship at Buffalo University. I had never before held a salaried position, but had subsisted, albeit frugally, from both the just rewards of my labor—musical composition—and from handouts here and there. Now, the academic contract specified that (a) I give eight public lectures, and (b) that these lectures be accompanied by concerts of my own contrivance.

I was apprehensive. What did I know about music, except how to write it? I had never put my musical ideas into any kind of verbal order, and had certainly never taught anyone anything and been paid for it. But I *had* kept a journal since adolescence which gave me a sense of words, and did have friends, like the experienced critic William Flanagan, and my own father, who showed me how to mold the "sense of words" around subjects on which I purported to have a singular slant. The eight lectures flowed without a hitch, and I turned them into essays.

Five years later my first book, *The Paris Diary*, was published, which is what made me a professional—that is, a commissioned and printed author. The book was taken for publication by George Braziller because of whatever cachet I may have had as a composer, though I've since learned that the reading public seldom overlaps with the much smaller listening public. My literary career quickly took off on its own, as a sideline, so to speak—or so to write. The mild success of *The Paris Diary* allowed Braziller to publish the eight essays under the title of *Music from Inside Out*. These essays in turn led to invitations from periodicals as diverse as *Christopher Street* (in which I had a music column for several years), the *New Republic* (likewise), *Commentary*, the *New York Review*, *Vogue*, *Saturday Review*, the *Village Voice*, the book review sections of all our major cities' newspapers, and virtually every American magazine, of which there once were plenty. Unlike musicians, authors don't get instant applause, but they do get recognition. My parallel lives were just that, parallel, never connecting.

I wrote not just about music, but about fashion or language or death, or whatever Leo Lerman or John Cage or Joyce Carol Oates asked of me. Sometimes, and I take pride in this, I would conclude a whole article without once having used the personal pronoun "I." (The "I" was for diaries.) My fifteen minutes of self-confidence reached their peak, or rather their nadir, with a piece in *Harper's* called "Critics Criticized," a model of unearned huffiness.

After perhaps 150 essays, things eased off in the eighties. The essays were collected over the years in various volumes. This makes fourteen books, including the present one, that I've published since 1966. But I am less in demand today, times change, trends pall, the young have their own ideas. So it is nice that Simon & Schuster is willing to chance that most unmarketable of commodities: a collection of nonfiction vignettes.

In rereading them last week I was impressed at how I repeat myself—special obsessions, more often *bons mots*—sometimes quite literally. Perhaps the editor will weed these out. Then again, perhaps not. We are what we repeat. The same words, like the same musical phrase, acquire a new patina, even a new meaning, in new contexts. Then, too, sometimes readers don't notice. Elsewhere in these pages I quote from Cocteau's journal: "You can say to anyone anywhere something you've already written. It sounds new. People often advise you to write it down: for even those who read you remember nothing."

All the pieces included in the present assemblage were formerly in periodicals, but none has appeared in any of my collections. (Not quite true. Those on Auden, Coward, and Bizet were in collections now out of print. For reasons of balance they forced themselves back in here.)

While organizing the first section, which covers twenty-one years, I was struck by these facts:

Of the fourteen Book Reports, only four deal with musicians, of which three are female jazz vocalists, not hitherto my specialty. The remaining reports deal with authors; of those, only three are about authors' fiction—Ishiguro, Duras, and Salter. The other reports are biographical. Of the fifteen personalities discussed, I have personally known all but four, to a lesser or greater extent, although solicitors of book reviews theoretically steer clear of potential bias. In any event, the biographical subjects were all dead when the books came out.

I never met Marguerite Duras. But when the *Washington Post* editors in 1987 invited me to comment on her two novels, which had just appeared in English, they were doubtless swayed by my

French connection. Hitherto I knew only two of Duras's works: a play, *Le Square*, which I liked without admiring, and the movie *Hiroshima mon amour*, which I disliked but admired. Naturally I felt curious to read her nontheatrical prose, only to learn that whatever she wrote *was* theater.

Lillian Hellman was among the playwrights whose biographies I was asked to review. The plots of her plays were tight, at least in *The Little Foxes* and *The Children's Hour*, and she was able to see beyond her navel. But her nonstaged prose, in stories and memoirs, was inferior, at least in comparison to someone like Tennessee Williams. As a person, however, she was easier to talk to. My words on her biography were in the *Washington Post* in 1988.

I knew Auden least, yet felt closest to him from having set so much of his verse to music, prior and subsequent to the present article, written in 1981 for the *Chicago Tribune*.

Josephine Baker I knew not at all, although—and this is the case with every performer, as distinct from the composer they perform—her purpose was to make us feel we experienced her very flesh. (She sings for me alone!) This 1989 report on her biography in the *Boston Globe* was thus like a letter to an old friend.

Libby Holman, on the other hand, *was* an old friend. And although "to know well" has more to do with intensity than with longevity, I treasure her on both counts. She too—the fact of her— was meant to be known: that is the *raison d'être* of interpreters. When her biographer came to grill me, he was like a lovesick child dreaming of the dead Laura. His resulting book was pretty good, better than the exploitative others that emerged in her wake. My review was in the *Boston Globe* in 1985.

Sitting here in Nantucket last month, twiddling my thumbs, humming "I loved long and long / And grew to be out of fashion / Like an old song," and feeling wistful that it had been thirteen years since the *New York Times Book Review* had asked me for anything, and longer since I was a darling of *Vogue*, I reasoned that Culture no longer existed, and that Learning, hand in hand with Nuanced Creativity, was hiding underground, where it would lie for the next few centuries. Then the phone rang. It was *Vogue*. Would I review the new Ishiguro novel? Long pause. They named a fee. I said yes, read the book, wrote the piece, sent it off. *Vogue* promptly turned it down; it was "too personal." Which both contradicts and corroborates that notion about Culture: *Vogue* just wants puff pieces, or so I reasoned, licking my wounds, insisting nonetheless on the full fee. (It is the only unfavorable review in this collection, nor is it pleasant to pen unpleasant reviews.) For the record it appeared in the *Yale Review*.

Now the phone rings again. The *Times Book Review* wants a review of the Billie Holiday item. Again I say yes. And yes, I knew her too, though she scarcely knew me.

James Salter is an acquaintance, and fellow protégé of the lamented North Point Press. We met, I think, through Robert Phelps. Before this, back in 1965, I wrote my first blurb ever, to adorn the cover of *A Sport and a Pastime*. ("To be read with the heart, the head, and with one hand"—something like that. I've since perfected the craft of blurbing.) Phelps himself was a precious friend, for reasons attested to in these pages, and so was Paul Goodman. James Lord in faraway France remains nearby in my feelings. It is a joy to write enthusiastically about all four of these men.

The two Cocteau pieces are not, properly speaking, book reviews. They were composed in 1986 as prefaces, and hence were themselves subject to review. Well, I've always preferred good reviews to bad (though no reviews are worst of all). Good reviews I will read once, bad ones twice, for if they stick in the craw they also instruct. Thus when the translation of Cocteau's journal, *Past Tense*, came out, I was interested in Michael Feingold's comment in the *Village Voice:* "Ned Rorem's flossy and misguided introduction (the American edition's only real mistake) unwisely tries to link Cocteau's work to the great French tradition of diary-keeping, summing up Gide and Mauriac, arrogantly throwing in excerpts from Rorem's own diary as an uncalled-for *bonne bouche*." When *Jean Cocteau and His World* came out seven months later, Fiengold wrote: "the introduction, inevitably by Ned Rorem, is superfluous and narcissistic, like all of Rorem's writings."

Except to correct errors of fact, it is unseemly for an author to defend his works against critics; the work itself must do that. Certainly my prose, in style and content, does seem to make many a reader climb the wall, especially when it deals with my own effete self, or with someone like Cocteau (is anyone "like" Cocteau?), whose own content and style either drive readers up the same wall, or inspire within them a protective, even proprietary stance. But what could I learn from Feingold's words? Sometime later at a party we were introduced. We chatted amiably for twenty minutes, during which neither of us alluded to his words. At the time I felt proud of this, indeed like a European, as opposed to itchy Americans who won't differentiate between professional and personal slights, and thus refuse to speak to their best friends who give them lousy write-ups. In retrospect, shouldn't I have asked Feingold to define his terms? Cordially.

The paragraphs on Noel Coward's diary were commissioned by the *Chicago Tribune* in 1982, those on Joe Orton's diary were for the *Advocate* in 1987, and those on Benjamin Britten's appeared in *Lambda Book Review* in 1991. How contrasting are these three Britishers: the urbane wit, the plebeian satirist, the reclusive genius. Yet how alike in their undeniable charm, without which the greatest art is less great.

Like all composers, I have been interviewed frequently over the decades, sometimes on the phone by ill-informed sports critics in Midwest journals, prior to a recital to be proffered in their town; more often in person by canny specialists for articles on, say, my flute or organ music, choral or chamber music, songs or operatic music. The best of such interviews are generally for well-researched doctorates to be included among monographs on Contemporary Trends.

But I have never interviewed anyone else. Except once. In May of 1985 Tom Steele, editor of New York's gay biweekly, *The Native*, incensed by drama critic John Simon's recent much-publicized homophobic wisecracks, asked me to tape a conversation with Simon. It was thought that since I knew Simon, I might be more clearheaded than the general gay community, which was up in arms. Not for a moment had I ever found John homophobic in private, but he did enjoy controversy and would say anything, including irrelevant wordplay, just for the pun of it. As I recall, John and I did the taping on a Friday (the previous evening we had attended together Larry Kramer's new play *The Normal Heart*, during which John was moved to tears), and the transcription and editing occurred over the weekend. On Monday our interview hit the stands as a cover story, and immediately sold out across the land.

In the text as I reread it now, I seem more the gay activist than I actually was. Three years later I again played the devil's advocate, but in reverse, when Larry Mass (physician and noted AIDS researcher, immortalized in *The Normal Heart)*, feeling that I was not politically "out" enough in my musical statements, talked with me for his thesis, *Homosexuality and Music*. Our words later showed up, along with other interviews on the subject—most of them quite solemn—in a volume titled *Queering the Pitch*.

Cole Gagne, who in 1982 published *Soundpieces: Interviews with American Composers*, produced a responsible and caring sequel eleven years later. This sequel contains eighteen discussions *à deux*, including mine.

Because I've always preferred the cathedral to the gargoyles, the dance to the dancer, I've never been an opera buff, at least not a bel canto buff. Though the composers may have planned it themselves, the *bis* in midstream insults them. As a composer myself, I find interpreters but a means to an end; today, alas, they are more glorious than those they interpret. (An opera superstar can earn in one evening what a composer is paid to write a whole opera.)

Nonetheless, as a sometime opera composer, I try to keep up, and used to write annually for *Opera News* until the editor, Robert Jacobson, died in the mid-eighties. Since then I have written several times for his successors: *"Bluebeard* and *Erwartung"* appeared in 1988, apropos of the Metropolitan Opera presentation of this double bill, and "Eight Looks at American Opera" in 1991, which won ASCAP's Deems Taylor Award the same year.

The other piece in this section is also from that magazine. "Considering Carmen" dates from 1978 and, except for an article on Mussorgsky, represents my sole piece ever about 19th-century music.

The epitaphs speak for themselves. It remains only to list their birth dates.

"Bernstein" was in the *New York Times* the Sunday after the musician's death in October 1990. "Copland" was in *Opera News* in December 1990. "Thomson" was spoken at the American Academy of Arts & Letters in November 1989. "Phelps" was given at a memorial for the writer in November 1989. "Plaut" was delivered at a memorial for the photographer at Yale in August 1988. "Ames" was in the *Yaddo Newsletter* in July 1994. And "Pastor" was read aloud at the Curtis Institute in 1994.

Similarly, the items in Part V speak for themselves. "Lenny on My Music" was written for the Bernstein Newsletter, *Prelude, Fugue and Riffs*, January 2, 1992, apropos of Bernstein's recording of my Violin Concerto, with soloist Gidon Kremer. "Childhood Reading" was a reply to the *Washington Post*'s solicitation to many artists, in May 1985. "Sarah Orne Jewett" was a reply to the *Times Literary Supplement* question, two months later, about "neglected" authors. "Myrna Loy—A Fragment" was destined for the *Boston Globe* in 1987; this is the only commission I have ever failed to deliver. *In medias res* I realized that, precisely because I knew the subject personally, I could not be sensibly objective. (Incidentally, I first met Myrna Loy, in passing, at a party at Libby Holman's, probably in 1958 or '59. I assumed they were good friends, both having been mother hens for Montgomery Clift, etcetera. It turned out they had never met before, and never saw each other again.) "Carnegie Hall" was a centennial homage printed in, I think, *Keynote,* in 1990. "Jane Bowles" appeared in a program for a revival of the author's play at Lincoln Center in the summer of 1993. "Ravel and Debussy" was delivered onstage at Symphony Space three minutes prior to my accompanying baritone Kurt Ollmann in two cycles by the two composers. "Who Is Sylvia?" was spoken at a festive dinner party, in December 1990, to honor lawyer Sylvia Goldstein for her fifty years of service with the music publishers, Boosey & Hawkes. "Being Sixty-five" was printed in *Keynote* in 1988.

Finally, "Out of Nantucket" appeared in *Geo* in October 1984. The island has changed in the intervening years.

So have I changed, not so much in the opinions evinced in this book as in their mode of expression, and in the examples summoned to buttress them. (Is Antonioni's name any longer on the tip of our tongues? or Marcuse's? Carson McCullers's? Janet Flanner's? Walter Cronkite's?)

All my prose, I guess, is a diary, in that both the manner and the matter are dated. By that token all art is a diary, since everything dates from the moment it occurs. That sentence is one of this book's Repeats. Have I said all I have to say? (Another Repeat: Even the most fertile artist says all he has to say quite early, then spends the rest of his years saying it again and again, in his unique language but with different accents, novel formats.)

Is music too a diary? Yes, by the above definition. It relates a composer's feelings, although the composer would be unable to tell you, in words, what those feelings are. "Music can be translated only by music," said Oliver Wendell Holmes, of all people. "Just so far as it suggests worded thought it falls short of its highest office."

Is this book then about music? Well, two-thirds is about general musical matters and about humans who deal in music, but not about structure, esthetics, or method, while the other third is about literary folk, with footnotes on places (Yaddo, Carnegie Hall, Nantucket).

What, then, shall this book be called? Now that 150,000 words are behind me, the peskiest choice lies in the title. For if a book can't be judged by its cover, the title can be judged by the book.

How about *The Present Prolonged?*, I ask people, quoting my own words: "Music exists—not on canvas nor yet on the staff —only in motion. The good listener will hear it as the present prolonged." No! answer the people. It's too arch, and anyway the book's not supposed to be confined to music.

Then how about *Notes Without Music?* That's pretty good, except that Milhaud used it for his autobiography—albeit in French.

Perfect Pitch? Slonimsky used it for *his* autobiography. (*Relative Pitch* might work.)

What about *That Was Then*, since the present is so quickly the past? No?

Courageous Coward might fit, since most of the artists mentioned are just that; indeed, the title defines The Artist . . . Hmmm . . .

There's always *The Unquestioned Answer*, offsetting Leonard Bernstein's Harvard Lecture series called *The Unanswered Question* after Ives's short orchestra piece.

Or *Form to the Trumpets*, culled from Cocteau's phrases: "The spirit within me is not a tender one. It cares nothing for sickness, nothing for fatigue. It profits by my talents. It seeks to give form to the trumpets."

Or *Learning to Forget*. Or *Remembering to Forget* . . . No, and no.

Which leaves *Words Without Song*, echoing as it so liltingly does, Mendelssohn's suite of piano solos named *Songs Without*

Words, which the French translate as *Romances sans paroles. (Romance Without Parole*—hey, that's not bad!) So far I like that best, partly because such modest reputation as I may have was originally based on my songs.

In any event the subtitle will be *Collected Pieces,* despite the noun's ambiguity. Or maybe *Essays,* because in the truest sense these pieces are essays, personal attempts, passes, tries. Accuracy is next to Godliness, and I have tried.

I am beholden to Chuck Adams for his patient editorial skill.

As for the dedication, that goes as always to James Holmes, with love now and forever.

—NR, 1996

PART ONE

Book Reports

Two Novels of Marguerite Duras

L'Amante Anglaise
The Vice-Consul

1987

Barbara Bray, translator of *L'Amante Anglaise*, has solved the problem of the title by leaving it intact. If English lends itself to palindromes, French lends itself to the *olorime*, a sometimes elaborate word game consisting of homonyms strung together in parallel lines, and appealing to the subtlest psyches. Thus Victor Hugo could compose an alexandrine couplet of which the verses, identical aurally, are optically related only by sense:

> *Gall, amant de la reine, alla, tour magnanime*
> *Galamment, de l'arène à la Tour Magne, à Nîme.*

And thus *L'Amante Anglaise*, which to the eye means one thing (the English girlfriend), to the ear can mean quite another *(la menthe en glaise*—the mint in clay).

There is no mention of an English girlfriend in Marguerite Duras's melancholy étude, and the sole allusion to mint falls in passing, when we learn that a character named Claire, who is probably insane, writes to garden magazines for advice about growing the herb indoors. But Duras, with her multiple Rashomonian perspectives focusing on a single occurrence which determine both the shape and substance of this work, has confected a sort of massive *olorime* no less tantalizing than Hugo's.

Claire, a middle-aged middle-class wife in the middle of rural France, has murdered her female deaf-mute cousin, hacked up the corpse, and disposed of the pieces by dropping them from a viaduct onto various passing trains. After a week, only the head remains unrecovered, and Claire rather dispassionately admits to the deed. A journalist comes to town hoping to unravel the tale behind the crime by taping interviews with Claire, with her husband (who may or may not have had an affair with the victim, who was his wife's housekeeper for many years), and with their best friend, a café owner. Each of them, in conversation with the writer, gives an account of the same happening. What is uncovered becomes a depiction of the mores of one small town as well as of the universally dangerous emotion of love. But a solid motive for the killing, and the whereabouts of the head, are never disclosed, perhaps because there are no final answers.

The book is composed entirely in spoken dialogue without editorializing or description, a mode uneasily close to Robert Pinget's *L'Inquisitoire* on the same subject a decade earlier. But the mood remains identifiable as Duras's own. Her art here lies not in how she reveals the heart of a murderous woman, but in how she reveals the heart of the murderous woman in you and me, all in her usual glacial and madly logical tone.

Glacial and logical is the tone for her other book too, despite the torrid Indian temperatures evoked and the kaleidoscopic ambiguities. Like *L'Amante Anglaise*, *The Vice-Consul* is built around three characters. The former French vice-counsul at Lahore, a virgin in his middle years and a social misfit, is now in Calcutta biding his time after having been fired from his post because of some shameful comportment (did he or not shoot randomly into a garden filled with dogs and human lepers?). He is shunned by most of the colonials, with the exception of the seductive, no-longer-young wife of the French ambassador, who vaguely leads him on. Their story is counterpointed by that of a deranged and starving beggarwoman, banished years ago by her family when she became pregnant, who now wanders the country, haunting the heroes in the malodorous shadows of lavish diplomatic feasts. In a land of pariahs the vice-consul too is a pariah, like the beggarwoman, or indeed like the colonials themselves who long for home.

The *Vice-Consul*'s fluctuating and unresolved patterns, like those of *L'Amante*, finally come to rest through sheer exhaustion. Both books are painful, *L'Amante* perhaps less so, since the worst is over by the time the interrogation, in its icy compassion, takes place, while in *Consul* the unabated anxiety seems a perpetual becoming. Both contain a semivisible character, an author, who does and yet who doesn't propel the narrative, in search of a definition for madness and a motive for unexplained killings. (Duras seems to be telling us that there is no *crime gratuit*—that there is in fact an assassin fundamental in us all.) And both retain their tight formal integrity by syntactical device, one being totally in dialogue, the other totally in the present tense—devices at once effective and affected.

The overall output of Marguerite Duras, now seventy-four, is firmly enough jelled for one to affirm that these two examples, each twenty years old, are typical—typical in that they deal, yet again, with violently untrammeled instincts surging beneath a calm and often banal surface, and in that their format is stageworthy: with little nudging both books become scripts. Most of her early novels have been adapted by herself and others, and she often conceived the same work simultaneously in several forms—as a novel, as a play or teleplay, then as a film scenario. With the success of *Hiroshima mon amour* in 1959, she began writing directly for movies, stressing text over camera work even when she herself turned director. But though the visual derives always from the verbal, not the reverse, any of her novels are a cameraman's dream, emphasizing as they do the elasticity and endless repetitions of time moving backward and forward, at different speeds, beneath human episodes that appear as waking dreams.

Still, with all its exterior panache and perception, there is something about the *oeuvre* I can't quite buy. Is it the manner over content, even in so lauded a prose work as her recent *The War* with its unique pathos in describing the aftereffects of a concentration camp on an inmate and his wife? Is it the brittle, the cool, the—dare I say it?—Frenchness of her protagonists? No. It's that her work, with all its imagination, is without much charm, and charm, despite its bad odor in some intellectual cliques, is a key ingredient of the highest art.

Duras is a first-class second-rater. Although she was clearly born with pen in hand (her phrases flow, her tropes convince, her structures sustain), and although her subject is eternal (life, love, and politics seen as horrific, erotic, and unselective), her protagonists are clinical and faceless—they are Everyman, or rather, Everyghost. Nor has she a need for suspense or sentimentality, the old-time virtues still celebrated by, say, Françoise Sagan, whose cast of neurotics is maybe more upper-crust and shallow than Duras's (though the persons in *The Vice-Consul* are pretty insular and let-'em-eat-cake-ish) but they do weep and sing and jump off the page.

Pantheon's policy of issuing in English the complete works of Marguerite Duras, lifting them intact from the Hamish Hamilton editions of 1966 and 1977, is commendable and overdue. Just as Duras introduced a new dimension to literary France—a dimension that flirts but does not, thank God, blend with the sterile solemnity of the *nouveau roman*—so that dimension now may alter the consciousness of literary America. The alteration is abetted by the translations' Britishisms (Eileen Ellenbogen's job on *The Vice-Consul* is no less seamless than Bray's), which, to Yankee ears, emphasize the sense of word game. For Duras's main device is the presenting of situations, including the situations of war and peace, as puzzles with unlimited solutions none of which will ever be *the* solution. Portraying situations per se, rather than the people caught up in them, is the method by which she holds our excruciated attention.

Lillian in Love
1988

John Cheever used to call her a BMOC. Viewed from afar, her feet square on the ground, grand but granitic, ubiquitous cigarette punctuating imperious utterances, slow to permit contradiction, angry, heavy, intimidating, an icy battle-ax sheathed in the reassuring glamour bestowed by at least two world-class plays, Lillian Hellman did indeed seem every inch the Big Man On Campus. Yet when I came to know her slightly during her last few years, I found her, if not exactly wreathed in charm, at least accessible, even vulnerable, beneath that toughness. She had labored (as distinct from, say Clare Boothe Luce) for her successes but appeared less marked by them than by her failures. Her sense of herself, as observed in a male ambiance, was as a businesslike flirt, and quite old-fashioned—a perhaps not unusual stance for one dealing in the fancy of the stage, nor unhealthy for one seeking to survive past her prime. If she was less than pretty, frankly plain, remember that the greatest courtesans have never been the finest beauties so much as stimulators of the imagination. But now her stimulation was dependent far more on her social persona than on her formal talent.

No American playwright born in this century has, after the age of forty, been able to match his earlier glory in this specialized métier, and Hellman was no exception. Still, like Tennessee Williams who held a trump card in his gift for fiction writing (rare in dramatists), Hellman was habile in reviving the past, *her* past, in prose, and this she did in three salable memoirs during the mid-1970s. Even those were overshadowed in the end by her notorious legal battle, begun in 1980, over Mary McCarthy's slander on Dick Cavett's show ("Every word [Hellman] writes is a lie, including 'and' and 'the' "). That swipe, along with her famous stand before the House Committee on Un-American Activities in 1952 ("I cannot and will not cut my conscience to fit this year's fashions"), seems liable to take precedence forever in the public ken over any scene penned in Hellman's dozen theater pieces.

Like another alcoholic Southerner, Truman Capote, whose total oeuvre was also small and uneven and who had tried to coin a form of fiction as fact—or fact as fiction—Hellman, at her death in 1984, became quickly better known for her life than for her work, although paradoxically the life could not have been publicized except for the work. (Is not such publicity quintessentially American? Is there one European writer more famous than his writing?) The most ugly type of the publicity fertilized the field for at least two full-scale best-selling biographies.

Isn't all that one might wish to learn about Lillian Hellman already available? Is her unquiet ghost rich or odd enough, and is her certain artistry varied or even good enough, to bear further investigation? Peter Feibleman thinks so, especially about the ghost. Maybe he is right insofar as he avoids analysis or championship of the artistry and, to set matters straight, purports to show the woman's true and human side through a series of painfully personal memories.

"To love intelligent women," said Baudelaire a century ago, "is the privilege of pederasts," and the quip still has its points. One of the points is David Plante's wildly original *Difficult Women*, portraits of three literary viragos (Germaine Greer, Sonia Orwell, Jean Rhys) by one who lived in compassionately dispassionate contact with them. They could not have been composed with the same clinical depth had the author been heterosexually involved with his subjects, nor, one suspects, would a "straight" man have had the patience for such overwhelming egos. Feibleman's *Lilly* resembles Plante's book not only in being an appreciation of an intelligent and difficult female (in this case a likable picture of an unlikable creature), but in keeping the lens in such unalleviated close-up that there is seldom room for another mortal within the frame. Except

Feibleman himself. His "pederastic" credentials, if any, are hard to deduce. Open though he is about Lilly's sexuality (she and Dorothy Parker "took to fighting about which one had slept with the lowest down men"), he is guarded about is own ("I like Los Angeles the way I like brothels"—what brothels, in this day and age?), with a single hint about "a young man," many hints about other women, and the open implication that Lilly's chief rival was his mother. But Lilly was not a collector of gays: when referring to them she generally used the mean term "fag." Surely the great love of her life, Dashiell Hammett, was above reproach. Yet she never cohabited in any sense with anyone, including Hammett, who seems to have been as much a mentor as a lover. Reports—hers mostly—of their intertwining lives read as though the two were acting out a Hemingway script (though maybe all love is playacting), and a similar arch tone is taken in the Feibleman rapport. Theirs was unequivocally a mother-son relationship, in which Peter was the mother, Lillian the son.

They met when she was thirty-five, at Peter's upper-class father's New Orleans house, where Lillian, also an upper-class Louisianian, was a dinner guest. She asked his age. "I'm only ten." Lillian said, "I don't know what you mean by 'only.' Ten isn't so young," and walked off. ("She was sexy, and there was a shower of sparks under the flint of her voice.") Peter was hooked, grew up fast, and by late adolescence, now a Manhattan Rastignac on his way to becoming a semisuccessful novelist, playwright, filmscripter, and actor (mainly in Spanish movies), he aggressively cultivated the older writer's friendship, retaining it with many a row and a rift for the rest of her life. The friendship melted into what in this context must be termed a love affair during May of 1963. That date is the only one cited in this purposely ambiguous document; it also signals the moment upon which the document apparently began. The form is a grab bag of devices: narrative filler, journals (of both parties, plus those of a secretary), press clippings, dozens of letters, statements from friends and foes, and especially tape transcriptions. The tape deck was set in motion capriciously, initially, one suspects, to capture secrets of creation or anyway a tone of voice, but the sessions often dissolve into querulous boozey exchanges about fidelity or recipes, sometimes uttered in bed, and always garnished with the parenthetical aside *"sound of Lillian coughing,"* which might have made an apt title. She was forever obstreperous, he forever patient.

Peter's patience extended through the accident-prone Lilly's multiple hospitalizations for broken bones, minor strokes, blind drunkenness, literal blindness from glaucoma, emphysematous conditions from chain-smoking, and the routine hiring of round-the-clock nurses who quit like clockwork because of their charge's crude irascibility. Her obstreperousness is tempered by the *billets doux* mailed from afar—generally signed "Miss H."—so tender, abject, clever yet childlike as to seem schizophrenic in tandem with Lilly's on-the-spot witchery. These leading roles are so throbbingly vital they leave no room for others. Hellman was terribly social ("names" are thrown out like chicken feed), but the vitality of her famous intimates—Mike Nichols, Leonard Bernstein, John Hersey, Claudette Colber, Jules Feiffer—is taken on faith until they speak their graveside eulogies in the appendix.

One or two vignettes do catch fire. It is interesting to learn, for example, that while Lilly was always financially well-off, she had visions of the poorhouse. (Her tenacity in the costly McCarthy lawsuit, which she agreed to drop only on the condition of a public apology, was surely due to a lawyer friend who donated his services.) Thus it came as a thrill when Elizabeth Taylor announced her stage debut in *The Little Foxes,* a venture that would net Lillian almost a million and a half in royalties. The description—snapshot, really—of Taylor herself shows a movie star unaccustomed to the exigencies of the stage, or even to the basics of bourgeois life. " 'Elizabeth's never been to a supermarket,' Lillian said one day in shock. 'She's never in her life stood in line to use a public anything. It's like deprivation. Elizabeth's a true innocent. Every time she gets laid she gets married. Nobody ever told her you can do it and stay single . . . I like her. It makes it hard. I don't like liking people, it's a waste of time.' " At the gala in Washington, when told that the Reagans would come backstage, Lillian agreed to behave. But discovering that her old friend and cast member Maureen Stapleton —who had once been married to a man named Max—was on a first-name basis with Nancy, the livid Lillian threw a tantrum, *"You know her, you know her."* To appease the playwright, Stapleton said simply, "I don't know her. Max fucked her," and Lillian "laughed so hard her crutches went flying." Libelous or not, that is a sample of the book's wit.

Feibleman writes sentences with professional flow and personal warmth, and manages to bind disparate scraps with inevitable-sounding panache. But his paragraphs are too long and there are too many of them. Forty examples of giggly bickering are proffered where twenty (or seven, or one) would do. Not until page 162 is there a hint that these two adults have any perception of theater or literature or, indeed, any art (like many authors they seem to be deaf to music); even when finally there is talk of métier, it often comes as whitewashing: " . . . [I]t never occurred to me . . . that people would take all the details of [*Julia*] for the literal truth." "She'd discovered a new form for herself in writing, a form that was neither fiction nor memory but a combination of both, which is probably what most recollection is." There is nothing about what it means to be a Jew, for either of them, in the gentile South or in the literary world, except in relation to food (in 1984 they would write a cookbook together, Lillian's last gasp), which Lillian divides neatly into "Goy drek" and "Kike drek." Her notorious lies, feuds, rudenesses are treated here as childlike, even lovable, flaws. As for the Mary McCarthy debacle, it is dismissed as "regrettable, but not without precedence: taking potshots at a celebrity, and so gathering some of the limelight, is hardly a new game." Threading the chapters is the motif of the Anonymous Caller: for years, but conveniently never in Peter's presence, Lillian receives intermittent phone messages from an unknown informant who reveals details of Peter's unstable character. Does the reader truly believe Lilly wouldn't simply hang up? At the end, when she says, "Nobody can come between us now—no more anonymous calls—nothing," and Peter replies, "There were no anonymous calls were there? You made them up," we see that Peter himself made them up as a novelist's prerogative. But this is no novel.

On page 376, after the careful scaffolding of authenticity has reached its claustrophobic peak, Peter divulges: "Before it's said by others, let me say it for myself: some of this book is invention." And the walls come tumbling down. What can we trust of the saga we have nearly finished? Is Peter even honest when he writes, "When Lillian died I forgot about her immediately, [but soon] the attacks on her had doubled in the press—the attacks she had predicted—not only on her work but on her life. After the dust had settled I was still angry [at her for leaving me] but by that time the anger was different"? It rings true. And this even truer: "Her will had made life comfortable for me . . . for two or three months I thought more about money than I thought about Lillian, that's how shallow I am . . . I've never had a clean thought in my life that didn't have another thought like that one beside it . . . I wonder whether I would have been so loyal if she hadn't been going to leave me money."

Yet his loyalty prevails. "It seemed that everybody in the world had written about her lately except me and all of them had been out to get her." Well, Feibleman "gets her" too, and manages convincingly through the vast labor of contriving this book. "Every Southern lady has a right to believe that one Southern gentleman will stand up for her when she's assaulted." He feels her to have been "larger than her own life . . . a great boom of a woman [whose] lasting voice, when all the storms in all the tiny teacups are done . . . will still be heard." Whether or not he convinces us of Lillian Hellman's lasting voice, his own voice convinces us of his own conviction, and that is the admirable purpose of this book.

An Auden

1981

Frank O'Hara once recalled showing his verse to Wystan Auden. Said the master: "You've got to be an Auden to get away with lines like that." An Auden! the younger poet marveled, taking in the prunelike lips dribbling vodka onto a sweater unchanged for weeks, the tobacco-stained thumbs and the urine-stained pants, the seedy carpet slippers (which because of chronic corns Auden wore everywhere, to the drugstore as to the opera), the whole pontifical form slumped like a mummy in a gutted sofa whose dust beclouded a setting no less gorgeous than the Collier brothers'. This portrait of the artist as an old mentor, corroborated by all who met him, is but the rough side of the canvas, for Auden was the most disciplined, the smoothest, and maybe the greatest English-language poet of our time; O'Hara had seen him as he saw others:

> . . . I imagine you before my eyes
> Flushed with the wine I ordered and my wit.

A product of industrial England—he was born in York in 1907—Auden might nonetheless be placed intellectually somewhere between Jean Cocteau, eighteen years his senior from a country he avoided, and Paul Goodman, five years his junior from a country he adopted.

Like Goodman, Auden was a clearheaded formalist in a distressingly unhygienic body, a rude bully who was momentarily kind, profoundly homosexual, but a champion of the family as stabilizing unit. (When Cyril Connolly learned that Auden, who

adored anagrams, had turned T. S. Eliot into "toilets," Connolly
turned Wystan Auden into "a nasty unwed." Yet Auden's wedding
in 1935 to Thomas Mann's daughter was legal and lifelong, though
of strictly political convenience—they never lived together. But his
thirty-year union with Chester Kallman was, at least on Auden's
side, modeled on bourgeois values. After Erika Mann died in 1970,
and Chester was far away, Auden proposed to other women, including Hannah Arendt, to her purported embarrassment.) Both
Auden and Goodman reveled in music but played the piano
thumpingly, confusing love for ability; expert at hearing others,
they couldn't hear themselves. Both were professional and caring
teachers, periodically looked upon as arbiters, wielding no less
influence through sociological belief (Auden liberal-conservative,
Goodman regimented-anarchist) than through verse forms. Yet
both were finally forsaken by the young; while planning to live
until eighty, each died in his sixties of overwork and disen-
chantment at having evolved into the obsolete species of Educated
Poet.

Like Cocteau, Auden was an aphorist who monopolized conversation with quips that brooked no argument. Cocteau too, vastly
"official" in his waning years, had been spurned by the very generations whose style he had shaped, and he died, successful and sad,
in a mist of self-quotation. When Auden had become a monument
he welcomed the interviewers he had shunned for years, but spoke
to them solely in epigrammatic non sequiturs. ("As a poet, my only
duty is to defend the language from corruption. . . . History would
be no different if literature had never existed; nothing I wrote
against Hitler prevented one Jew from being killed. . . . I live by my
watch. I wouldn't know to be hungry if I didn't have my watch.
. . . Italian is the most beautiful language to write in, but terribly
hard for writers because you can't tell when you've written nonsense. In English you know right away. . . . I don't go along with
the generation gap. We're all contemporaries, anyone walking the
earth at this moment. There's a certain difference in memories,
that's all. . . . Art is our chief means of breaking bread with the dead
—you can still enjoy the *Iliad*. . . . I like to fancy that had I taken the
Anglican Holy Orders, I might now be a Bishop.") Like Cocteau,
Auden was a jack-of-all-trades, authoring not only haiku but very
long poems, plays, librettos, screen scenarios, translations from

many a language popular and obscure, and the most original essays of our century on subjects far from his "specialty." Like Cocteau, Auden was also a professional actor and a social star, but while both were wildly candid in the parlor they were circumspect in print: when their respective forays into so-called pornography, *Le Livre blanc* and *The Platonic Blow,* were stolen and published, they were nervous. Because Cocteau's musicality was less proprietary (music was the one art he did not presume to practice), his collaboration with musicians was more expert: he did not, as did Goodman and Auden, concoct "settable lyrics," but left musical decisions to the composers. Nor did he fall into the fatal trap of the others who, during later years, revised early poems, making changes for change's sake, always to the disadvantage of the original. To Cocteau revision was a moral error; the old poet is not the same person as the young poet although they bear the same name.

Auden's thoughts on Goodman aren't recorded. But as early as 1929 he asked himself, "Do I want poetry in a play, or is Cocteau right: 'There is a poetry in the theater, but not of it'?" Neither he nor Goodman ever created for the stage with the inborn panache of Jean Cocteau, probably because, too literarily convinced of what theater *ought* to be, they grew hamstrung before the fact. Auden did translate two plays by Cocteau, of whom he wrote: "The lasting feeling that his work leaves is one of happiness; not, of course, in the sense that it excludes suffering, but because, in it, nothing is rejected, resented, or regretted." That is the only good word he ever had for any Frenchman of any period. He loathed France, the French, and, as he termed it, Frog culture.

The foregoing play of comparisons could seem extravagant but for the lingering influence of Humphrey Carpenter's definitive thesis, of which each infectious page echoes the games of the protagonist, forever sizing up society and art through contrast and metaphor, and emphasizing that the best reviews are made from quotes. The very fact of the new book is itself an exercise in contradiction, Auden having claimed that "the biography of an artist, if his life as a man was sufficiently interesting, is permissible, provided that the biographer and his readers realize that such an account throws no light whatsoever upon the artist's work." He did add that "more often than most people realize his work may throw light upon his life"—this, despite earlier admonishments that his letters be burned. Such admonishments, of course, always mean "Don't burn my letters." So he had his cake—for posterity to eat. Now Carpenter has made an elaborate icing to Charles Osborne's memoir of 1979 (most of the anecdotes are identical, but the tone is less chatty, the narrative more thorough), serving also as complement to Edward Mendelson's historical interpretation of the poet's work up to 1939, *Early Auden.*

The youngest of three sons, Auden grew up in a secure and musical milieu, behaving ever afterward like a precocious favored child. His lapse at fifteen from the Anglican church ("people only love God when no one else will love them") coincided with a growing homosexual awareness, which in turn concurred with his emergence as a poet. The emergence came in a flash, fired by the offhand question of a chum at Gresham's boarding school:

> *Kicking a little stone, he turned to me*
> *And said, 'Tell me, do you write poetry?'*
> *I never had, and said so, but I knew*
> *That very moment what I wished to do.*

Until "that very moment" he was pondering a future as a mining engineer, and until he died he remained less drawn to the Mediterranean décor that was his eventual home than to the northern melancholy of factory neighborhoods which shaded so much of his work. As to stylistic landscape, he underwent the necessary influences—Frost, Hardy, Dickinson, Owen, de la Mare, Riding, Eliot—but achieved his own mature voice quite early. "An incurable classic," he labeled himself, and like a true classic—Ravel, for example—he can't be relocated by "periods": he sprang full-blown from the head of his muse, his coolly intelligent timbre altering little with the decades. Since the French are nothing if not also coolly intelligent (what did he think of Ravel?), Auden's Francophobia seems to have stemmed mainly from revolt against the Francophilic generation immediately preceding him. But he was also anti-Romantic, notwithstanding an abiding attraction to Freud (nothing if not Romantic), and given to psychoanalytic quips, both toward his own guilt about not feeling guilty ("And that Miss Number in the corner / Playing hard to get; / Oh I'm happy I'm not happy, / Make me good, Lord, but not yet"), and toward the psychosexuality of others, e.g., "Ackerley did not belong to either of the two commonest classes of homosexuals, neither to the 'orals' " (among whom Auden placed himself) "who play son-and/ or-Mother, nor to the anals who play Wife-and/or-husband. . . . " Indeed, in the interests of high camp he often replaced "I" with "Mother," either to set matters straight (from the audience to a lecturer on Debussy: "Take it from Mother, *Pelléas* is shit!"), or to jar an oversolemn subjectivity ("Mother wandered lonely as a cloud").

At Oxford, despite doing badly on exams ("There is nothing a would-be poet knows he has to know"), he was already the famous leader of a gang that included Isherwood and Spender. To the latter he wrote: "My dominant faculties are intellect and intuition, my weak ones feeling and sensation. This means I have to approach life via the former; I must have knowledge and a great deal of it before I can feel anything."

"Feelings," began to turn up, along with a knack for suppressing them, in Berlin where the newly graduated Auden plowed the terrain before Isherwood made it notorious. There the poet became dazzled by one John Layard, a sort of precursor to R. D. Laing, and by his own notions of psychosomaticism which seemed to cover anything. "Rheumatism is simply a refusal to bend the joints, and therefore an indication of excessive obstinacy. Abnormal tallness such as Stephen Spender's is an attempt to reach heaven. Cancer and homosexuality are caused by the frustration of the wish to have a child."

Returning from Germany to Larchfield Academy in Scotland, later to Downs School at Colwall, he was, in the guise of schoolmaster, about to spend the most contented five years of his life. As eccentric ham and practical joker, as one who talked to all people on his own terms and not theirs, he was a born instructor. Like Kenneth Koch today, Auden showed schoolchildren that "poetry" was no more and no less than "memorable speech. We shall do poetry a great disservice if we confine it only to the major experiences of life . . . Poetry is no better or no worse than human nature." Teaching also afforded him the leisure for book reviewing and essay writing ("It's awfully important that writers aren't afraid to write badly . . . The moment you're afraid of writing badly . . . then

NED ROREM

you'll never write anything good"), for he hadn't previously developed a prose style. As for poems, his first collection was published in 1930 by T. S. Eliot at Faber & Faber which remained his English outlet until the end.

By 1932 his Communist sympathies allowed him to declare that "unless the Christian denies the value of any Government whatsoever, he must admit . . . the necessity for violence, and judge the means by the end," a viewpoint he would refute. Later he would refer to "the intellectual Communism" of his youth as "old-fashioned social climbing," though he was never embarrassed that his poems of the earlier period preached ideas to which he did not readily subscribe, for in poetry "all facts and beliefs cease to be true or false and become interesting possibilities."

In 1935 he switched careers dramatically, becoming scenarist for Government documentary films in which he collaborated regularly with Benjamin Britten, his first real work with a musician. Yet he was always a bit lofty about movies, and interrupted the work to cowrite three plays with Isherwood, and to travel in Iceland, land of his forefathers, from where the news about Spain brought him back to the "real" world.

Before leaving for Spain, where he felt duty called, he wrote the best known and last of the lyrics whose subject is no longer explicitly homosexual, but on the impermanence of all interpersonal rapports: "Lay your sleeping head, my love / Human on my faithless arm." The Barcelona of 1937, with its open Communism, elated him less than the closed churches depressed him; how could his "side" stop people from doing what they liked, "even if it is something silly like going to church?"

The next year he traveled with Isherwood to China as professional correspondent, and, as with Iceland, made a book from it, *Journey to a War*. The two men returned to London by way of America where they were wined on red carpets, provided with "blond boys," and offered high fees (by British standards) for their writings. Neither of them put it immediately into words, but each one planned in his heart to emigrate, which they accordingly did the following January on the eve of World War II. The poet Richard Eberhart announced prophetically: "Auden's coming to America may prove as significant as Eliot's leaving it."

So much for the first half of the poet's life.

America offered Glory and Great Love. Glory, of course, had strings attached. "One makes more money by lecturing on poetry than by writing it." And there is evidence that had he bent to the Swedish Academy's demand that he retract remarks to the effect that Dag Hammarskjöld took himself for God, he would not have had to say stoically in 1964, and every year thereafter: "Well, there goes the Nobel Prize." It might be argued too that there was a decline in the energy, the *necessity*, of the later poems. Auden did have a trump card denied most poets: his prose, which increasingly and dazzlingly took over.

The Great Love also had drawbacks. Chester Kallman, a quick-minded student ("far cleverer than I"), a poet, very blond, son of an immigrant Latvian Jewish dentist ("It is in you, a Jew, that I, a Gentile, inheriting an O-so-genteel anti-Semitism, have found my happiness'), age eighteen, appeared at a time when Auden, at thirty-two, was fed up with one-night stands. If the older man enjoyed the Socratic role, he in turn learned from Chester who was a marvelous cook (though sloppy to a fault), a connoisseur of camp (everyone was "Miss this" or "Miss that"), and, most importantly, a devotee of bel canto, which Auden adopted completely ("No gentleman can fail to admire Bellini") along with Chester's aversion to Brahms. Chester meanwhile took on Auden's most dubious points, but his loud, drunkish opinions lacked authority because he lacked Auden's supporting gifts. Arrogance without talent is galling, but when certain friends recoiled from Chester—among them the gentle Britten, and even Auden's father—Auden credited their dislike to anti-Semitism and dropped them. Chester was cavalier with Auden as well, calling him "Miss Master," and, more gravely, halting permanently their sexual relationship while flaunting his own promiscuity. Their "marriage" was ultimately founded on the sympathy of mutual work which they accomplished while cohabiting, for better or worse, for three decades. One cannot know to what extent Auden's librettos, assuming he would have written any, might have been different had he worked them out with someone else—with Isherwood, for instance, who is unmusical, and so would not have let his text adapt an untheatrical preciosity due to "musical considerations." Nor can one know to what extent the librettos themselves might not be largely the work of Chester. Auden had answered Stravinsky's invitation to write the book for *The Rake's Progress* with: "I need hardly say that the chance of working with you is the greatest honour of my life." The work itself, while surely honorable, is hardly the greatest effort of either man (though it's Stravinsky's longest by far); but the real collaboration was between Chester and Auden, which Stravinsky used as a *fait accompli.* The fact remains that innumerable operatic adaptations of classics, plus four major operas—one by Stravinsky, two by Henze, one by Nabokov (none of whom had English as a mother tongue)—would never have existed, whatever their worth, were it not for the Kallman-Auden union. When Auden died, Chester survived him by little more than a year, stating that "my criterion is gone."

The remaining chronology is divided by Carpenter among six subjects:

CONVERSION. In 1940, aghast at what he perceived, in the Allies as in the Axis, to be "this denial of every humanistic value," he returned to the church. Long after the war when Auden, declaring himself an "old hand at this sort of thing," agreed to write a text for Stavinsky's elegy to Kennedy's memory, the composer said to Robert Craft: "Wystan is wholly indifferent to J.F.K.; what he cares about is form. And it is the same with his religion. What his intellect and gifts require of Christianity is its form—even, to go further, its uniform." Another musician, Marc Blitzstein, remarked: "Wystan doesn't love God, he's just attracted to him." Such *bon mots* in retrospect seem more glib than the poet. Auden had immersed himself in Kierkegaard ("the individual must either abandon himself to despair or throw himself on the mercy of God") who influenced his epic *New Year Letter* ("versified metaphysical argument is very difficult"). In the face of England's annoyance with his defection in time of war—Harold Nicolson called him "a disgrace to poetry"—Auden felt that "aloneness is man's real condition . . . At least I know what I am trying to do, which most American writers do not, which is to live deliberately without roots." Those "American writers" with whom he lived, literally under one roof on Middagh Street in Brooklyn, were Gypsy Rose Lee and Golo Mann,

Paul Bowles and Jane Bowles, Carson McCullers and George Davis, and also his countrymen Benjamin Britten and Peter Pears. Auden played Mother Superior to the motley household, presiding at meals and ordering punctuality, but kept private his weekly excursions to the Episcopalian Mass.

CRISIS. Another motive for the return to God was his breakdown at discovering that Chester had taken another lover, a person whom he seriously planned to murder. The situation was aggravated when Chester's affair withered into a series of casual adventures which were to endure forever after. "His promiscuity is harder to take," Auden confided, "because it fills one with jealousy and anxiety for his spiritual welfare while a genuine love fills one with jealousy and respect."

> If equal affection cannot be,
> Let the more loving one be me.

. . . And he survived, as he always had and would, through routine: "The surest way to discipline passion is to discipline time."

TEACHER AGAIN. Routine, no matter how innovative his curriculum, is the teacher's sine qua non, and Auden relished his 1941–42 stint at Ann Arbor. He refused courses in so-called Creative Writing and modern poetry—"Poets who teach should keep as far as possible from their own field of work"—launching instead a syllabus ranging from Aeschylus to librettos, and forbidding his class to take notes, since "one person cannot really communicate anything specific to another." As usual, he arose each dawn to pursue work on *A Christmas Oratorio* as a memorial to his mother, the only work in which he used Christianity as a direct subject, for "culture is one of Caesar's things." In 1943–44 he taught at Swarthmore; in 1945 returned to Germany as a bombing research analyst; in 1946 became at last an American citizen, went briefly to Bennington, had an affair with his secretary (female), spent a long season on Fire Island (" . . . where nothing is wicked / But to be sorry or sick"), visited Tanglewood to hear Britten's *Peter Grimes*, which left him lukewarm, and with whose composer he had a permanent falling-out due partly to the failure of their operetta, *Paul Bunyan;* then moved back to Manhattan, living this time at 7 Cornelia Street where, when Spender once tried to let in some daylight, the curtains fell down ("You idiot! In any case there's no daylight in New York"). In 1947 *The Age of Anxiety* won the Pulitzer Prize. Auden was indifferent to the Bernstein-Robbins ballet composed on this long poem, but was overwhelmed when Stravinsky, the same year, approached him for a libretto. Thus began a permanent change of inventive focus, and the first of his long chain of co-billings with Chester.

ISCHIA. The 1950s saw Auden ever less in the United States. The decade began with *The Rake's Progress* Venetian premiere. Despite its success, Stravinsky never worked with Auden again (possibly because Auden announced far and wide that Britten, who had seen the score, liked everything except music). Auden and Chester summered in Ischia now, and commuted to their new and final American apartment on Saint Mark's Place in New York. The Latin sunshine, some say, contributed to Auden's premature and bizarre wrinkling ("my face looks like a wedding-cake left out in the rain"). After a residency at Oxford, he finally removed his summer abode, in 1957, to Kirchstetten. To live within reach of the Austrian opera houses attracted both Chester and Auden, who also relished the prospect of a German-speaking community. Yet Auden—and here is a paradox among great artists with an "eye" for words—had scant talent for either talking or writing foreign tongues. He was deeply moved at finally owning a home of his own ("what I dared not hope for / is, in my fifties, mine"), and although he never regretted quitting the Italian island, he wrote:

> *. . . though one cannot always*
> *Remember exactly why one has been happy*
> *There is no forgetting that one was.*

"A MINOR ATLANTIC GOETHE." While working on translations of Goethe, Auden came to think of the German poet as a "dishonest old hypocrite," and yet "Great Mr. G" grew into an image of what he himself hoped to achieve at this period of his life. His enduring prolificity and fame led Chester, now middle-aged and balding, to vanish for periods into Greece to lead his own life. Auden was lonely, drank, was obsessed about money, returned to Iceland and otherwise traveled widely as lecturer, revised his old works and worked unstintingly on new ones. He and Chester continued to work together on musical projects. But by the 1960s the world saw Auden as an unquestioned Absolute, a sort of Anglo-American Aschenbach as well as a deteriorating specimen on whom liquor, cigarettes, and the airless years had taken their toll.

RETURN TO ENGLAND. He remained listed in the Manhattan phone book. When an anonymous caller announced, "First we will castrate you, then we will kill you," Auden was delighted by his quick reflex: "I'm afraid you have the wrong number." Yet he was increasingly unnerved by American violence. Though far from senile, he seemed incapable of give-and-take conversation; though far from self-pitying, he feared a coronary which might leave him dead and unapprehended on the bathroom floor. He arranged, for his own safety and for reasons of nostalgia, to become writer-in-residence at his alma mater where he moved in 1972. The move was a mistake, the old Oxford days were gone. As irony would have it, the dreaded heart attack occurred not in Oxford but in a Viennese hotel room. By further irony, however, it was not a chambermaid but Chester himself who found the body. The body is buried in his beloved Kirchstetten, and the lane where he lived is now named Audenstrasse. On the memorial marble in Westminster Abbey are engraved these lines from his elegy on Yeats:

> In the prison of his days
> Teach the free man how to praise.

Anyone who uses the phrase "Great Artist" must surely thus qualify Wystan Auden. Not only is his verse as strong, original, and influential as any in English since Eliot, his work has a breadth generally linked to the notion of Great. As a man of the flesh Auden was a Master, insofar as the term obtains to those Romantic creators whose personae were no less viable than God or State: he was for half a century an intimidating and coercive leader, a well-trained organizer of the intellect and, not incidentally, a maker of Masterpieces. Two shortcomings, however, denied him the wreath of what the French call Sacred Monster. First, his sense of frivolity: the public of the Great frowns upon Charm. Second, he was just too young: the period of the Masterpiece, which ran roughly from Beethoven to Proust, could in a pinch be stretched to Mann or Picasso or Stravinsky, but ours is no longer an age of worshiping individuals, when even rock superstars are promoted as being like you and me.

Humphrey Carpenter's survey is a model of scholarship. It is virtually without editorializing, and almost willfully without style, a wise choice—if indeed choice is involved—since to write with style about style is to becloud the issue. If the book lacks the color and compassion of Millicent Dillon's concurrent biography of Jane Bowles (yes, the same Jane Bowles who in the famous house on Middagh Street served briefly as Auden's stenographer), that's because Auden was not a walking wound; he kept his wound at a distance as something to write a letter to (his chronic anal fissure became the object, not the subject, of a lengthy piece—"you are taking up more of my life every day"). If on the face of it Auden seemed invulnerable, it's that like many an artist with an iron will he could hold his vulnerability in abeyance, check it at the studio door.

Carpenter's book, considering its great length, has only the minimum of redundancies, mistakes in French, and juxtapositions of chronology which disorient the reader. If the book errs—and I'm of mixed feelings about this—it is that Auden's ongoing libidinous history threads the pages as prominently as does his poetry. Are documenters of heterosexual poets—of Wallace Stevens, say, or William Carlos Williams, or even the rakish Dylan Thomas—as prone to detailing not only each gloomy romance but every casual pickup? When Carpenter goes beyond this, he has a knack for entering that studio door without calling attention to himself, and of collecting what he finds on the other side. The result is a treatise that appears all that will ever be needed on the remarkable subject.

Josephine Baker

1989

As a kid I not only loved Josephine Baker, I wanted to *be* her when I grew up. Her records permeating our Midwest parlor with that humorous whine, or her movies at the local art cinema displaying that mocha-hued glamour, lured me with the thought of expatriation in a Latin land. If I never quite became her, maybe I never quite grew up. Or was it that, when I settled in France during the late 1940s, the mystique of Josephine Baker had been replaced by the more sophisticated Edith Piaf (naive now, she too, with the passage of time), if not by more sophisticated notions of negritude?

In any case, today, sixty-five years after her spectacular Parisian debut ("She made her entry entirely nude," wrote Janet Flanner, "carried upside down and doing the split on the shoulder of a black giant . . . Whatever happened next was unimportant. She [had instantaneously become] a new model that to the French proved for the first time that black was beautiful"), and ten years after her death, Baker is distant enough to reappraise with an unjaundiced eye.

That her book might justify her cover is surely one hope of Phyllis Rose, author of *Jazz Cleopatra*. Before turning to page one we behold an unclad seductive wide-shouldered female standing on a rock, spangles about the neck, clasped hands from which depend yards of pearls and a lamé sheath hiding the torso's salient features, an unsmiling but joyously self-assured face with Kewpie doll lips and a perfect straight nose, sunken cheeks, and huge eyes that meet you straight on with a naughty twinkle befitting any

Wasp darling of the faraway twenties. Except this darling is black. The picture offers all anyone need know about the star—as a professional effect.

But the title is misleading. There was little of the tragic Egyptian stateswoman in the semicomical public aspect of the American personality. Nor could the music Baker interpreted be properly termed jazz; jazz is a music first created by Afro-Americans, while Baker's repertory stressed Gallic ballads like *"C'est lui"* (a spin-off of *"Mon homme,"* immortalized as "My Man" by Fanny Brice), or her theme song, *"J'ai deux amours,"* whose evocation of Paris would inspire a chorus of sobs from homesick French troops when Baker entertained them in Morocco during World War II. The subtitle, *Josephine Baker in Her Time,* is apt insofar as the narrative refracts a vanished epoch through the current ethos of feminism and black pride. Ms. Rose, who is white, chose her subject "as instinctively as when you fall in love," and her love's object "was someone so different from myself that she borders on being another species."

Biographies of even the subtlest performers are a more viably final genre than biographies of creators, about which there can never be a last word. The present book's content provides as much as we'll ever need to know about what lies beneath that image on the cover: Josephine Baker's private and public life were one. In her last days Baker "told the story of her life so many times and in so many ways that one wonders what she was trying to get straight," writes Ms. Rose, who earlier tells us about herself: "Somewhere between my registering with a certain pleasure the French infatuation with black America and my realizing how much fantasy there was in the infatuation, this book was conceived." This book itself is in large part a fantasy built on speculation, and one imagines Josephine lifting a quizzical but approving eyebrow at this brainy sociological thesis—a fantasy about her fantasy.

Born in 1906 of Indian-Negro blood and raised in the poverty of Saint Louis, Josephine Baker learned to dance by watching kangaroos at the zoo. At thirteen she was a professional street musician touring the Southern black vaudeville route, her "first real school." By fifteen she had been twice married (to wastrels), and was a success in Eubie Blake's *Shuffle Along* wherein she upstaged the other chorus girls by crossing her eyes and moving her rear end "like an instrument." By 1924 she was well-paid and well-known in New York's Plantation Club, which starred Ethel Waters, ten years her senior but whom she resembled like the laughing side of a tragic mask. Next year she sailed to France, ostensibly on a brief tour as a featured attraction in *La Revue Nègre*. But her ferocious nude prancing and gorgeous ebony body, which the vicarious French found "savage," were such a sensation that overnight she became the celebrity, and soon after the European citizen, that she would remain for the rest of her life. She also became the chief resident of the Folies Bergères where her signature costume was nothing but a girdle of diamond-studded bananas.

Her erotic exoticism as contrasted with her wistful singing voice, and projected by her friendly approachability on stage (she was never off), in a country without—not yet—race prejudice, combined to make her the most famous performer on the continent, the darling of society high and low, the model for great painters, the example for great couturiers, and a satisfied woman. Her notorious "free love" included a fling in 1926 with her equally highly charged secretary, the yet unknown Georges Simenon, who declared her "the only woman who matched him sexually." ("They enjoyed a weekend reunion a good forty years after their original affair, both of them as passionate as they had been before, [although] she was not eager to display a body that had been operated on so many times.") During the 1930s she starred in two movies—one with Jean Gabin—as a hot-natured "native," sang the lead in Offenbach's *La Créole,* ran nightclubs, toured the western world in vaudeville (which the French quaintly call *Le music hall*), and was an inspiration for American blacks. During the war she worked indefatigably as a sort of Mata Hari for the French Resistance under De Gaulle, who later decorated her, and toured with the military.

Like all dynamic entertainers she gave the impression that you alone were her audience. Indeed, she adored *you* as she adored all creatures, surrounding herself not only with fans and lovers but with pets, including at one point a leopard. In 1940, when she went to North Africa in her guise of nomadic spy-dancer, she couldn't leave without her three monkeys, two white mice, and a Great Dane. (Ms. Rose: "She knew that if positions were reversed, they wouldn't leave without her.") The following year when she entered a Casablanca clinic to have a stillborn child (sired perhaps by her mentor El Glaoui, the vastly rich and very old Pasha of Marrakech), medical complications ensued. Maurice Chevalier, whom she despised for his *collabo* politics and refused to see, gave out the story that she was dying, and Langston Hughes's first job for *The Defender* was to write her obituary. She reemerged nineteen months and endless operations later and quickly resumed work. But if the stamina remained the beauty had waned; for the next thirty years it was the illusion of Josephine Baker that she projected.

After the war she adopted twelve children of various nationalities, her "Rainbow Tribe," and raised them on a vast estate which was also a fairground open to the public, donations going to good works. Excursions to the United States were both happy and sad. If in 1951 she set a precedent, in her intense efforts at world integration, to change racially restrictive terms in her Florida contract; a few months later at Manhattan's Stork Club a racial slight, real or imagined, by the management earned worldwide publicity. With various fortunes gained and lost she was generous to a fault, supporting her tribe, a flock of servants, and a number of family members, including two more husbands (both of whom acted capably as impresarios), and donating to civil rights causes.

She never stopped working, but her popularity ebbed in ever wider curves: she went broke, was "forgotten," got evicted from her château, yet always cannily rallied the press to photograph her misery, resulting in regular comebacks supported by a seemingly endless group of sponsors. A spectacle called simply *Joséphine*— scenes from her life—was mounted in Monte Carlo, thanks in part to Princess Grace. It reached Paris in April, 1975 (the fiftieth anniversary of her beginnings there), received raves, and was sold out for weeks in advance.

The day after the opening Baker took a nap while waiting for a journalist, and never woke up. She was found in bed surrounded by newspapers, presumably looking for more good reviews. If officially she died of cerebral hemorrhage, some said she died of joy. The nationally televised state funeral at the Madeleine was unprecedented for an entertainer, with twenty thousand mourners crowding the streets outside the church.

Josephine Baker was nothing if not a camp—the somewhat dated gay-lingo noun (and verb) used uneasily by the author, but only when hiding behind the clout of Susan Sontag's twenty-five-year-old definition, "theatricalization of experience"—which in its get-them-before-they-get-you defiance, applies to the exaggeratedly formal self-presentation of any persecuted minority. (What term but "camp" describes her Folies turn as Mary, Queen of Scots, singing Schubert's *Ave Maria* on the way to the scaffold? When the ax falls the stage is transformed into a cathedral, dancers in stained glass costumes become an honor guard, and Baker, "swathed in a cape so as to appear headless, continued to sing *Ave Maria*. She now represented Mary's soul on its way to heaven.") Ms. Rose goes so far as to paraphrase, without credit, the late Parker Tyler in depicting Baker, like Mae West and Marlene Dietrich, as "an impersonator of a female impersonator." But except for her passing mention of the star in 1973 attempting to "target the gay community," or the questionable and irrelevant aside that a certain dancer "charmed Langston Hughes into the one heterosexual romance of his life," Ms. Rose never refers to homosexuality. Rose's Baker does not drink or smoke, and, except for an unbridled libido, seems as normal as you and me.

If in sanctifying the beloved by showing her as a nobody who became a magnanimous somebody (though Baker herself declared, "Even generosity can be a form of egoism"), and by waiting till the final pages before administering even a minor slap ("Both Josephine and Evita [Perón] did things on a large scale with no thought of accounting"), that is a lover's prerogative. Ms. Rose's chief problem, and perhaps chief asset, lies in using Baker as an unquestioned major artist as springboard for a sociohistorical tract. For the tract is no less a study of international class struggle than it is a biography. Pages and pages sweep solemnly by with no mention of Josephine, so ardent is the author's Freudian case for French fascination with things African. But was Picasso, for instance, who demonstrably launched with *Les Demoiselles d'Avignon* a vogue for African art, all *that* aware of Josephine Baker? She was not African but American; and though much of her appeal surely lay in her coloring, a case could be argued that the negritude itself, for the blasé French, was appealing for its very Americanness, like the "childlike" brashness of Gershwin, Hemingway, Disney, and Jerry Lewis who, white as snow, are still the most famous U.S. names in France. Wasn't Baker really less an artist than a phenomenon, and a twenties phenomenon at that, whose innocent American vitality wowed Europeans as, in the thirties, the experienced European languor of Dietrich and Garbo wowed Americans? Paris in my heyday swarmed with every class of Nigerian and Senegalese, but none was canonized. Billie Holiday, a far deeper artist than Baker, came through town without leaving a dent; if Katherine Dunham impressed, it was solely in comparison with the fact of Baker.

Like Marilyn Monroe, Baker's whole life was one of being publicized. She didn't create any viable literature, or have any created for her by the High Artists of the time—as Cocteau and Poulenc created for, say, Edith Piaf. She was a gaudy presence with mediocre material and essentially an optimist, as distinct from Piaf, who was a mousy presence with a major voice and essentially a pessimist. If, like Monroe, she wasn't "very good" as an actress, her "every move and phrase was timed for maximum effect," in the words of Phyllis Rose, repairing an earlier statement that "improvisation mobilized her best energies in life as it did in art."

Her life was far from improvised. Her staying power no doubt resides, in life as in art, in her involuntary blackness and voluntary likeability on stage, and off stage in her tireless fight for civil rights in general, and for the downfall of Walter Winchell in particular (who she felt had betrayed her) and by extension of Senator McCarthy. "That her success was entwined with the perception of race in ways she preferred not to explore is part of the story I have told in this book," writes Rose, "which is as much about the European exoticism that embraced her as about the American-style racism she sought to escape." And, I might add, about her ability to reanimate posthumously the enthusiastic child in us all.

Dreams That Money Can Buy:

The Tragic Life of Libby Holman

1985

The subtitle is deserved. Insofar as she loved not wisely but too well, despite being an absolute monarch who changed forever the way America sings and was then forgotten, Libby Holman was a heroic artist who fell from high.

It's depressing, in this age of talentless superstars, how few of even our middle-aged connoisseurs recall the name of Libby Holman, she whose way with the blues caused the term "torch singer" to be coined, and whose publicly private life caused the terms "black angel of death," "champion of the underdog," "Her Highness," and "giver of intense pleasure" to be uttered by such a diverse assembly as Clifton Webb, Coretta King, Tallulah Bankhead, and Alice Toklas. Yet only yesterday, it seems, my parents were discussing the scandal of her husband's ghastly death in 1932, while I, awed by such glamour, began amassing records from the years of Holman's greatest glory (1927–31): *Moanin' Low, Body and Soul, Love for Sale, There Ain't No Sweet Man That's Worth The Salt of My Tears,* each intoned with a boisterous bass whine, lewd intelligence, and weird knack for elongating consonants and for wringing sense out of even articles and prepositions. She was the first among female pop singers—canaries, as they were called in the Jazz era—to exploit the husky purple depths of her vocal register rather than (like Helen Morgan or Ruth Etting) the squeakily poignant top. And she was the first who, by the squarely-on-pitch purposefulness of her delivery, gave the illusion of being master, not slave, despite the abasing texts of her white composers—Oscar Hammerstein,

Johnny Green, Howard Dietz—in that prefeminist period ("When I got no man to mess me around / I'm a poor lost mare a-pawin' the ground"). Also exploited, though not by Holman herself, was the impression that so many of her lovers, female as well as male, came to unnatural ends, with the implication that she was somehow responsible. The impression has dogged other artists (think of Cocteau), coloring, often overshadowing, their true value. The process, though unfair, is virulently romantic and I was not immune.

The world of so-called classical music, because I was already of it, seemed less mysterious than the world of jazz. Classical interpreters were a mere means to an end, and that end was Mozart or Debussy who were personally unavailable because their flesh—thus their magic—was long underground. Popular performers, like movie stars (or in Europe, like royalty) were an end in themselves, thus meant for worship, usually from afar.

In May of 1938, age fourteen, I ventured with my friend Bruce into Chicago's loop for a matinee tryout of Cole Porter's *You Never Know,* starring Libby Holman in what would be her last Broadway show. Hecklers in the audience (like those years later in a London theater where Gielgud played soon after his publicized arrest on a morals charge) were evicted, while Bruce and I thrilled to the very fact of her, especially after the show when we saw her emerge through the stage door, plump in a red and black bolero, hatless, with dark frowsy hair that framed her full face which was forever so highly tanned that she frequently "passed for black." Did it occur to me that I would one day know Libby Holman?

In the mid-fifties we met through another childhood friend, Gerald Cook, who had become—and would remain until she died—Libby's pianist and chief musical advisor. (When a young editor on the Sarah Lawrence weekly asked if Libby searched for meaning in her songs, she answered, "Yes, I do, and when I find it, Gerald plays it and then I vomit around it.") We became fast friends—were there other kinds? Because of hard dieting, drinking, and repeated ulcer operations, the plump face and figure were now bony, and the dark frowsy hair would soon be tinted with silver and white, but the dynamism remained. Indeed, she was one of the three most dynamic women I ever encountered (the other two, both French, were Nadia Boulanger and Marie-Laure de Noailles). The dynamism stemmed from the contrast between the chaotic violence with which she studied her craft, and the orderly violence with which she presented that craft to the public, a presentation both histrionic and intimate, and more than communicative: contagious. The contagion tinged her social stance too. She entered rooms as in a cyclone, and the cyclone, though it could abate somewhat, shuddered always there as Libby listened (like all good talkers she knew how to listen), and while listening concentrated utterly on you, without glancing over your shoulder at someone more important.

Even at that late date a friendship with Libby could raise eyebrows. Whoever still knew her as an artist knew her too as that branded creature. Virgil Thomson, for example, otherwise a level-headed bohemian, took a dim view of my enthusiasm, and a still dimmer view of the opera Paul Bowles spent a decade in composing for the star. "Whenever a man in her life dies," quipped Virgil, "she gets richer," as though that were reason enough for him to steer clear. As our acquaintance grew I witnessed the cyclone—her bell jar—rage ever more insidiously about her until, in the summer of 1971, it tore her apart.

Anyone worthy of a biography has, by definition, long since expressed that worth as exquisitely as possible; biography is therefore superfluous. "But I ascribe motivations," protests the biographer. Motivation is in the eye of the beholder. Libby Holman had been innocently overwhelming her audience for half a decade before that audience decided her voice contained the potential for murder. A biography, like a piece of music criticism, may sometimes be a work of art in itself, but the art doesn't explain anything except itself. Nevertheless, Jon Bradshaw's study is quite an experience— a terrific book about a terrific woman; a book which paradoxically told me a lot about someone I knew all about.

Born in 1904 of poor but proud Jewish stock in Cincinnati, Libby Holman was by the age of twenty-five the most famous musical light of Broadway, and by extension of café society where her gaudy style and self-lacerating romances were aped and admired and loathed. The fame soured into notoriety when in 1932 her husband of six months, Smith Reynolds, heir to the Reynolds tobacco fortune, died by gunshot during a small party on the young couple's estate in Winston-Salem. Holman was suspected of murder, and news coverage of her became second only to that of the Lindbergh kidnapping, but her case's most crucial details—like Lizzie Borden's—were never clarified. Instead of going to prison she was acquitted, the powerful Reynolds elders, appalled by the whole affair, allegedly having bought off the prosecution. The accused woman received a generous settlement in the form of a trust for her still unborn son; but although she was rich now, and to grow increasingly richer, the scandal shed a sordid glow over the remaining forty years of her life. (Libby once told me that she was so drunk on that terrible night that she didn't know whether she'd killed her husband or not.) Transcripts of the hearings, which took place in the staid South, show them to have been anti–"free love," anti-art, anti-gay, and above all, anti-Semitic, with inferences that Smith may have committed suicide because "he had just learned that Mrs. Reynolds was a Jewess."

Before the event, she had appeared in eight hits, most notably *The Little Show* and *Three's a Crowd;* after the event, she starred in two more, then quit Broadway for good. The rest of her stage life was devoted to concertizing, first in nightclubs with black guitarist Josh White, for whom she renounced Torch in favor of Folk, later with black pianist Gerald Cook, whose suavely rarefied accompaniments were perfect frames for the new, less flamboyant, and vaguely intellectual notion the singer had of herself. The public appearance of these two black men with the white femme fatale provoked, even in the 1940s, problems which at the very least were inconvenient. Holman eventually created a foundation (in the name of her son, Topper, who had perished in a mountaineering accident) to promote civil rights as well as environmental causes and disarmament. (Of the various endowments awarded, Libby was proudest of one granted in 1958 to the then obscure Martin Luther King.)

The "vaguely intellectual" notion of herself was honest and earned. Libby was a voracious reader, of classics, of "good" poetry, and later, of Eastern philosophies which she followed, somewhat pathetically. (Chablis and tofu don't mix.) The notion was even productive—although the opera fashioned for her by Paul Bowles from Lorca's *Yerma,* about an adolescent virgin who longs to become pregnant, fell flat when finally produced at Denver University. Libby, just turned fifty-two, was beyond the role, but the music is of abiding beauty.

Yerma's yearning had long been Libby's own. In the 1940s she adopted two sons, her second marriage, to Ralph Holmes, having failed to produce offspring. Holmes, like his brother, the movie actor Phillips who had also been Libby's lover, was neurasthenic, alcoholic, and successfully suicidal. Phillips in the 1930s was the spitting image of what Montgomery Clift would look like fifteen years later—Clift, who, like Libby herself, was troubled and driven and sexually ambiguous and shy and exhibitionistic and madly gifted and deeply drunk, but less of a survivor, and who would become her lover, and finally perish after "the longest suicide in history," leaving her to declare him the one great passion in her life.

Was she a survivor? Clift's friend, poet Jack Larson, said, "Just as rats sense a sinking ship and rush ashore, Libby always rushed to get aboard." After Clift died Libby deteriorated: most of her stomach was excised because of the ulcer; then came suicide attempts, then unavailing lithium treatments. Her dear friend, the wondrous author Jane Bowles, who like Libby had always been uneasy about being Jewish and was herself a model of instability, said wistfully, "Don't leave me alone in my Jewishness."

Meanwhile, she had married a Jew. At the end of 1960 Libby took her third and last husband, who appeared in all ways different from anyone she'd known. Louis Schanker, older than she by one year, was a roughneck abstract expressionist, a first-rate second-rater whose heyday had been the thirties (although he was unaware of the Libby legend), doggedly heterosexual, gross and plain and pipe-smoking and solid, but not without charm. Theirs was a love-hate union which endured until Libby's death in 1971. Legally the death was by her own hand; within these pages there is more than a hint of foul play.

Schanker, who outlived his wife by ten years, refused to be interviewed for this biography. He is the one character, among the several oafs and philistines, who is portrayed without a redeeming feature. Bradshaw's necromantic passion for his subject, on the other hand, continually gives her the benefit of the doubt. Because he never knew her, he is free to envision Libby, like Laura or Rebecca, through is own fantastic lights. Still, his enthusiasm is based on factual research as well as on the more urgent and still throbbing proof of her artistry: a discography of fifty-two entries. His book is not, perhaps, high literature so much as rapid-fire journalism. The first third is especially compelling as it recounts, via alternating chapters, the simultaneous but separate existences of Elizabeth Lloyd Holzman (rags to riches) and Zachary Smith Reynolds (wealth to wastrelsy), the chapters converging only after their meeting, marriage, and murder trial. That trial, related ex post facto, is as engrossing as *Rashomon*—if not *Reckless*, the misbegotten 1935 "musical" based on the affair, starring Jean Harlow, with a title song by Hammerstein! Bradshaw's prose infelicities (he often has Libby enamored "with" people; writes "vulgarity" when he means "obscenity"; refers to "the El Minzah Hotel") turn to assets in that they reflect subliminally the singer's own earthy tone. He is deferential in detailing her aspirations to "higher" things (e.g. singing lessons which led her to *talk* operatically); like Marilyn Monroe she didn't know that what she did *was* among the higher things.

There are some fine-hewn cameos, notably of Lucius Beebe, Tallulah Bankhead, and of Louisa Carpenter, Libby's rich and likeable sapphic love of forty years. Who knows where Bradshaw learned such details as that Libby never had an orgasm, although "her lovemaking was fantastic, beyond your imagination," but the revelation is not so apt as her own, made at twenty-two: "Singers don't have romances, they inspire them."

"It's just not good enough," she keens throughout these pages, the phrase referring not to insatiability but to standards. The mediocrity of our globe is what felled her. If one definition of a practicing artist is "he who knows how to go too far and still come back," Libby Holman fills the bill. As a woman, though, she went too far and fell over the other side. Still, maybe that's not quite true. Her essence remains.

Billie Holiday

1995

On the day she died in a hospital room, age forty-four and hounded by cops, penniless yet world famous, Frank O'Hara, who glimpsed her face on the *New York Post* while buying a carton of Gauloises, ended a poem thus:

> *and I am sweating a lot by now and thinking of*
> *leaning on the john door of the 5 SPOT*
> *while she whispered a song along the keyboard*
> *to Mal Waldron and everyone and I stopped breathing.*

Fifteen years earlier, in 1944, the surrealist poet Charles Henri Ford noted:

> *The distress we feel in your presence is like hearing*
> *footsteps that will take us away,*
> *or reading a threat in an unknown handwriting . . .*

Elizabeth Hardwick in a memoir:

> Night—working, smiling, in makeup, in long, silky dresses, singing over and over, again and again. The aim of it all is just to be drifting off to sleep when the first rays of the sun's brightness begin to threaten the theatrical eyelids.

Of her sold-out Carnegie Hall concert in 1948, just after her release from prison where she had served a year and a day for drug abuse, novelist Carl Van Vechten wrote in a letter:

... that seesaw motion of the arms, fingers always turned in, that swanlike twitching of the thighs, that tortured posture of the head, those inquiring wondering eyes, a little frightened at first and then as the applause increased they became grateful. The voice the same, in and out between tones, unbearably poignant, that blue voice.

The promoter of the concert, one Ernie Anderson who had not met her before said she asked for some comic books. "I went out to Times Square . . . and bought a huge stack . . . but it made me very sad. Here was this great contemporary artist and the only education she ever got was on Harlem streets."

How did Billie Holiday feel about her literary groupies? Or about why their metaphors for what is already a metaphor, the intoned rendering of verse, should be any more valuable than comic books? Her manager Norman Granz doubted that she ever read her ghostwritten autobiography, *Lady Sings the Blues*, in 1953 —that she was concerned only with the money and the publicity the book might bring in. Still, groupies she had all her life, and all my life I've been one of them.

Like most classically trained American composers of what ASCAP defines, for lack of an apter term, "serious music," I was as a kid no less interested in Louis Armstrong and Cole Porter than in Arthur Schnabel and Igor Stravinsky. Yet oddly, despite what would eventually become my specialty, the setting of preexisting words to music, I was more drawn to ends than to means—to songs than to singers. True (though none of us gave a thought to opera divas or lieder singers), we did adore Mildred Bailey and Ella Fitzgerald; but the adoration stemmed as much from their virtuosity as background to our jitterbugging as from the grace of their mostly unproblematic lyrics. (By "we" I mean the smart spoiled children of cultured white liberals.)

Then, fifty-six summers ago when I was fifteen, the disk of "Strange Fruit" was released (with, on the flip side, Billie's own iambic pentameter "Fine and Mellow," one of the few blues this jazz artist ever sang), and our world changed forever, The graphic couplets about a lynching, grotesque and hopeless, rhythmless and dangerously slow, declaimed in a vulnerable velvet whine, were like nothing ever heard before. Who knows what the basic tune was: I would come to learn, hearing her in more familiar territory (despite her reputation as a spokes-artist for "her people," Billie's repertory was essentially "white" from Tin Pan Alley), she would always distort the melodic line, not by adding but by subtracting. Her way with a tune, rather than the tune itself, permanently affected the way I deal with vocal swerve, whether composing songs on poems of Sappho or John Ashbery, operas on books of Gertrude Stein or Elliott Stein, or church litanies on Latin or French texts.

When she toured to Chicago that summer we trooped down to the Panther Room and sipped Tom Collins as she, in black satin and sporting the signature gardenia over her left ear, motionless but for the gently snapping fingers, keened "Jim" and "Night and Day," and finally, in darkness with just a spotlight on her closed eyes, "Strange Fruit," which everyone was waiting for. This morbid record had launched her nationally, even as the jolly "A-Tisket A-Tasket" had launched the younger Ella Fitzgerald the year before. These women were reverse sides of one Janus mask. Ella, with her nimbler vocal cords, came through as optimistic even in her plaintive songs; Billie, with her more limited tessitura, came through as plaintive even in her optimistic songs. Each interpreter was blessed with target-sure pitch: in Ella's case this was the pitch inscribed by the composer, with Billie it was whatever pitch she chose to hit.

During the coming years in New York I grew to know her well (ah, but did she know me?), frequenting those 52nd Street dives where she held forth. Since her sole frame of reference was the jazz milieu, about which she did not intellectualize, there wasn't much to talk about. Yet how about that midnight when Ralph Kirkpatrick took her back to his flat and played Scarlatti on his harpsichord! Billie's eyes glowed with awed pleasure. Or the afternoon when Lenny Bernstein at the empty Onyx Club tried to teach her his "Big Stuff" by rote as she prowled about with her boxer hound! The recording of "Lover Man" (where she was to be backed up by strings, of all things) was as eagerly awaited as Copland's *Appalachian Spring* that same season. And wasn't the bleak "Good Morning Heartache" the impulse for Paul Eluard's *"Adieu bonheur, bonjour tristesse"* which Françoise Sagan would adopt for her first novel?

As though she were next of kin we followed the glories and horrors of Billie Holiday's career, from her various arrests, her jail term, her good and bad trips abroad, her elaborate concerts, her notorious undependability, legal taboos, and dubious marriages, until she died, sordidly and young, on Friday, July 15, 1959.

Forgive me for so conspicuously intruding into this review. But a certain handful of glamorous victims—Sylvia Plath, Marilyn Monroe, Dylan Thomas, Jane Bowles, James Dean, Billie Holiday—make one feel proprietary. So at first I felt edgy about Stuart Nicholson venturing into my domain. In fact his book is caring, intelligent, well-written, maddeningly thorough, and, for the most part, responsible. Is it a biography? Nicholson's structure is built around Holiday's music from which her life emerges, rather than around her life from which the music emerges.

Here are the bare bones of that life:

Born, Baltimore 1915 ("Mom and Pop were just a couple of kids when they got married. He was eighteen, she was sixteen and I was three"), Eleanora Fagan only acquired her professional name years later. Racial injustice, dirt poor, raped at eleven, moved with mother, Sadie, to New York where both worked in a whorehouse. (Sadie was Mildred Bailey's maid for awhile, but dismissed for drunkenness.) Began early to entertain in Harlem hangouts, influenced in style if not in content by Armstrong and Bessie Smith. Taken up by big bands, black and white (Benny Goodman, Count Basie), toured uncomfortably for years. Lived more or less regularly with Sadie, on whom she doted, until Sadie died in 1945, leaving her bereft and with no further firm attachment. Slept around, misused by lovers, managers, and two husbands, most of whom drained her financially and morally, in return for which she was kept in drugs and drink. Sex life not dwelt upon in these pages, though affairs with three, and only three, white persons are hinted at: Benny Goodman, Tallulah Bankhead, Marlene Dietrich. Social life (except for a trillion passing fans) exclusively with black pop musicians. Wined by the rich, but not dined. Didn't read, attend theater, or listen to classical music. (Indeed, the one classical composer in the book, William Grant Still—misspelled as "Stills"—is mentioned only as a Negro whom Artie Shaw, in his fight for racial equality, featured in his band.) She was combative yet passive, irresponsible, self-destructive, as seductive of her person as in her moaning laments, and very expensive—as when she would not show up for long-planned recording sessions. The adventuresome and compassionate impresario John Hammond, who for a decade did more than anyone to advance her fortunes, finally gave up. When she went downhill she went fast.

"The great paradox of Billie Holiday," writes Nicholson, "was that the very singer who could freeze an audience into their seats with the emotional power of her singing struggled throughout her life with deep emotional problems of her own that she could not begin to understand." In the same breath he adds, "It is not what happens to us so much as how we handle what happens to us that decides our future."

Nicholson, an English jazz journalist, broadcaster, and biographer of Ella Fitzgerald, says that Fitzgerald "had to endure a family background and social conditions not greatly different from Billie's; . . . Ella was almost certainly sexually abused as a child and she too hung around a whorehouse in early adolescence. Each was the product of a broken home, each suffered years of poverty and each stared racism square in the face in the musical milieu of the 1930s, 1940 and 1950s. Yet Ella worked her way to Beverly Hills luxury and was still singing in the 1990s, while Billie Holiday was never able to come to terms with her personal demons. Much of her private life was spent running from them, retreating into the pursuit of pleasure, something that was in conspicuously short supply during her childhood."

He might have gone on: The mystery was not that these two contraltos from near-identical backgrounds ended up so differently, nor that they became singers—much less *good* singers—in the first place. Many vocalists come up the hard way, and are as good or as bad as those who always had it easy. The mystery is that they are each one of a kind and irreplaceable. The author concludes: "Today [Billie Holiday] has been so consumed by her image that it has rendered her a victim at the expense of her music, the one thing that made her unique."

Upon this excruciating canvas Nicholson has sketched, by enumerating with comment, seemingly every public appearance of Billie Holiday's career, from the dives of Baltimore and Harlem (with

61   *NED ROREM*

names and addresses), through the Apollo Theater and the down-town clubs (mainly the two Café Societys), to Carnegie Hall and the spots all over America and Europe after she was denied a cabaret license in New York. Similarly Nicholson lists nearly 150 recording gigs, with time of day, personnel, and names of tunes, from 27 November 1933 ("Your Mother's Son-In-Law," Benny Goodman Orchestra) to 25 May 1959 ("I Can't Get Started," Mal Waldron and others). His remarks are often original, always cogent. A few random quotes:

"The Baptist holy-roller tradition produced extrovert singers like Mahalia Jackson, Sarah Vaughan, Aretha Franklin [while] the tradition of religious music Eleanora came from was conservative, an important consideration in defining what would ultimately be-come her undemonstrative style. The Catholic Church, with its ecclesiastical chants in Latin where vowels are more important than consonants, places great stress on pronunciation . . . Gregorian chants embodied two other factors that helped shape her style; they were performed *sotto voce* and used a minimum of melodic motion."

"She had some kind of wisdom she didn't understand herself."

"She once said that she could never sing the same way twice: 'I can't even copy me.' However, evidence of her live recordings tells a different story."

"Even though her voice was half gone . . . this performance, and the rest that make up [her final] album, remain one of the saddest things that ever happened to a great artist as she sang of her fate at the moment it was overwhelming her."

Elsewhere his claims are hickish: "Often Billie was confronted with songs that did not fall into the standard thirty-two-bar ternary AABA format. But even its more sophisticated variations, such as ABCD or ABAC, for example, posed no problems for her . . . Her grasp of form and structure were such that they also brought great symmetry to her vocal variations, and the best are minor miracles of organizing harmonic and rhythmic ideas." Such claims are irrele-vant, being attributes of composers, not interpreters. Singers don't have a "sense of harmony"; and a "grasp of form" has nothing to do with performing, only with making. (Did Billie even play the piano?) Any virgin listener can catch the rhythmic eccentricity of, say, a Gershwin tune without tears. "She had a remarkable ear and almost certainly possessed relative pitch"—as though any kid who can carry a tune doesn't possess the same.

What he excels in is describing song after song after song, with their interjected cooings and adulatory supportings by this or that instrumental soloist who shifts his colors behind the tragic empress who, even when stating a theme, paradoxically states the theme's variation. For she was a radical in the truest sense, altering the root of any song she touched. Nicholson puts order into Billie's chaos by dissecting every artistic move, with lists on the number of times certain hits were recorded, on the number of live broadcasts between 1948–59, graphs on the relative speeds of various tunes—fast, medium, slow. Two family trees. Can, finally, a book about a performer, as distinct from a creator, come to life? Like Diana Ross's filmic version, everything about it is right, except *it*. The "it," of course, is Billie's way with a song.

There are misspellings ("Piaff" for Piaf), grammatical lapses ("who" for whom), misuse of words ("libretto" for lyric, "retrospective" for retroactive), and misprints ("22 June" for 22 July, as the date of her Requiem Mass at St. Paul's Roman Catholic Church on Columbus Circle). The first two lines of the prologue alone contain three geographical blunders: "The rue Saint-Benoît in Paris begins at the rue Marbeuf and ends a block away in a cul-de-sac. Situated at the end of this little Montmartre street used to be the Mars Club." In reality the rue Saint-Benoît is in Saint-Germain-des-Près, two miles from the rue Marbeuf on the Right Bank (which Nicholson calls the West Bank), and both streets are a full four miles from the nearest border of Montmartre.

This is nitpicking. What is easier than to say what a book is not? Still, there is one vast lacuna. Nowhere in the morass of statistics can one find organized information on the composers without whom Billie Holiday's repertory would not exist. Admittedly, composer and performer are more intertwined in the pop world than in the classical world where one always knows the dancer from the dance. Jazz interpreters are allowed leeways of variation inconceivable on the so-called recital stage where even a soloist's transposition of key, let alone an added hot lick, is considered an apostasy. Still, it would be nice to know who, for instance, composed "Gloomy Sunday," which Billie sang hundreds of times, or "I'll

Look Around," or even the famous "Body and Soul." I do know who wrote "Yesterdays," another of her standbys, but I didn't learn it from this book, where Jerome Kern is named only in connection with an award he once bestowed. Yes, one Lewis Allen is cited as the author of "Strange Fruit," but did he compose both words and music? was he black? was he an educated professional? The lack of any finite compositional identity fosters the public's notion—if they even have a notion—that vocalists make it all up as they go along. And yes again, there is a lit of eighteen songs composed or cocomposed by Lady herself, including the memorable "God Bless The Child," but this is lagniappe, not an essential.

I've just put on a Holiday record, "The Moon Looks Down and Laughs." In a trice I glide back to high school. The room here seethes with her essence, as another room seethed long ago. Immediately these words, and Nicholson's words, seem superfluous. What would Billie herself make of this bookish realm? Is the self-awareness of nightingales enhanced by their reading Audubon?

There comes a point when musicologial wisdom, history, analysis, canny comparisons, and psychological insights pile up, not into an illuminating blaze but into an ever-darkening maze with ever-fewer corners to turn. At that point the music simply speaks for itself.

Notes on Ishiguro
1995

A composer is forever bemused to learn how outsiders view his world. Not just in old movie gems like *Humoresque* (Joan Crawford: "The music I like? Some symphonies, all concertos") or *A Song To Remember* (Chopin, to Madame Sand: "Say, George, here's a new nocturne"), but in treatises by literary giants like Gide or Pound who tell us, albeit in polished prose, what anyone can glean from a textbook. Even Proust and Mann, in their fictional biographies of composers, wrote "around" the issue, rather than perceiving music from inside out. Curiously, just recently, Joyce Carol Oates, Frank Conroy, and James Hamilton-Paterson, in a whodunit called *Nemesis,* a saga called *Body and Soul,* and an imaginary portrait of Elgar called *Gerontius,* each focused on great musicians with rapt awe. (Curiously—because these are sentimental anomalies in an increasingly uncaring world.)

When composers themselves write about music, their own or other people's, it is never with rapt awe. Their tack is either critical, analytical, or anecdotal; their awe goes into their art, about which they are no more verbally clear than are laymen—they just know how to create it. For music is too precise for words, rather than too vague for words; if it could be depicted in words it would not need to exist.

Naturally I am speaking of serious concert fare, not pop genres, which have all but effaced, even in the ken of sophisticated nonspecialists, the fact of current classical music. The fact must be stressed because, in the past decade, classical music commentary has vanished from even our most intellectual periodicals. Except for *New York Magazine,* and to an extent *The New Yorker* and *The Village Voice,* no major American weekly or monthly any longer carries an active classical column—not *The New Republic, The Nation, Harpers, The Atlantic, Playboy, Esquire,* nor indeed *Vogue,* though they do hire pop music reviewers. The living classical (wrong term, yet the only term to be understood in this context) composer is not even shunned, for to shun something, that "something" must exist. The classical composer today is invisible.

These musings were noted while waiting for *Vogue* to deliver the galleys of Kazuo Ishiguro's vast new fiction, *The Unconsoled,* published last spring in England and due here this fall. The magazine felt that since the book was "about a musician" I might be a logical choice of reviewer. I had admired *The Remains of the Day,* was struck that such a diffident and elegant novel, with nary a misplaced word, could also be such a public success (translated into twenty-two languages and a Merchant-Ivory film) in these philistine times, and that the success could guarantee the author an advance of half a million for the upcoming tome. Now, after eight years of silence, how would the subtle Ishiguro, in his fourth book, write "about a musician"?

The galleys were accompanied by a thick sheaf of British reviews, profiles, and other advance hype which I read with an ever-sinking heart. The biographical interviews (born in Nagasaki, raised in England, bilingual but with no knowledge of written Japanese, son of an oceanographer, well-off, married, and living far from the madding crowd) all mention that the young Kazuo adored baseball, movies, the guitar, and aspired to be a rock star but didn't have what it took. "A lot of things writers work through, I did in my songs," says he. "The phase when I just wanted to show off some newly-acquired technique: the big purple phase. By the end I got it down to something simple, with deep melodies and sparse lyrics—I suppose somewhere near the starting point of fiction." He composed more than a hundred songs and "dreamed of becoming a new Dylan or something." But neither he nor any critic mentions the *type* of musician who appears in *The Unconsoled,* though there are hints that the music might prove as loftily shapeless as a Yanni improvisation.

Elsewhere the forty-one-year-old author explains: "My first three books were related in style, theme and technique. I felt I had come as far with them as I wanted to. I was also conscious of getting older and that if I was to write a really good book it would have to be now." Good means long. *The Unconsoled* weighs in at 535 pages, yet the impression is that nothing is said that couldn't be said better at half the length.

"*The Unconsoled* is as calculated as anything I've done." Maybe. Yet what writers say about their work and what the work says about itself aren't always the same. "I don't want to repeat myself," announces many a sophomore genius. But what he wants and what he, in fact, produces don't always jibe. Even the most variegated of the unpredictable pathfinders—Stravinsky, Joyce, Picasso, Schoenberg—have no more than five or six crucial ideas in a lifetime. (Such ideas are named "periods" by historians.) They seize the idea and mold it big, small, square, in watercolor or marble or as a novella, for violin solo or symphony orchestra or opera stage. After wringing it dry they proceed to the next idea. Even when they tackle a new language, they speak it inevitably with their own accent. That accent is their signature, and is involuntary. Originality cannot be willed, nor is it in itself a valuable quality. To be different does not mean to be better.

Anyway, Ishiguro does repeat himself, as I discovered on finishing the sheaf of hype and beginning his new book. The rare best of the new book seems an echo in the same tonality as *The Remains of the Day*, while the huge worst echoes many an earlier "symbolic" author, mainly Kafka.

From the outset we are drawn into a nightmare of frustration which prevails to the last page. The hero/narrator, "the greatest pianist in the world," had come to a provincial mid-European city—Brno perhaps, or Pécs—to give a recital (or is it a concert with orchestra? or a lecture?) next Thursday, before going on to Helsinki for a similar appearance. His nationality is never revealed, though he may be Anglo-Japanese, since England is often evoked and at one point he says to Sophie, who may have once been his wife, and Boris, an obnoxious kid who may be his son or stepson, "I still have more trouble with French than I do with Japanese." As for his name, Ryder (no first name is ever mentioned), since every paragraph is rife with metaphor (or so we must believe), is it meant to evoke the painter Albert Ryder? or Djuna Barnes's novel of that name? or simply one whose existence "rides" on the good faith of others?

Those others are indeed of good faith, but it comes to naught. From the obsequious porter to the venerable conductor they worship Mr. Ryder, yet are forthcoming in nothing. He is told of his heavy schedule, yet never learns what it is. He is told he will be given a piano for practice, yet the instrument, after hours of searching, is in a public washroom with doors that restrict his arms. He is buffeted from one well-meaning but self-absorbed townsperson to another; every corner he turns, each corridor he enters, leads to another unnamed street, another room with no issue. Anybody who asks is granted unlimited time to recite a litany of petty grievances, or the story of his life—oh, always with deep respect—and Ryder forever succumbs. Exhausted, he nonetheless falls in with the non-sequiturial stance of the citizens, never questioning their sanity, or his own, unlike, say, Alice in Wonderland or Dorothy in Oz. At one point he attends a party in his honor dressed only in a nightshirt. Of course, this is standard dreaming for any public artist. (Myself, I'm expected to perform *Aïda*, though I am stark naked, not a woman, can't sing, and don't know the score. As the curtain rises I wake up.) The event on Thursday at which he is eagerly awaited? Because of the wall surrounding the colosseum he arrives hours late, but does manage to observe some peripheral proceedings through a hole in the roof. When able to appear himself, after many more stultifying misadventures, it is apparently next morning, and nobody remembers him.

This résumé is as clear as it can ever be. The situation, a bad dream from which Ryder will never awake, is Kafka in reverse. In *The Castle* the little man never attains the faraway goal where presumably the rules are made; in *The Unconsoled* the big man is himself thwarted constantly by the status quo. "I wrote the whole thing as a kind of dark comedy," its author explains, "but people don't find it as funny as I do. I get the impression they think it's very solemn." Kafka too, who told Max Brod who told Manuel Rosenthal who told me, expected readers to slap their thighs at his pessimistic fables. But at least Kafka is concise and visionary where Ishiguro is directionless and undifferentiated. It's hard to laugh when oppressed by tedium. Only one reviewer suggests that the book's greatness will shine through on careful rereading. Has his brain been washed in the same laundry as the emperor's new clothes?

Everyone of every class speaks with the same formal diction, with everyone calling everyone Miss Collins or Mr. Ryder or Dr. Lubanski or Mrs. Tilkowski. Though presumably speaking in the tongue of their land, they all say "okay." Certain anglicisms are retained in the American edition (e.g. "marvellous" and single quote marks for speeches), while the smooth professionalism of the narration is sometimes jarred by overuse of the adverb "then." And surely it is an editorial oversight rather than a surrealist nuance that repeatedly credits Clint Eastwood, not Keir Dullea, as protagonist of *2001: A Space Odyssey;* or that has instrumentalists enter the orchestra pit while the conductor advances across the stage.

Toward the end comes a gorgeous passage—twenty self-contained pages quite independent of the hero's ongoing anxieties—reminding a bewildered reader that Ishiguro can still be an economically touching master playing the Proustian game of evocation and nostalgia. The passage also contains the sole references to sex. Brodsky, formerly a noted conductor, now the town drunk, longs to resume with his long-ago love, Miss Collins. His "wound," like Cocteau's *Blood of a Poet*, stands in his way. "In Poland . . . when I was a conductor, even then, I never thought the wound would heal. When I conducted my orchestra, I always touched my wound, caressed it. Some days I picked at its edges, even pressed it hard between the fingers. You realize soon enough when a wound's not going to heal. The music, even when I was a conductor, I knew that's all it was, just a consolation . . . " The elderly Miss Collins softens. Chapters later she reneges. "Your wound, it's nothing special," she tells him. "In this town there are many people with far worse . . . You'll never be a proper conductor . . . You'll never be able to serve the people of this city . . . because you care nothing for their lives.

Alas, the populist notion of art as a selfless service may be the author's own, and thus account for the oversimplified, ultimately senseless, discussions of music. Bach's name is dropped once or twice, indicating a "serious" milieu. All other composers seem to

69   *NED ROREM*

be "moderns" who use outré titles like *Epicyloid,* and are dealt with either mockingly by the writer, or with head-in-hands respect by his characters. Examples: "I've decided to play Jean-Louis La Roche's *Dahlia.* I'm just an amateur and you'll have to be very tolerant." "Then on to the modern stuff. Grebel, Kazan, Mullery . . . Sublime sensitive adagios . . . " "Mother's been looking forward . . . to hearing me play Kazan's *Glass Passions.*" ". . . the realization that I had not prepared the piece that I was to perform before them . . . Was it Yamanak's *Globe-Structures: Option II?* Or was it Mullery's *Asbestos and Fiber?* . . . all I knew was that my parents were already in the city." ". . . as the elongated discords stretched into the sixth and seventh bars . . . the twelfth bar when the notes burst and come fluttering down." "The modern forms, they're so complex now. The likes of von Winterstein, the Countess, . . . they're completely out of their depth . . . They can't distinguish a crushed cadence from a struck motif. Or a fractured time signature from a sequence of vented rests . . . It's not their fault music has become so difficult and complicated."

This high-sounding gobbledygook is as deep as Ishiguro dares go into music. Is it ignorance, poetry, satire? Certainly it is aimless. Like Ravel's *Boléro,* which the composer subtitled *An Orchestral Tissue Without Music,* Ishiguro's entire book has the unvarying meter and rhythm of the Chinese water torture. Unlike *Boléro,* which increases in both timbre and dynamic with each repetition before finally exploding in orgasmic release, the book remains static, without climax, heading nowhere except back into itself.

If in the end *The Unconsoled* signifies nothing, neither is it filled with sound and fury. Ryder may be the world's greatest pianist, but for the reader he remains a cipher. Let his nightmare be *his* problem. For nothing is more boring than another person's dream. When that person is himself a bore, the result is fatal.

Salter's Stories
1988

Although still something of a cult figure, James Salter, because of his short fiction, inhabits the same rarefied heights as such establishment idols as Flannery O'Connor, Paul Bowles, Tennessee Williams (whose stories are superior to his plays), and John Cheever. Like the first three, his style is opulent and his content agonizing; like Cheever, his characters are mostly well-off youngish suburban American Wasps who spend time in Europe. Beyond this, I'm at a loss for literary comparisons.

I have always avoided linking the arts. Despite Pater's—or was it Goethe's?—"architecture is frozen music," the arts are *not* interchangeable; if they were, we'd need only one. Yet at times, confronted by James Salter's unique verbal world, I find myself involuntarily turning to music and movies for my similes. His prose is true prose—cliff-hanging prose—not poetry, but its spell stems less from a gift to spin yarns than from rhythm and echo, from color in the guise of "dark" vowels and clipped consonants, and from tunelike phrases with their repetition and variation— aural attributes ringing through the pages with a sensuality as continual, and as impossible to depict in words, as the continual sensuality in, say, Debussy. His prose is also visual, deceptively unplotted, elliptical, with "silent" spots where we can nonetheless "hear" what's going on for long periods without dialogue, as in an Antonioni film. Indeed, as with Antonioni, décor *chez* Salter, if not actually a hero, is at least a catalyst; with a few deft strokes the sun and shadow of Barcelona, Rome, Long Island, West Point, southern

France or central Germany are evoked as tellingly as any of the unsettled humans that dwell in his paragraphs.

At other times his pen seems dipped in what some liberationists used to call—without defining it—gay sensibility (he focuses on expensive soap or women's clothes with an unapologetically delicate relish that would be shunned by a Mailer or a Wolfe, lest we get funny ideas), except that Salter is not gay. Definitions are elusive, and shift with the times.

Rather, his sensibility is French. That is, his perceptions are superficial in the best sense—crucially "impressionistic" like a Monet lily caught in a fugitive second and imprinted on our brain forever—as distinct from Teutonically profound, digging deep but in just one hole, like a Beethoven motif badgered to death. French sensibility, rare in America, falls like dew into Salter's sentences, emitting a specialized flavor without, thank heaven, being "experimental" or even quirky.

Dusk, an assemblage of eleven stories just issued on lasting creamy stock by the proud North Point Press, represents more of a continuation than an evolution in Salter's relatively spare catalogue. He does not improve (do even the greatest, after a point, really improve?), but merely recasts his always perfect notions into alternative shapes. His ideas, ebbing and swelling with messages of sex and death, never much change with the passing tides. Each of the first five stories, by design or not, portrays male-female intercourse with a carnal urgency that throbs on the page. The remaining six contain nothing sexually explicit, although they're "about" sex, or the pangs thereof.

Salter's early novel, *A Sport and a Pastime*, published twenty-three years ago, is, in skill of diction and in erotic intent, identical with the first story here, "Am Strande von Tanger," recounted all in the present tense. It displays the delusion of the creator spirit in an expatriate American, "an artist in the truly modern sense which is to say without accomplishment but with the conviction of genius."

Polish is the keynote of a Salter melody—the polish of an exquisitely necessary trope which in a measure or two can set the tone, desperate or wistful, of a whole little work gleaming with the economy of a good song; indeed, this garland of stories, at its best, resembles an elegant cycle of songs which could hardly be changed for the better. So it's jarring when Salter occasionally errs. Some of those exquisite tropes are repeated once too often ("air thin as paper," "tea" and "camel" used as hues), along with mistakes in foreign tongues and lapses in English grammar. If, however, there were to be a twelfth or thirteenth offering, one could ask for something giddy, for Salter, long on wit, is short on humor.

What lingers? This:

If James Salter steps sideways rather than forward, he's on the path of many great artists. His writing, as it's being read, feels abstract (but music is always abstract) until in quick retrospect it settles into a stream of pure narrative. The narrative is generally of failure, a writer's failure, and one guesses the writer to be *our* writer. Now in reality Salter is a success, in the only way that any artist need be: he is appreciated by people he does not know. Still, no serious artist, no matter how appreciated, thinks of himself as a success; he knows wherein he has *not* succeeded and that knowledge obsesses him. The writers about whom Salter writes, write of the senselessness of writing, and yet, in the face of all odds, and whether or not they are "any good," they persist. This paradox— writing about the writing about that which may not be worth writing about—is in the final analysis elating and hopeful. Hope is what lingers.

Rediscoveries:
Paul Goodman,
James Lord,
Robert Phelps
1983

My definition of love is: *the need to live with,* and it pertains no less to pictures and poems than to people and pets. All love is at once gracious and stingy, and all lovers—be they begetters of recipes or harems—long to share the notion while retaining the fact of their passion. Too much braggadocio and you risk seeing your mousse devalued on some other table or your lover in some other bed. Thus with books. Rare favorites, once divulged, seem less rare. Yet who can resist? The very act of divulging endows us with a halo, while deep down we know what's too hotly coveted finally dribbles through the fingers like sand. So, lest it vanish forever, I herewith bestow on you some coveted sand, in three little buckets.

I say "little" advisedly. My infatuations, in literature as in music (and who knows? perhaps in affairs of the heart), have always been with the *petits maîtres.* If these are perhaps not substantial enough for a desert island (where like everyone else I'd take Shakespeare, and where anyway there's always plenty of sand), I nonetheless, here on Manhattan island, turn to them often for the solace a Greek finds in his worry beads. Each of my three books, according to the terms of this column, is in some sense neglected; each is elegantly brief (together they come to half of *Hamlet*); each is by someone I have known well; and each is to me musical. They are Paul Goodman's *Hawkweed,* James Lord's *A Giacometti Portrait,* and Robert Phelps's *The Literary Life.*

•

When he died at sixty Paul Goodman had finally seen glory—so long deserved, so long withheld—come toward him, then fade away again. He was the first real live author I ever met, and he remained always the one who most dazzled me. I was fourteen in Chicago, and Paul for the next thirty-five years became the poet to whom I, as a composer, most often turned for song texts. Indeed, he is primarily a poet in my mind; in his own mind too he was the Poet Who Philosophized rather than the Philosopher Who Versified, although to the world he is recalled mainly as the writer of *Growing Up Absurd*. The fame which that relatively complex treatise (and by extension the reprints of earlier sociological volumes and a fiction trilogy, *The Empire City*) so quickly brought to him was almost as quickly dissipated when Youth, his chief audience, turned to the easier formulas of McLuhan and Marcuse. Paul survived to hear his own concepts, hardened through overuse into clichés, flung back at him by people who ignored the concepts' origins. But if his obituaries, in recapitulating his career, made no mention of his poems, it might still be argued that without them there would be no New York School of Poets, no James Schuyler as we know him, no early John Ashbery, no colloquial Kenneth Koch. In taking urban romance and horror as his theme, in filtering this through his bitterly sexual ego, and in voicing his ego in what must paradoxically be termed a "literary vernacular," Paul Goodman introduced a dangerous esthetic—aggrandizement of the daily self. Dangerous, because what seems to fall so trippingly is in fact quite rare. As with Frank O'Hara, his chief protégé, who left in his wake a hundred widows of every sex scribbling O'Hariana in their versified diaries, there was really only room for one Paul Goodman. The room has yet to be acknowledged. But because they so faithfully fill my musical needs—not to mention for sentimental reasons—Paul's poems make him, for me and a few other lunatics, the speaker of a generation.

Alas, at the time he died Paul had just finished editing his *Collected Poems*. In so doing he committed the fatal error (which Auden committed before him, and Henry James before Auden) of updating his life's work. Such updating is always, always, for the worse: no artist speaks with the same tongue young as old, nor is he always "better" old than young. In gentrifying or vulgarizing his youthful *oeuvre* to suit a later purpose Paul left a doting audience holding the bag. Much of his poetry, meanwhile, in its first version, had been made into songs with their own integrity.

Last night while rereading some excruciatingly contagious lines from Paul's short volume *Hawkweed* (a volume he never, thank God, found time to revise), I came upon these sad words

> *Ajax is dead our pet white rat*
> *he died during the night*
> *and Minos his identical twin*
> *in the cage never before alone*
> *will not live very long.*

> *I have brought the body in a box*
> *to throw it in the river*
> *a dirty end for rat or man*
> *but it is still my lordly Hudson*
> *and solemnly I bring the body here.*

and they brought back other words from the height of Goodman's strength when, as the French extol in their pop tunes the crannies of Paris, he deliriously praised his native city and provided me with the substance of my very first song which begins:

> *"Driver, what stream is this?" I asked well knowing*
> *it was our lordly Hudson hardly flowing.*
> *"It is our lordly Hudson hardly flowing,"*
> *he said, "under the green-grown cliffs."*

I met the novelist James Lord in 1949 during my first months in Paris, where he had lived since the end of the war, and where today he stays on—one of the rare Americans who still cleaves to the legend of fertility in foreign soil. We continue as casual friends, or rather as staunch acquaintances, although when I quit France for good in the late fifties he took over my role of official American in the entourage of the lamented but ever-inspiring Marie Laure de Noailles. During those young years, once when I was unhappy, James penned some consoling stanzas and hid them under my dinner plate as an entrée to appease my fever. I set them to music. But they, I believe, are his sole poetry. Unlike Paul Goodman, James Lord is not a born rhymester. Perhaps not even a born novelist, although *No Traveler Returns* (one of a hundred fictions about an uprooted American so popular in the 1950s) was deftly composed, and might have survived had not Vidal's *Judgment of Paris* and Baldwin's *Giovanni's Room* edged it from the charts. What he is, is a friend of graphic artists and a documenter of their works, having, among other triumphs, won a Légion d'Honneur for the reconstitution of Cézanne's studio in Aix, and later becoming the chief biographer of Alberto Giacometti. On the latter subject I discuss him here.

In 1963 James Lord posed for his portrait by Giacometti during eighteen sittings in as many days. Before each sitting he took a snapshot of the previous day's work. In the evenings following—and sometimes surreptitiously during—the séances he made notes about the painter's conversation and about the painting's progress. Notes and snapshots are reproduced in a small eighteen-chapter book. Less fawning than Boswell, though no less astute, Lord has done what all artists finally do (i.e., what cannot be done!), in this case depicted the evolutionary process of a picture *as it is taking place.* That the picture is of himself seems, in a sense, merely coincidental. Nor does it matter that when Giacometti finally finished—or, as Valéry would say, abandoned—the portrait it did not, in my view, resemble the model. What matters is that the writer conveys the unique sensation, passive and active, of that model who gradually becomes the core of another's attention, and of a joint ceremony that will engender an offspring which, like a mule, will never reproduce.

Now, James Lord is comparatively obsure while Giacometti is an international fact of life, yet I find the book about the painter more important than the painter. If Lord is appalled by this judgment, let him know that his portrait of the portraitist has only reinforced, not provoked, my feelings about Giacometti himself. Yes, Lord's book could not have existed did he not apotheosize, oh so coolly, the painter Giacometti; yet Lord's high opinion is irrelevant to his "device." He has made a work of art out of describing the creation of another work of art, and the two works are mutually independent. Lord's chore would have been no less or more successful had the painting so magically described turned out a failure in the eyes of the world. Every word in place, he shows Sisyphian patience with Sisyphus himself. The limning of Giacometti, the artist who also *plays* the artist (ah, suffering and pseudosuffering—which is more painful?), is a demythologizing catharsis for those who think "creation" is ever the effect of divine afflatus. Indeed, Lord's essay could well be renamed *The Case Against Inspiration*.

In movies there was once a similar achievement. Clouzet's 1957 film, *Le mystère Picasso*, used a camera, placed against the back side of a transparent canvas, to record every hesitation and blotch and sign and separate advancing stage of Picasso's anguish in realizing to their finish eight paintings from scratch; we actually witnessed art in the fluid process of becoming rather than in the static version of having become. But in literature there has never been anything resembling the truth of James Lords's accomplishment.

Nor does anything quite resemble Robert Phelps's *Literary Life*. I first met Robert at Yaddo where he showed up in 1960 with his spouse, Rosemarie Beck (one of our most undersung and disturbing narrative painters), and we hit it off instantly, being precious Francophiles—a remote breed then as now—in a hotbed of Teutonic Faulknerites. During the next years Robert single-handedly choreographed the advent of my career as composer-turned-writer. His viewpoint on me was—is—the same as on everyone: that of voyeur. In assuming always the role of sycophant (or as he calls it, of follower) Robert writes from the spacious vantage of his biases. What James Lord did with Giacometti—forming a work of art out of an artist—Robert Phelps has done, over the decades, with Colette. By excising from context unrelated paragraphs of that autobiographical creature who never wrote autobiography, by larding these with his own wise and Wasp aperçus, and by sewing the whole together chronologically, Phelps "invents" the memoir of another. He did it with Cocteau, and even, to a lesser degree, with Janet Flanner when, for my sole use, he created from Flanner's "Letters from Paris" a garland of vignettes to be sung by a mixed chorus.

In 1968, with photographer Peter Deane, Phelps published a luxuriant scrapbook called *The Literary Life*, an almanac of the Anglo-American cultural scene between 1900 and 1950. Hundreds of photographs are surrounded by cross-references, pithy quotes, and classy gossip, so that for any given year we discover that what we always knew we never quite knew. Take 1913. Did you realize that while Gertrude Stein was struggling with the rioters at the Paris premiere of *The Rite of Spring*, Edith Wharton was divorcing —which even Henry James regarded as "the only thing to save her life"? That *Swann's Way* and *Death in Venice* were rolling from the presses as Tagore was accepting the Nobel Prize? That Baron Corvo and Ambrose Bierce were dying as Ravel and Falla were polishing "Trois Poèmes" and "La Vida Breve"? That Chaplin was shooting his first film as Virginia Woolf, having finished her first novel, was suffering a nervous breakdown? And that the Federal Income Tax Amendment became law in the U.S. despite the fact the Robert Frost was declaring: "A sentence is a sound in itself on which other sounds called words may be strung"? Frost's definition is exemplified, more shimmeringly than anywhere I can think of, in the sentences of this adorable conglomeration which, simply put, is useful information readably stated.

So much for my three loves. Whether they'd love each other, who can say. They have never met. Phelps and Lord, roughly the same age (my age), reside respectively on this city's 12th Street and Paris's rue des Beaux-Arts, while Goodman, who would now be seventy-one, has for the past eleven years lain underground in Vermont.

Beyond the binding cord of my taste, what have Paul's poetry, James's journal, and Robert's history in common? They have in common *economy* — the final ingredient of the best art, from the Sistine Ceiling to a Piaf tune. Their grammer and form seem almost commonplace, but their method and outcome are inimitable.

Cocteau in America
1986

The day he died in 1963 I wrote an essay called "I'd Take the Fire." The title is Jean Cocteau's answer—"*J'emporterais le feu*"—to the familiar question, "If your house were burning down and you could take away just one thing, what would it be?" My argument was that the culture of France (all aspects of it—novels, painting, dance, theater, music, even movies) had, since World War II, fallen from high and shrunk into an elegant parasite. Cocteau had ignited a France of his own, luring others to wax and glitter among his special flames which, for awhile, colored each corner of the land where now only an afterglow remained. He had indeed gone off with the fire. Yet on his tombstone is engraved the reassuring phrase, *Je reste avec vous.*

That he stayed with us, and that the fire left behind some unquenchable embers, seems evident today, although in what proportion is hard to assess, at least for me in America, America being under my nose and thus too near for focus. But now on rare trips back to Paris I find no cause to retract my statement of twenty-three years ago: there's an atmosphere that more than ever feels decadent in the true sense—a decomposition, imitation at its weakest, creativity at one remove. Structuralism turns out books about books, IRCAM turns out music about music, everything is intelligence, nothing is passion (except TV serials from the USA). Yet there seems to be a revival over there of Jean Cocteau sparked by the posthumous publication of his diaries, and the revival bubbles where it counts, among the young. Reading those diaries, and reindulging in his plays, films, poems, and so forth as incentive for these pages, I find revived in me a France of another time, and especially the America of my youth.

Some free associations:

Cocteau is everywhere. A ten-minute survey of my American library shows his named dropped by the most disparate authors: Edith Wharton (1912: "a passionately imaginative youth to whom every great line of poetry was a sunrise, every sunset the foundation of the Heavenly City"), Aldous Huxley (1920: "a man of fabulous cleverness, but not serious"), James Agee (1945: "Still photographs of motionless objects have a very different quality from motion-picture photographs of motionless objects; as Jean Cocteau observed, time still moves in the latter"), Judith Malina (1952: "There is no other person in the theater with whom I should care to work save Cocteau"), Pauline Kael (1971: "Julie Christie had the profile of a Cocteau drawing—tawdry-classical"). Anecdotes emerge from Alice Toklas, Gore Vidal, Tennessee Williams, Truman Capote, Louise Bogan, Lincoln Kirstein, and even such rugged types as Hemingway and Pound (though not from Charles Ives or Martha Graham). There are poignant references by composers as diverse as John Cage, Elliott Carter, and Paul Bowles, and by such non-French Europeans as Hindemith, Weill, Henze, Britten, and Varese, who have written background music to his play, songs to his words, or, in Carter's case, used the device of the "timeless" crumbling tower at the start and close of *Blood of a Poet* as structure for a string quartet. (*Blood of a Poet* was the subject of a study by Sigmund Freud as well, or so Cocteau once told me, though I've never pinned down the source.) You'll find Cocteau's name in any book about Mishima, Dietrich, Diaghilev, Spender, and a hundred others.

Last week in Maurice Messegue's health-food treatise, *Of Men and Plants,* I came across a twelve-page homage to the master. (The faddist arrived at Cocteau's country home by accident a week early, introduced himself to the poet, who was on a ladder decorating the ceiling with images of the very flower that Messegue planned to use in an infusion for the ailing artist, and was told, "I was expecting you.") Just yesterday, in *The Village Voice* (May 6, 1986), in a column by one Freda Garmaise who laments the passing of true gossipmongers: "Cocteau knew that startling news didn't have to

NED ROREM

be Stravinsky sleeping with Chanel, but could be any revelation of a habit, a fixation, or opinion which would cause us to reflect on the person, if not human nature in general." And this very morning, perusing for the first time the utterly French *Monstres Sacrés* of 1939, I'm struck by the plot's uncomfortable resemblance to the utterly American *All About Eve* of 1950. Could Mankiewicz have known Cocteau's play? Of course, where Cocteau gave he also took. His sacred monsters are allowed to utter many an uncredited *mot:* "Happiness is a long patience" comes from Balzac, not Florent; "All my life I've heard, 'Wait 'til you're older, you'll see,' and now I'm fifty, I've seen nothing" comes from Satie, not Esther; and "I don't seek, I find" is Picasso, not Liane.

Yes, "Cocteau is everywhere," I noted those three words in my diary eleven years ago on returning from a first exposure to the self-proclaimed originality of Robert Wilson's *Letter to Queen Victoria.* I went on: "Part One, a discourse between two motionless women repeated verbatim at different speeds, reminded us (visually) of the conversation between Oedipus and the Sphinx in *The Infernal Machine.* Part Two, in an aviator's prison (I think), where the actions of smoking and sleeping and dying are repeated verbatim at the same speed, reminded us of the Mexican execution in *Blood of a Poet* . . . Music is omnipresent like the dancers [and] parodies eighteenth- and nineteenth-century classics as counterpoint to the ultramodern doings on stage. (Again Cocteau: the film *Les Enfants terribles* and the ballet *Le Jeune Homme et la mort.)*" That same week I took Molly Haskell to task for her hackneyed put-down of how "known" homosexuals treat women in the movies: "It does seem unbalanced to refer to the nonwomen of the Inge-Williams syndrome without once breathing the name of Cocteau in a book that purports to be inclusive. Jean Cocteau was not only the single most influential *cinéaste* in France (Truffaut, Resnais, Genet, Godard, Reichenbach would never have been as they are without him), and by extension in the whole 'experimental' world since 1931, but a compassionately original creator of feminine roles. Think of those women of all ages and styles that Cocteau put on the map: Lee Miller, Gabrielle Dorziat, Josette Day, Yvonne de Bray, Juliette Greco, Berthe Bovy. Even Jeanne Moreau owes her stage debut to Cocteau in *La Machine infernale.*"

●

My first exposure to (should I say my first injection with the benign but permanent virus of?) Jean Cocteau took place in 1938—I was fourteen—when David Sachs, fellow Chicagoan and seventeen (today Professor of Philosophy at Johns Hopkins and still a staunch acquaintance), lent me, with whatever motive, an English version of a novel whose untranslated title was *Les Enfants terribles*. (Rosamond Lehmann would eventually render it as *The Holy Terrors*, although *The Problem Children* too is apt.) Authors we love we "relate" to, we think we'd get on with them, yearn for their living contact. I didn't know it then, but across the ocean *Les Enfants terribles* was provoking this yearning, among the young, more than any book since *The Sorrows of Young Werther* 150 years earlier, and as *Catcher in the Rye* would in America twenty years later. As unsolved crimes are often confessed to by innocent old ladies, or as New York bars still harbor octogenarians who swear they are "layers" of Djuna Barnes's model for Doctor O'Connor in *Nightwood*, so the city of Paris once swarmed with siblings claiming to be the original *enfants terribles* from whom their fabulous friend had fired a masterpiece. Such claims are usually unproductive and always fallacious: "People do not read but read themselves." After the fact and by association the models (and I was one) base themselves on the masterpiece, forgetting that the writer is only a writer when he's writing—that "awake" he's as ordinary as anyone.

Except Cocteau, as I would later learn.

My second fix came through *Blood of a Poet* in New York in 1944. Unbeknownst to us the film had been doubly censored. Among the original occupants of the opera loge, applauding the snowy death scene, were the Vicomte and Vicomtesse de Noailles who had financed the venture. When Noailles, because of the equivocal tone of this film as well as Buñuel's anticlerical *L'Age d'or* which he had also subsidized, was given an ultimatum by not only the Catholic Church but, far worse!, the Jockey Club, the scene was reshot with actors, including the Texan trapese artist, Barbette, *en travesti*. Meanwhile, the Hayes office in the USA toned down the blood in the death scene and the "sex" in the hermaphrodite scene simply by slashing the film stock—which accounts for the jerkiness in the incidental music, a jerkiness we had taken as a *trouvaille* of Georges Auric.

Auric also composed the score for *Beauty and the Beast* which showed up on our shores in 1946, subtitled by Irving Drutman, with the heartbreaking Jean Marais (Garbo, moved by the ugly creature, was disconcerted when Marais at the end turns into his beautiful self: "Give me back my beast") and the heartwarming Josette Day (who had previously been seen only in Jacques Deval's trashy *Club de femmes*). With the privilege of retrospect it is now clear how these people—the fleshly actuality of them—would become enmeshed in my existence during the next decade. If I was gifted and personable on showing up in Paris in 1949 it was less for these traits than because I was versed in *their* traits—a versification that seemed to the French a rare contradiction in terms, Yankees being, now as then, a breed that had "passed from barbarism to decadence without an intervening culture"—that launched me. All through the fifties I dwelt chez the Vicomtesse de Noailles, better known as Marie Laure, whose only previous American friend was the painter Tom Keogh. If I was the one American musician of Auric's acquaintance, what others were there to know? Yes, Marais's dearest friend was an American dancer, George Reich, at the time we worked together on the ballet *Dorian Gray* in 1952, but that was a fluke. As for Cocteau, his sense of America was as bizarre as Kafka's, judging by the cool *Lettre aux Américains*, and the sole Americans he ever evoked were Glenway Wescott and Monroe Wheeler. (Incidentally, except for Marie Laure who learned it on her nanny's knee, none of these people knew English. Cocteau had the gift of gab, but not the gift of tongues.) I'd have thought I was run-of-the-mill; in fact, the Americans who knew the general arts of France during those first postwar years all knew each other too—all twenty of them! Meanwhile, back in an earlier Manhattan I was learning the specific arts of Cocteau (like learning a foreign language) just well enough to sometimes miss the point.

"All love is a little death, and great love is suicide," groaned Tallulah Bankhead from the proscenium of the Plymouth as we, that April 4 in 1947, thrilled to the verse of the man for whom even death was chic. How could we know, in our zeal to find Cocteau all-knowing, that this "truth" (which makes as much sense as "a little bit pregnant"), penned for another character but confiscated by Tallulah, was invented by Ronald Duncan for his poeticized Englishing of Cocteau's prose play, *L'Aigle à deux têtes*, mistranslated as *The Eagle Has Two Heads*? (Elsewhere Duncan unaccountably omitted one of the quainter *répliques* of the original: *"Un peu trop, c'est juste assez pour moi!"*—"A little too much is just enough for me!") The previous year we witnessed Marc Blitzstein's outrage at Cocteau's modernizing of the Tristan legend, *L'Eternel retour*, when the dwarf Pieral pours out a love potion labeled Poison. Marc, nothing if not left-wing, found such games "aristocratic" in the light of the workingman's plight. Yet he was not anti-Cocteau, and claimed that while in France during the war he played his music for the author, who especially admired a little waltz which later became part of his opera *Reuben Reuben*. Marc's the first person I ever knew who had met Cocteau, although Cocteau told me, years afterward, that he didn't recall. (Both were telling the truth.)

He didn't recall Paul Goodman either, yet I myself recall, bright as this morning, the two of them chatting at the Gotham Book Mart on January 8, 1949. Not many guests showed up, and Cocteau himself was an hour late to the little reception. The rest of us gawked as the two great poets made little headway at mutual comprehension. Paul had once composed a ballad in Cocteau's honor, and had adapted at least one play by the Frenchman who now expressed merely lukewarm curiosity, seemed worn out, and was soon wafted off by his hired translator, Patrick O'Higgins, who would eventually write a memoir of his permanent employer, Helena Rubinstein.

The following May I sailed for France, ostensibly for three months, but remained seven years.

On French soil my perspective on his fame shifted radically even as today's hindsight has shifted my perspective on his worth. He was hardly as rare a bird in Paris as he had seemed, I now realized, in Chicago. Just as when, as a boy, I had assumed all the other boys went home as I did after school to practice Griffes and Ravel on their pianos (I'm still not cured of the trauma of discovering that most people—even wise and educated people—just don't care about the serious music of their time), so I assumed those boys longed to model their social style on the imaginative bohemianism of *Les Enfants terribles*. In fact, there were probably no more than two dozen of my contemporary adolescents in the whole United States who had even heard of these problem children. And if the film *Blood of a Poet* did have a run in New York during most of the

1940s, that run was neither as permanent nor as widespread as its maker would have had us believe in his aimiably petulant *Letter to Americans;* it was a strictly local on-and-off affair, being confined to a now-vanished revival theater on lower Fifth Avenue where it was inevitably screened, always to a scant house, co-billed with something called *Lot in Sodom.* And if *The Two-Headed Eagle* had dazzled us on Broadway, we did not view it in the context of failure, evidenced both by its so-brief life and its bowdlerization. (Cocteau unjustly laid the blame. In 1953 when Tennessee Williams declared that Garbo, who had never appeared in legitimate theater, could have been our greatest stage actress, Cocteau added, "My bad luck was that she wanted to play in *The Two-Headed Eagle,* but Tallulah got there first and made a mess of it." Then why didn't Garbo do it if she wanted? Meanwhile, Cocteau never saw Tallulah, who in my opinion was ideal in the role.)

Here now in Paris was the uncut version of *Blood of a Poet* still playing to full houses, but co-billed with *Blood of Beasts,* a cruel documentary on slaughterhouses by Franjus, replete with a Trenet lovesong as background music to animals being rent asunder—a communist antidote, I was told, to the effete Cocteau. The "effete Cocteau" was more than a household word, he was a crucial woof in the fabric of our collective unconscious—crucial enough to be despised. Just as in music, Youth, which calls the shots, had in postwar France begun to replace what it called the veneer of Poulenc with the depth of Boulez, so it was replacing the fancy of Cocteau with the intellect of Sartre, of Camus, and of even Jean Genet. (But if Camus and Sartre were, in their icy philosophy, in direct contrast to the gaudy warmth of Cocteau, Genet was nevertheless a sort of Cocteau of the lower depths: his earliest novels owe much to *Le Livre blanc,* as do his erotic alexandrines and the little movie *Un Chant d'amour.*) Not that Cocteau wasn't as famous as any movie star; indeed, despite protestations that his outward glory blinded the public to the nuance of his oeuvre, he allowed newsreels to depict him *in the act of not being famous* as he painted or wrote in various sequestered nooks. But he was out of fashion. When in my innocence I professed to admire this or that of his works, the French adopted the same hopeless shrug as when we Americans spoke—as we all did then—in Freudian jargon. "We've had all that," they implied, although in fact psychoanalysis would inflame France in the sixties as it had inflamed the States in the forties.

Although we ourselves have placed them there, we can grow to resent and thence to crush theatrical idols for their stance upon the pedestal. If this has not been the case for such moral irreproachables as Shaw or O'Neill or Arthur Miller, it has been the case for Wilde and Williams and Jean Cocteau. A 1952 production of *Oedipus Rex* reunited Cocteau and Stravinsky after many years. Cocteau not only declaimed the speaker's role, he refashioned the twelve-foot puppets of Remo Bufano. We saw him, as well, before the dress rehearsal happily hammering at the props. (Paris stagehand unions are more lax than ours.) But Cocteau, being that season out of favor with the fickle French, was not to be loved. At the gala the elderly perfumed public, laced with Camus-oriented youth chained to an outmoded ritual, jeered each appearance of Cocteau until he raised a famous hand to stop the orchestra. "If you don't respect me and my work," he pleaded, "at least respect Stravinsky who is a great composer." The hall grew still, the music started up, Cocteau sat down again on the little stool at the edge of the stage, motionless and crestfallen. Nobody missed the irony when he pronounced the final lines—the very lines that Stravinsky once discounted as superfluous—when the King finds himself snared in his own trap: "He falls. He falls from high . . . Farewell, poor Oedipus, we loved you."

Yet four years later Cocteau was embraced like a king by the ultraestablishment arms of the French Academy. His entry costume was designed by Lanvin, and thus garbed he was pictured, with the customary jewelled sword, on the cover of every European weekly. During these years he produced, on the one hand, two collections of essays and two book-length poems, all of great power, economy, and originality, and on the other hand, dozens of prefaces, blurbs, and salutations (for Lanvin: "Mesdames, your legs are poems—bind them in Lanvin hose"; for Marlene Dietrich: "Madame, your name starts with a caress and ends in a whiplash") mostly off the top of his head, refusing no one, forever approbatory. This untranslatable catalogue remained unknown in the United States, even to rabid coctolophiles who, while influenced by the *maître*'s more famous films, necessarily ignored his complex non-fiction and high-camp pronouncements.

He continued (as Nadia Boulanger—the grandest musical pedagogue of Paris, formerly of the world—continued) to have an almost radioactive effect on specialized foreigners like myself who passed through town, but the overwhelming majority of French youth, who don't like kings, had abandoned him. Now, Youth is the sole public a successful artist craves in his old age. Six years later Cocteau died, as most people do, of a broken heart.

More free associations:

So, Jean Cocteau is not a fact of cultural life in America any more than, say, John Cheever is in France. True, Cocteau has more than triple Cheever's listings in *Books in Print,* but ask your literary friends to name three Cocteau novels and see where you land. True again, Manhattan now boasts a theater named the Jean Cocteau Repertory in the Bowery, but how many of his plays are mounted there? (Half his plays have yet to be translated.) His name does not appear in the extended entry for French Literature in our *Academic American Encyclopedia* although lesser lights like Aragon, Giraudoux, Malraux, Céline, even Butor and Sarraute, are given long shrift.

Perhaps Cocteau's nonexportability lies in his quintessential Frenchness. Except for movies and dress design, nothing French has had much impact on America since 1960, and during the previous generation a novelist like Thomas Mann eclipsed even Gide on our shores. In the so-called New Romanticism of American music today there is no hint of even Debussy and Ravel as mentors: nothing's transparent, direct, superficial (in the vast sense that Impressionism is superficial—a split-second glimpse of a rose at twilight, a secret overheard on the subway); all is murky, Mahlerian. (Minimalism's simplicity comes from the East, not from France.) What we know of Cocteau is the tip of the iceberg, except for his films.

His films, starring Jean Marais, chief protégé and interpreter, did, when they first came out, draw mobs to the provincial nabes throughout France. But if Marais himself, for two generations the most popular film idol in his country, has yet to make a movie in Hollywood, as have Jourdan and Boyer and Aumont and even Gabin, is it worth adding that Marais is the sole homosexual of the group—and unashamed at that? More likely it is—was—his, to

Americans, precious image as friend to Jean Cocteau. Cocteau was never invited to Hollywood either, while Noel Coward, nothing if not gay and outspoken, was the toast of the town. In a way, Cocteau was the dark side of Coward: the two were the only successful jacks-of-all-trades in their world, and both were court jesters. But Jean was the pessimist's Noel, and America prefers the upbeat.

Important to note here that, despite his reputedly outrageous public behavior—a behavior which I, however, was unaware of during the (admittedly late) years in which I knew and watched him—never in his works, except for the pseudonymous *Livre blanc*, did Cocteau use homosexuality as subject matter, as did the more circumspect Gide and the more sullen Genet. If, as a "male couple," Marais and Cocteau were sufficiently notorious in their homeland —as Benjamin Britten and Peter Pears were in theirs—to become the brunt of popular jokes, the unions in both cases resulted in the highest art, altering forever the nature of opera and cinema throughout the globe.

Important also to add that nothing is as it seems. In a recent memoir Jean Marais makes an extraordinary declaration while describing his early acquaintance with the poet. The year is 1937 and Marais is about to be cast as the star of Cocteau's *Knights of the Round Table*, his first big part. Hitherto the two men have been on terms of professional *vouvoiement*. One night Marais is called unexpectedly to the Hotel de Castille (where coincidentally the previous summer I, age twelve, spent a fortnight with my mother, father, and sister), wherein Cocteau then resided in a semipermanent fog of opium. Terrified that his hard-earned role has been taken from him, Marais, on the edge of tears, rushes to the hotel where the ashen Cocteau tells him quietly: "There's been a catastrophe. I am in love with you."

"This man whom I admire," writes Marais, "gave me what in the world I had most wished for, asking nothing in return. I don't love him. How can he love me . . . me . . . it's impossible.

" 'You see how I live. I must be saved. Only you can save me.'

" 'I love you too,' I said. I lied. Yes, I lied. It's difficult to explain this lie. I had a huge admiration for Jean Cocteau, but it was a respect which did not correspond to his sentiments. I was flattered too. To think that a nobody like me could save this great poet! At precisely that second I must have turned into a sort of Lorenzaccio.

From that moment on I wished to give happiness—to 'give flight to sorrow, friend of poets,' as he later wrote me."

Later still, Cocteau wrote that opium smoking, the least vulgar of pursuits, forced him into the most vulgar of company, i.e., the police, and for that he finally renounced it. In fact, Jean Marais would seem to have been the right person at the right time, and has remained his friend's greatest champion to this day. For some deeply touching and previously unpublished lyrics of love slipped nightly beneath the bedroom door of the actor by the older man, see the appendix of Jean Marais's *Histoires de ma vie* (Editions Albin Michel, 1975), if you can find it.

These have been thoughts on the occasion of a new picture book compiled by my friend, Arthur Peters. I've sought to render a flavor of the French magician—without relying too much on what I've written elsewhere—and to stress how he appears to American eyes, yesterday and today. Now I see I've not managed to weave into the fabric certain observations penciled on my cuff—for example, that Cocteau never wrote about food, or even talked about it. Or that he never stopped working (Colette: *"Tu es un mauvais oisif"*), even, one supposes, while making love, or, as he later claimed to prefer, "making friendship." Or that he never stopped talking, his conversation, although based largely on mere anecdote and epigram, being a threat to even such a salon stylist as Anna de Noailes who, it's said, when she found the young *arriviste* on her left at dinner, stopped his lips with her left hand so that he wouldn't take over her monologue as she paused for a spoonful of soup. Or that the first time I ever met him he gave me a French lesson by showing that every line of *Au Clair de la lune*, if read with the proper innuendo, was obscene.

He could charm the birds off the trees. Which is maybe why, at the close of *The Knights of the Round Table*, we hear: "Look Segramor, you know the language of the birds. Now couldn't you listen and tell us what they say?" "The birds are saying: Pay, pay, pay, must pay, must pay." Or why, in the otherwise mawkish *Letter to Maritain* (though less mawkish and a good deal more gorgeous than Maritain's pallid reply; if we don't for a minute believe in Cocteau's godly "redemption," we do believe in his belief in other people's belief, but we hardly care that Maritain believes he's made a convert), he recognizes a brother in the Chicago murderer Loeb, who trained birds in his prison cell.

Like Oscar Wilde (and how few others), he was, in France, exactly as famous as his work—not more famous, like Truman Capote, or less, like perhaps Ferdinand de Lesseps who built the Suez Canal. He may not be the most important artist of our century, in the sense that Picasso is, but he is one of the most subliminally influential—more influential, surely, on an international front than Eisenstein or Gertrude Stein (unknown in France) or Balanchine or even Henry James. He may foment in the collective unconscious, but he's not our daily fare; a cult figure, he nonetheless overflows that category, like an aristocratic Allen Ginsberg, beguiling those who heed him by the utter intimacy of his every statement.

Unlike Orson Welles, a Yankee counterpart and generally deemed our premier moviemaker, yet who in his last thirty years couldn't procure even minimal backing for his ideas, Cocteau managed to make a final film, but only with the personal finances of a younger colleague, director François Truffaut. *The Testament of Orpheus* turned out to be a deenergized rehash of his former mythologies. The master, who would be ninety-seven today, might acknowledge this with sadness, he who once wrote, "Don't look back, or you risk turning into a statue of salt—that is, a statue of tears."

Cocteau's Diary

1986

The distinguishing feature of a diary as opposed to a memoir is on-the-spot reaction, the writer's truth as he feels it, not as he felt it. If that truth is no more "truthful" for being in the first person, it does contain the defining character of immediacy. The intimate journal is a literary form used almost solely by the French. They kept it as a sideline—a book about how hard it is to write a book —fragmentary by its nature, forever unfinished. Not only France's authors, from Rousseau, Baudelaire, and Amiel to Charles Du Bos, Jules Renard, and Julien Green, but her other artists and even politicians—Berlioz, Delacroix, de Gaulle, Poulenc, Malraux—have made literature of their lives. The genre has never been popular with non-French continentals, still less with the British, who prefer autobiography, and (at least until recently) is virtually unpracticed by Americans who, with all due emancipation and collective carnality, do retain a decorum toward their personal selves. We know less about the daily grind of such graphic romancers as Philip Roth or Edmund White than we do about that circumspect *littérateur*, André Gide. Gide, the modern world's most famous diarist, was so enmeshed in the genre that he not only published quadriannually throughout his life a journal documenting his existence, but in his only novel he allows his alter ego, Edouard, to keep a diary whose entries are interpolated like ballast to stabilize the various frantic plots of *Les Faux-monnayeurs;* simultaneously with his novel Gide kept a special diary called *Journal des Faux-monnayeurs* detailing his problems—and Edouard's—in developing the novel; and in his regular journal he detailed the problems of composing the *Journal des Faux-monnayeurs*. Claude Mauriac, in *his* diary, describes a charmingly strained postprandial hour in the country home of his famous father, François Mauriac, where the two had persuaded Gide to spend a weekend. The trio of authors are clearly anxious to retire to their rooms, ostensibly for a nap, actually to confide to their separate Rashomonian journals the literary lunchtime remarks before they fade from memory.

How is it that Jean Cocteau, of all people, during this long display of intimate self-promotion among his peers, never kept a diary? Was he not the most public, the most spellbinding, creature of culture in Paris during the first half-century? If Diaghilev's demand to the young poet, "Astound me," had in 1912 unleashed a talent which proceeded to thrill every caste with its ballets, monologues, paintings, drawings, plays, novels, essays, poems, choreography, and even church murals (as a musician Cocteau did lack a voice, but compensated by "inventing" Satie and the Groupe des Six), was Jean-the-man any less formidable? Had he not inherited from Wilde the title of "world's most dazzling talker" and from De Quincey that of the world's most conspicuous *opiomane?* Was he not dogged by the suicides of many whose strength was unequal to his? Had not *Le Livre blanc* pseudonomously described his bouts in the all-male brothels of Toulon, bouts depicted visually a decade later in his melancholy lithographs for the novels of Jean Genet (the Cocteau of the working class)? Had he not attended operas with Barbette, the Texan trapezist in drag, and created (some say destroyed) names now more legendary than his own—Jean Marais, Edith Piaf? Had he not been glorified by Proust as Saint-Loup, by Gide as the Comte de Passavant? Was not the sight of those long hands, that rebellious hair and tapering nose, an almost daily fact in the press for fifty years? Could it not be argued that insofar as cinema has now become our most expressive, our most *telling* art, and that insofar as his nine films were the most influential in Europe and by extension the world, Jean Cocteau was the most important artist of our time? And finally, was he not infatuated with this very importance?

Yes, why had he never kept a diary?

Well, Jean Cocteau did in fact publish a sort of journal, *Opium* (1930), albeit on the specific subject of disintoxication, just as the

Journal de la Belle et la Bête (1946) and *Maalesh* (1949) were day-by-day reportings on the specific subjects of filmmaking and theatrical touring. But he never kept a journal on his more generalized quotidian doings, although he did over the course of the years pen many a retrospective self-portrait as well as historic portraits of famous friends, vignettes which served as the sole quotable matter for his various biographers during the thirteen years after his death.

Now it turns out that for the thirteen years before his death he did keep a diary—a voluminous one at that. This long-secret fact, now revealed, has caused a resurgence of all his work in France. The opening pages would seem to coincide with Cocteau's permanent removal from Paris to the Midi where, in the lavish Villa San Sospir at Cap Ferrat, he passed his remaining days with two friends, the actor Edouard Dermit and the wealthy Francine Weissweiller. The book cannot be said to be any more or any less a bid for immortality than the bulk of Cocteau's earlier vast and varied oeuvre, and its inception predates by four years his official "immortality"—the 1955 reception into the Académie Française.

This first volume came out in Paris in the early fall of 1983, twenty years to the day after the poet's death. Surely his will would have stipulated the discreet period so as to impose a proper distance and to avoid problems with living persons, yet not so discreet (like Mark Twain's fifty-year stipulation) as to divest his papers of gossip value and to allow the chief actors to dissolve into limbo. Cocteau himself chose the name *Le Passé défini* (how prettily the grammar balances with Noel Coward's *Present Indicative*), suggesting he did intend publication posthumously, the title is so clearly *après coup;* the book's not about the definite past at all, but, like every diary, about the present. Given his flamboyant reputation (one can't help but take lightly Cocteau's contention that reputations of public figures are made by their public more than by themselves), the book promised to be succulent, especially since Cocteau himself had once said—and this, despite the ongoing appearances of the diaries of so many of his quick and sober colleagues—"A diary should appear only after our death. Who cares about entries like, 'Reread *Andromaque*. Lunched at Madame So-and-so's.' "

I devoured *Le Passé défini* on the spot and made entries in my own diary.

27 December 1983. Went to bed with Cocteau, vaguely disappointing, except for the close (to me) vitality: the journal covers eighteen months, beginning in July 1951 (six more volumes are promised by Gallimard during the next years), in which nearly every entry brings home an event at which I was present. But the fragmented philosophical gems were all later polished and reset more tellingly elsewhere. What blinded me yesterday is frayed today—the constant harping on being read and then forgotten by those few who read. *"On peut dire à n'importe qui et n'importe où une chose qu'on a déjà écrite. Elle est neuve. Il n'est pas rare qu'on nous conseille de l'écrire. Même ceux qui nous lisent ne se souviennent de rien."* Maybe those readers are too polite to say that his conversation seems a replay of what they've already read. Or maybe, in different contexts, an old *tournure* takes on new light, even new sense. Don't I reread my own diaries having forgotten that I used a charmed phrase here, then reused it there? Cocteau was too quick to accuse his public.

In passing he writes of me in an episode which I too have described: our visit, with Marie-Laure de Noailles, to her mother's at the Villa Croisset in Grasse. I noted: "On arriving, Cocteau announced to Madame de Croisset, 'It seems like yesterday that I was bringing Marie Laure back from our outings.' (He'd not been in this house since the summers of World War I when the adolescent Marie-Laure began nursing the love-hate she never forsook.)" *His* entry, though, wilts when he tells us that, *"Comme je n'ai aucun sens du temps, j'ai l'impression d'y revenir après une promenade."* He forever states that he has "no sense of time," yet isn't it precisely because he does have a sense of time that he has the *impression d'y revenir?* Again he tells wrong (wrong theatrically) an anecdote—retold in my *Paris Diary*—about Garbo at the Véfour where clients mistook her for Madeleine Sologne. Isn't that irony sufficient? But Cocteau adds what mustn't be added: *"Le sens du légendaire est perdu."* Never apologize, never explain.

His pro-Stalin leanings seem naive even for then, as do his generalities about Americans: Americans hate Negroes, yet they all do their best to acquire a suntan.

Around that same season Boulez proclaimed: "Every musician who has not felt the necessity of the serial language is useless." (Omit the word "not," and I would agree.) Cocteau, who for the first time had no bandwagon of his own, jumped on that of Boulez, with statements like: "It is understandable that young musicians today take their stand on Schoenberg and find in him an arm against works which fear his science of numbers." But the "counter-charm" of which he was approving, was himself; nor is it probable that he would have recognized any work of Schoenberg. Dalton Baldwin recently told me that after a recital of French songs which he gave with Sousay around 1960, Cocteau backstage dismissed every work on the program—Ravel, Poulenc, Debussy—except Gounod whom he claimed the master of French song.

28 December. Cocteau's diary is hard to put down, not least because I'm continually comparing his version of this or that event with my version. For example, in December of 1951, the notorious debacle at the *Bacchus* gala when Mauriac, a few seats down from us, arose at the final curtain and fled, amidst a battery of flashbulbs and shocked gasps; and his vitriolic attack on Cocteau in *Figaro littéraire* on the 29th, followed by Cocteau's open reply, "Je t'accuse," next day in *France-Soir* (which Cocteau admits to having written *before* Mauriac's article appeared), both men tutoyering each other like beloved enemies. Indeed, I seem to recall—but where's the fact? I've searched everywhere—that he signed his public letter, *Ton ennemi qui t'aime.* This sort of front-page squabble between renowned intellectuals about religious morality versus artistic prerogative, though seemingly petty at the moment, is majestically stimulating on rereading, especially in the light of America's know-nothing journalism and a government that eschews literary argument.

Yet who will find himself now in the grip of such reading where Mauriac is unknown and Cocteau but a one-time moviemaker? If the diary were translated, would I myself feel uncomfortable at others reading this mess by an idol? Cocteau's need for love and acceptance is touching, and what I personally owe him is incalculable. Yet what once passed for insight now seems specious. At the very outset, look at this false analogy as he chides so-called existentialists: *"Ne rien faire et boire dans des petites caves, c'est existentialiste, C'est comme s'il existait à New York des 'relativistes' qui dansent dans des caves et qu'on croie qu'Einstein danse avec eux."* But there *aren't* any *"relativistes"* dancing in *caves* in New York. Existentialism is a philosophy and Einstein was a physicist, and physics, though open to misuse, cannot be misinterpreted and cultified in the same sense that a philosophy can. In this chaotic journal Cocteau resembles his Sphinx—"I secrete my thread, let it out, wind it back and spin it in"; most of those threads were deknotted into smooth essays the following year, notably in the *Journal d'un inconnu*. As with my unimpeachable Ravel, who dimly showed clay feet a few years back when Orenstein published a batch of his juvenilia, so Jean Cocteau changes—perhaps evolves, and for the better—to my ken.

His words on Proust (on "re-reading" Proust, as he puts it) do ring with the authority of One Who Was There. No such demystification exists in any other article on Proust . . .

29 December. Finished Cocteau. The man and his work will remain always among those three or four most influential upheavals to blind me against other esthetics, other voices. But if childhood loves can never be dislodged like wisdom teeth, they can still grow loose in their sockets in our old age. Cocteau, in repeating to exhaustion his every bon mot lest we may never have heard it, weakens, by revealing his tricks, the very foundation of his structure. Even Debussy, the nonpareil, when I examined the warmongering text for his very last work, *Noël des enfants qui n'ont plus de maisons,* became an average vengeful creature subverting his own art.

That was then. Today, nearly three years older, I'm also wiser for having read the vast second volume, and admit to an impatient thirst for the third. It is wrong to read Cocteau's diary for its art, for art is by definition sculptured, economical, with a planned ending, while this vulnerable and open-ended affair is a continually backtracking blueprint, as removed from the finished products being polished simultaneously as, say, Baudelaire's loose letters from his tight verse. *Le Passé défini* exudes the utter authority and utter insecurity combined in all true artists; indeed, it could only have been composed by a true artist although it is not itself art. By its nature it lacks the tailored care of the formal journals. It contrasts to the body of Cocteau's poetry, from the perfumed perfection of *Le Prince frivole* in 1909 *(Au revoir! il le faut, pour désunir les couples / Que je longe en glissant sur mes pieds bleus et souples . . .),* through the touching honesty of the still-uncollected love-poems to Jean Marais in 1939 *(Ah! je chante, je chante / Pour t'avoir le même demain / Car la vie a l'air trop méchante / Sans la caresse de ta main),* to the crystalline sadness of the hundred alexandrine quatrians in *Le Chiffre sept* (1952) which begin:

> *Voici que presque rien de ce fil ne me reste.*
> *Sa pelote était lourde et me bondait le coeur.*
> *Et le coeur si souvent a retourné sa veste*
> *Qu'il croyait ne jamais perdre de sa douleur.*

If the poems, and thus the whole catalogue (for Cocteau referred to himself as solely a poet, whether concocting a libretto, a filmscript, a pornographic story, or a woven rug) are as much style as content, the diary is mainly content with only passing stabs at style.

What is the tone of this content? Cocteau's diary is not what the French call a *journal intime* in the sense that it limns sensual or carnal reaction. Discretion reigns. The book seems out of the 18th century, like Mozart or the Philosophes, in that there's little talk of menus or of birds & bees, much less of romance or raw lust; and, despite the author's most frequent residence in the South of France, his subject is urban. Mentions of nice weather are rare, succinct, never descriptive, while mentions of work, friendship, and social life (the index contains close to two thousand names, half of them "dear friends") are the core of Cocteau's concern. Already in 1932 on the first page of *Essai de critique indirecte* he had noted, *Je me réserve de vivre et de faire l'amitié (plus difficile à faire que l'amour) . . ."* The mood is warm, sincere, tactful, thoroughly unbitchy even when directed toward François Mauriac whose mean and nagging assessment of Cocteau is a thorny refrain throughout these pages. *("Pauvre Mauriac. A sa mort il aura tout eu, sauf tout."* "Poor Mauriac. At his death he will have had it all, except it.")

Cocteau's homosexuality is often mentioned by others, and not rarely with miscomprehension, as by his biographers Steegmuller or Brown, or with a sneer, as by such "friends" as Igor Stravinsky or Coco Chanel, but it may surprise readers that it is never mentioned by himself. Whatever his public odor as a citizen, it was never abetted—as was Gide's or Jean Genet's—by his own writings or movies, and whatever his private leanings as an author, his diary is not a confessional. So his motive for caution, for posthumous publication, seems unclear. "The Gidean method consists of pretending to say all in order to hide all; a diary exists so that its writer can enter into it without reserve anything that goes through his head." So writes Cocteau in *Le Passé défini*, without reserve, but not divulging much either. Still, a diary is the sole literary form *sans* form—the one literary genre without guidelines. If as I claimed earlier, a diary is a book before it becomes a book, to some extent all art is a diary in that it reflects its maker's hidden nature despite itself. (A symphony is a diary in a code so abstruse that even its composer cannot decipher it. Unlike painters or writers, composers are seldom jailed for subversion.)

Cocteau all through this book seems anxious to be thought a Thinker. He did indeed have an original, active and fabulous mind, but a Thinker he was not—not in the sense of being (like for example Auden—is there any other among poets?) an intellectual, an analyst. His long speculations on Time, on Distance, or on other such scientific matters as the absolute reality of flying saucers, can be savored without embarrassment only if savored as fantasy, just as Freud today can no longer be read except as poetry. On the other hand, Cocteau's flair for the character sketch (of Picasso and his family, of Chaplin and his, or of the temperamental comparison between Spain and France) is as canny in words as on the drawing board. No less spirited is the description, unself-pitying, of his own ill health. How, during seizures of violent illness, he is able to *write* about them, as well as to write twenty letters a day and then to write about writing the letters, can be explained only by an indefatigable craving not to be forgotten. Glory, not power, guided him. Which explains the absence of malice, even when faced with huge disappointments, in all those longing to be loved.

When people ask me, "What was Cocteau like?," I'm always inclined to forget that I was only with him six or eight times during the thirteen years of our acquaintance. True, we corresponded regularly during those years; he designed covers for my music; I composed a ballet with Jean Marais in 1952 and thus was in steady contact with the poet by proxy. True again, to reside in France as I did during the 1950s when Cocteau was in daily evidence—pronouncing from the screen, over the air, and from bookstore *vitrines* —was to be, even for the peasants of Oléron, in his inescapable presence. And true, Cocteau had a habit of collective *tutoiement* so that in a room packed with people each soul felt singled out. To meet him once was to know him. His need to be liked made him give all, disseminating himself indiscriminately throughout the globe. Yet while you were with him you were seemingly the sole beneficiary of his charitable flood of fire. I've known few people in my life with such infectious charm; it may be affectation or opportunism, but it can't be faked.

Jean Cocteau's diary mirrors this personality so contagiously that twenty-two years after his death he, like Whitman, risks "springing from the pages into your arms." But does culture ever cross borders intact? Not even music is a universal language. Cocteau, who despite his contention (contradicting Frost's "poetry is that which can't be translated") that *"La langue d'un poète ne pouvant qu'être traduite,"* never, except for his films, quite "took" in the United States. Neither did Gide, until his diaries were translated here in the late forties. As with Gide—indeed, as with every French nonfiction writer—ninety-nine percent of Cocteau's literary and social references are French (with occasional exceptions like Shakespeare, Hemingway, Gershwin, and Garbo), yet Gide's dramatis personae has come to be familiar to two generations of international readers.

Will Cocteau's diaries, now that they are in English, help to make his entire catalogue a success over here? I do and don't hope so. Because I love the work of this wildly controlled, snobbish, adorable, frightening, irritating, unusual, haunting, and generous genius I want to share it with America. And because I love his work, I want to keep it to myself.

Courageous Coward
1982

On a cool but humid evening twenty-one springs ago I met Noel Coward in Paris's Club Elysée and we spent the rest of the night together. Next morning he listened carefully to my music, which, unaccountably, he termed "forbidding," although he hoped I'd make an opera from one of his plays. That afternoon he flew back to London, and I never saw him again. Yet twelve years later when I read of his death I felt deprived of a friend; and at the small memorial service to which, for some reason, I received a golden invitation, I shed the gentle tears of loss, although in that show-biz milieu I was a fish out of water. Now I have just read Noel Coward's diary which I began with the double interest of one who knew the man (would he mention me?), and one who would review his words (should I mention "us"?). It is a very long book. But I learned less about Noel Coward in these nearly seven hundred pages than during that brief encounter in 1961.

I recall a man with style, vulnerability, vast culture and, above all, with a talent for listening which only the securely famous— they are few—seem to afford. And I recall a man involved with the passion and risks of romantic love. His journals portray a person not so much of style as of manner, with few self-doubts, knowing all the answers yet closed to the crafts that do not touch him—that is, to the darker sides of painting and music. Although that person is clearly gifted in the art of friendship, especially if the friends are rich and royal and celebrated, he would seem to have no private life, no ardent attachments, no sex. In one trembling transient entry

102

he nearly succumbs to "that old black magic," but the tune is never taken up again. Indeed, his book would be just what Coward detractors might assume—brittle, sarcastic, straining for wit, a self-parody—were it not for the charm it exudes. Charm is the identifying escape hatch and valuable it is, for charm, even less than fame, cannot be bought. Charm, the ability to ingratiate without cloying, can be sold, however, and it was Noel Coward's chief barter.

No small part of his charm lies in his naiveté, though this greatest of all sophisticates might be stunned to hear it said. I don't mean merely that his diary shows him to be as starstruck as you and I, although stars are his sole society and he is himself one. Rather, it is his cocksureness in matters he knows little of. It is usual for us to admire jacks-of-all-trades in all their trades save the one we ourself practice. Among musicians I am surely not alone to wince when Noel Coward writes, "The music is pouring out and I can scarcely go to the piano without a melody creeping from my fingers, usually in keys that I am not used to and can't play in." Yet his score for *Bittersweet* is on a par with Gershwin who is on a par with Schubert. The paradox is that, on a ground where angels fear to tread, Noel Coward a half-century ago composed a sheaf of torch songs and waltzes more cherished than those of many a modern master of technique. I'll never forget Noel stating proudly that he, like Irving Berlin, was musically unlettered, or at least unnoted, "despite my magic tunes which now form part of the collective unconscious. I just play them into a dictaphone and they're taken down in shorthand by a lackey." Then: "Lenny Bernstein's one of my greatest fans, but must I take seriously his 'serious' music?"

About serious classical music, current and of yore, Noel Coward comments with forthright innocence, as though deaf to the diatonic logic of our most inspired composers. A few samples: "Britten's music is dull, without melody. It has the same effect on me as a Braque painting." "I hate Mozart and I loathed the libretto [Così fan tutte]." "I have taken to cooking and listening to Wagner, both of which frighten me to death." "[Menotti] doesn't seem capable of writing a true melodic line. It's all bits and pieces." "Madame von Karajan had kindly invited me to her box. [The Beethoven] was quite lovely at moments . . . until the choral part of the Ninth, when I got the giggles." From the mouths of babes: The giggles, in my opinion, are the proper response to this most overrated of masterpieces. Yet the response to the lyricism of the young German composer, Hans Werner Henze, is perhaps not quite thought-through: " . . . *Ondine* at Covent Garden in which Margot was superb, Freddie Ashton's choreography brilliant and the music tuneless and hideous." Of my music (for yes, he mentions me) Coward quaintly declares he spent "an evening with Ned Rorem, avant-garde American composer, amiable but a trifle too 'advanced' for me," when even the most reactionary critics have pegged me as backward.

Of serious musical performers he speaks even more strangely. Isaac Stern (identified in a footnote as "distinguished Russian violinist") is described as "brilliant, but looked dreadfully funny." "Dear Artur Rubinstein *[sic]* . . . played the Schumann Concerto with exquisite taste but he is, poor darling, looking a bit old." "I drove with the Queen Mother and we sat together in the first row. Rostropovich really was marvelous, thank God, otherwise there would have been grave danger of the giggles." He did admire Maria Callas as "one of the few really great artists that I have ever seen"—seen, not heard. The only other inclusions in this category are Laurence Olivier, and the author of *African Genesis*, Robert Ardrey, "the most extraordinary brain I have ever encountered." His crush on Joan Sutherland was colored by "how thrilling to hear that glorious voice singing my music," while the Beatles in 1965 were simply "bad-mannered little shits [about whom] it is still impossible to judge from their public performance whether they have talent or not."

If Coward's musical appraisals are the conventional ones of the ignorant literati, they reflect but a minor part of his concerns. But since they reflect on my major concerns I stress them, because nobody else will. As a diarist Noel Coward has every right, literary and moral, to whatever passes his fancy, even to enumerating his opinions on music and eliminating his lusts.

If the British prefer autobiography, some of them—Virginia Woolf, Harold Nicholson—have kept journals, presumably for their eyes alone. However, *The Noel Coward Diaries*, as they are posthumously named, were clearly penned for other eyes. His final written words in 1969: "I perceive now, 31 December, that there has been no entry since 7 September. With my usual watchful eye on posterity, I can only suggest to any wretched biographer that he gets my daily engagement book and from that fills in anything he can find and good luck to him, poor bugger." The poor bugger is Graham Payn, actor and longtime intimate of Coward, aided by Sheridan Morley, author of *A Talent to Amuse*. They might well have heeded an earlier entry: "It is a truly wonderful gift, my natural and trained gift for dialogue . . . Other people far less clever than I can often be dead right when I am wrong . . . I will never again embark on so much as a review sketch that is not carefully and meticulously constructed beforehand." Could the writer of those phrases have wished his book to appear as it stands? Except for about a hundred central pages Coward's diary is little more than a "daily engagement book." He drops names like old Rockefeller flung dimes to the rabble, meager tokens, promises of nothing. On V.E. Day: "Lunched at the Savoy with Lorn and we rested our poor feet. My Victory article appeared in the *Daily Mail* together with the King's speech and the Prime Minister's. Visited Mum. Went to Juliet [Duff]'s to have a drink and to see Georges Auric. Stayed on to dinner with Juliet and Desmond MacCarthy and took them both to see the Stage Door Canteen. Made a brief appearance and got a terrific ovation." Seventeen years later: "I dined one night with Ginette and George Axelrod. The next night with Dick Quine, Kim Novak, Bill [Holden], George [Axelrod], and Capucine, who is a dear. The third night by myself. Heaven. And the last night with George Cukor." The identities of—though not the anecdotes about—these people, and scores of others, are found in the endless footnotes which adorn every page. Jerky reading. What it adds up to can seem silly, though in deference to the author's value, one might call it profoundly shallow. Anyway, silliness is germane to the diary-as-genre; the self-congratulatory musings of an Anaïs Nin are no less cloying in their solemnity than Noel Coward's in their glee.

A diary is the only literary form without rules; like a life, a diary can be said to take shape only when it is ended—that is, when it has died. This one spans but half a life, having been started only in 1941 (Coward was born in 1899) and continuing until 1969, three years before he died of a heart attack in his Jamaican villa. The reader might bear in mind that most of the work Coward is remembered for was completed long before this diary began.

Those hundred central pages are compelling as backstage scenes composed by an authority of timing. Because he is as famous as he thinks he is, and because when he gets going about some of his famous friends (he has no others), Coward's thumbnail portraits are definitive. If as a feminist he's old-fashioned (on Vivien Leigh: "Enchanting women can certainly wreak havoc when they put their silly minds to it"), he's acute on the Lunts ("Lynn is mentally slow with flashes of brilliant swiftness; Alfred quick as a knife with flashes of dreadful obtuseness. They are deeply concerned with only three things—themselves, the theater—insofar as it concerns themselves—and food, good, hot food"), on sixtyish Clifton Webb's puerile mourning of his mother ("There is no future in the past"), on cities like Las Vegas which he loved or the Actors Studio which he loathed, or, indeed, on the demands of his immediate geography ("It is no use imagining I can escape the consequences of my own fame and that I am bound to be set on and exploited by people wherever I go"). As a pacifist I am personally nervous about his insights on the meaninglessness of war when they are balanced by blind patriotism—royalist to the core—and defenses of capital punishment "as a deterrent." But it's fun to hear about Marlene and Gertrude and Larry and Tallulah and Diana and Princess Margaret and Tony and Bob Hope and the Queen herself and all from the horse's mouth, and how they do adore him, and how awfully hard he works, yet travels incessantly despite his several lavish homes and his kidney stone, but his Big Opinions are generally bromides even on atomic energy or on the sickness of pals, although the tale of his mum's agony and death rings true in its terse excruciation. The rapports he claims to value most, however, are those, not with, say, the difficult Claudette Colbert, but with the wise Rebecca West who did join him at a Swiss clinic where they each had the hormonal youth treatment by being injected with the liquefied organs of an unborn calf, or something of the sort.

Who is this self-confident creature with the inscrutable mien of an oriental sage in white tie and tails, that we should devour his daily thoughts? Comparisons are fragrant.

In 1946 he makes his sole entry on Jean Cocteau: "we went to *La Belle et la Bête*, which I rechristened *La Belle et la Bêtise* on account of it being long, dull and badly constructed, but *d'un beauté [sic] formidable* every now and then. I wish creative artists like Jean did not consider it necessary to be 'precious', 'amusing' and 'different.' "

Well, it takes one to know one. Probably Jean Cocteau and Noel Coward were not much interested in each other—any more than the French and English ever are—each being so quintessentially of his country. Yet they are more comparable than any two artists of different nationality in our century, and no other *bricoleur*, not even da Vinci, has ever remotely resembled them. In an age of specialists they were general practitioners excelling in every area: poetry and playwrighting, essays and novels, moviemaking and movie acting, librettos and cabaret lyrics, oil painting and set designing. If Coward in being a composer—and a real one—went Cocteau one better, the latter was the more astute prosifier *about* music. Both were aphorists, and both made their personal selves—their very bodies—into public exhibits. Coward was Cocteau's junior by exactly ten years. Both died at 73 and the deaths in each case followed shortly after the highest national homage: for Cocteau an entrance into the Académie Française, for Coward a knighthood.

Diaghilev's notorious *Étonne-moi* which so shaped the future of Jean Cocteau could have been paralleled by an *Amuse-moi* to Noel Coward. One might reasonably argue that Cocteau represents Coward's deeper nature; that *Orphée* and *Blithe Spirit* are the somber and bright faces of the same medal; that *Les Parents terribles* and *Private Lives* are but the sad and happy versions of the same boulevard comedy; that their many solos for prima donnas were, so to speak, identical twins of opposite sex; and that, in short, Noel was the optimist's Jean. Both wore their charm as armor against a press which, though benign in their dazzling childhoods, consistently massacred their middle life, relaxing only for their triumphant comebacks in the shadow of death. If Noel lacked the imagination of Jean, and even the basic chic (Noel backward—*Léon*—is French slang for "hick"), neither was he ever the anxious sycophant that Jean could sometimes be. Cocteau's movies aimed higher and endured longer, while Coward's plays seem to have more staying power.

Cocteau's influential antecedents were on the whole inferior to him, and he worshipped them. (Montesquiou and Rostand *fils*, for example, were precious hacks.) Coward, on the other hand, descends from the great Oscar Wilde through Somerset Maugham. But Wilde for Coward "was one of the silliest, most conceited and unattractive characters that ever existed," while Maugham was alternately pathetic, entrancing, contemptible. If Maugham as a serious novelist embodied, in his own words, the best of the second-rate, Coward as a giddy dramatist was the best of the first-rate. Coward himself claims the nineteenth-century playwright Clyde Fitch, of all people, as predecessor. "His writing is undoubtedly trivial," Coward tells us, "and his view of life largely circumscribed by the times in which he lived, but they are full of entertainment value, well made and every now and then witty . . . Of course he was decried by the critics; anyone so immediately successful would be. There is a certain analogy between him and me, I think, except that my scope is wider and I think and hope that I have a little more depth, even in my comedies. In those days, of course, the theater was still a place of entertainment and not a platform for propaganda and orgies of racial self-pity." Yes, Coward was revolted by all the angry young men; yes, he was elitist ("I have no real rapport with the 'workers,'" he noted in 1942, "in fact I actively detest them *en masse*"); and yes, he was obsessed and devastated by reviewers who, despite his continued popular success, treated him as an anachronism after the war. "It is foolish for a writer constantly to decry the critics," he observed in 1964 for the thousandth time; "it is also foolish for the critics so constantly to decry anyone who writes as well as I do."

If I am ambivalent about him, seemingly unable to react except through my own piecemeal diarylike paragraphs, it's that I am ambivalent about myself. During my Chicago infancy Noel Coward was an idol, but he was not *my* idol; I never felt his spell as I did the vastly grander Cocteau's, and was repelled as much as attracted by his oeuvre. Like Auden who in 1926 was busy writing "unreal" plays and put down Noel Coward's realistic drama by asking, "Is it like this / In Death's other kingdom?," I seemed vaguely trapped in my generation, gazing at the indolent wit of the irretrievable past while simultaneously focusing only dimly on the dutiful violence ahead. I craved both luxury and sparsity in art, and Noel was only luxury. No ambivalence about Coward himself, though. Unlike the greatest artists, who are a sum of contradictions, sacred and profane, he was just what he seemed—his life and his art were one.

Uneasy as I was made by the superficiality of his book, I, who am morbidity incarnate and who also keep a diary, was nonetheless elated by his ability ever to rise above adversity, mainly by sheer conceit. Courageous Coward! (Some readers act annoyed at this conceit, as though the childlike honesty of it were not endemic to every creator, good and bad.) He had a lot of fun being Noel Coward, and I'm envious. When I asked him, on that evening so many years ago, what he thought the ideal life was, he answered simply, "Mine."

Revisiting Orton
1987

Twenty summers ago the young English playwright Joe Orton was violently slain by his closest friend, who then committed suicide. Because his career, though brief, was already studded with many an odd and glittering hit, news of Orton's death in London was greeted (as Mann said of *Death in Venice* fifty years earlier) "by a shocked and respectful world." Even *Time* magazine unsmirkingly offered a praiseworthy statement on the gifts of the thirty-four-year-old writer, and, without recourse to the noun "homosexual," mentioned "the lover" with whom he had shared a single-room flat for sixteen years. Suddenly Joe Orton made a living out of dying—uncalculated, of course, like Sylvia Plath's death which turned her into a "name" overnight and forever colored our reading of her poems. Orton's work too is retroactively shaded by his premature end; but while Plath's suicide resulted from long melancholy, Orton's murder occurred in a period of elation.

The sixties were an era of novel visibility for dramatists in the English-speaking world. If heretofore actors' names sold tickets, now in America the creators' names were taking precedence over their re-creators. Already since the close of the war Inge and Miller and especially Tennessee Williams were being touted above their interpreters. That was as it should be: the horse before the cart. By 1963 the epoch of playwright-as-star reached a peak. Edward Albee's name was (and remains) better-known than the names of his casts, or indeed than his very plays. Albee dethroned Williams as popular idol, but was himself dethroned a few years later by the

Absurdists. Likewise in Britain, big shots such as Osborne and the Angry Young Men, whose realism had already displaced Noel Coward's and Terence Rattigan's post-Sheridian suavity, were themselves being displaced by a local brand of absurdism in the macabre comedy of Pinter and Stoppard. The tone of their comedy was in turn borrowed from France where Beckett and Ionesco (neither of them French, incidentally) had been active since 1950. Their subject was hopelessness in a malignant world, their texture unsentimental and cartoonlike. The blend was a horrific wryness as befit, one may suppose, the unprecedented mood of our newly bomb-conscious globe.

Onto this stage of competitive foment entered Joe Orton in 1964. Born in 1933 to a working-class Leicester family, Orton was a so-so student who quit school at sixteen. Two years later he enrolled at London's Royal Academy of Dramatic Arts, where he met Kenneth Halliwell, several years his senior, who would become his roommate and inseparable companion for the rest of his life. The two collaborated on unpublished novels and unproduced plays. Halliwell, less aggressive and affable than Orton although more educated and literary, seemed to have come up with the structure, even the ideas, for these ventures, while Orton supplied the guts, the force, the flowing sap. In later years when Orton was "making it" alone, the older friend continued to furnish notions, titles, and polish—an assistance never hinted at in interviews as Orton grew more in demand. Meanwhile, in 1962 both were arrested for stealing and "willfully" damaging an array of library books, by replacing hundreds of plates in art books with suggestive images and written commentary. They were sent to separate jails for six months, an experience which embittered Halliwell but which Orton found firming and fruitful. In the next four years several pieces were sold to British Television. Then *Entertaining Mr. Sloane* and *Loot* were composed and mounted, both with decent runs (the former also on Broadway), while two major awards were won for Best Play. Joe Orton became a public figure.

His was a new voice, vital and sparkling. He wrote, yes, of despair, like everyone else, but despair turned upside down, high camp in the guise of low camp, with most of the (male) characters polymorphous perverse and emoting comprehensively in a working-class lingo that was very very funny and very very sad. Homo-

111   *NED ROREM*

sexuality—if you wish to call it that—was there for the taking, sans Tennessee's coyness or Albee's ambiguity, but quite unapologetic, quite natural, and quite crazy, like everything else. Joe Orton knew that the slight difference between Comedy and Tragedy lay solely in treatment of theme, and that the virtue of goodness lay solely in the eye of the beholder. Indeed, he planned for his collective oeuvre to use the famous epigraph of Juvenal, "Who'll guard the guardians?" (What a farce he might have drawn from our Poindexter and North!)

In his final year Orton wrote a screenplay for the Beatles (never filmed), two more stage plays, including *What the Butler Saw,* began a diary, took various trips to Tangier (which seems to have been as far as he ever got from home), then died, in full glory. Soon after his death two of the plays were filmed, and he excited another flurry of curiosity in the United States. Then the 1970s arrived. Time passed. New trends loomed, but the surge of international energy abated. Orton seemed long ago. The stage today has again grown devitalized, or so it seems to me, who seldom see plays anymore and have lost track of all my old friends from the theater. How, I wonder, does Joe Orton hold up?

In preparation for this review of a pair of just-published books, *The Orton Diaries* and an early novel named *Head to Toe*—books whose initial cachet rests in their having been penned by a once-leading dramatist—I reread Orton's seven plays. They hold up. They date, of course (all art dates, beginning with *Oedipus Rex,* from the moment it leaves its author's hand), but they date well. The plays *play;* what's more, they play themselves. Even with mediocre actors (like a Mozart sonata beneath the fingers of a hack) they do not derail, the logic and velocity seeming intrinsically taken care of. They're hard to sabotage. Without actors they can be read enjoyably in an armchair. They are not fantasies, they mean what they say, and what they say is hilarious, because the unembellished icy horrors of our world, when literally reinterpreted on the boards, *are* hilarious. The plays are also deft and professional.

Less deft and professional, even a dab amateurish (being sheer imagination unfettered, and also ungrammatical), is the posthumous *Head to Toe,* a Candide-style chronicle from 1961. A nonhero called Gombold suddenly finds himself in a forest, actually the scalp of a hundred-mile-high giant, and during eleven chapters he strays from one nightmarish adventure to another toward the toes, remounts the other leg, and ultimately, after a dumb and devastating war between the Right and Left Buttocks, disappears forever into the rectum of the ogre who now lies dead and rotting. If the immediate ambiance sifts Lewis Carroll with Swift and William Burroughs, the enveloping allegory—that we are all inescapably part of a greater whole, and that whole is Indifferent Wickedness—is surely Kafkian, if you're willing to accept Kafka's self-definition. (According to Max Brod, Kafka was a self-proclaimed humorist, "the Offenbach of fiction," who giggled wildly at his own black comedies, while simultaneously maintaining a classical distance from them.) The phantasmagoria lacks the warm honing of the plays, but at least there's a stunning objectivity; not for Orton the self-indulgent pronoun "I" which in first novels by Americans (he loathed Americans) so often leads us through a Sensitive Boyhood. Though lit with original fancy, the tale is too cold for comfort and cannot sustain itself. In its form lies its defeat.

In the formlessness of *The Orton Diaries*, on the other hand, lies its power. Open-ended though all journals by definition are, in this case the reader continually knows what the writer ignores—that the book will be cut short by its author's literal death. Our fore-knowledge casts an extraliterary thrill over every paragraph of this otherwise lighthearted notebook wherein Joe Orton inscribed his thoughts each day of his last eight months. I was fascinated by the diary, not least because Orton's rough and tumble stance is as far as you can get (oh, maybe Anne Frank is farther) from my own effete bid for style.

The publication's endpapers are examples of the clever collages from the "defaced" library books for which Orton was jailed. The central pages are a jumble of photographs of the author (a good-natured blue-collar masculine baby of a breed—frequent in London, rare in New York—which must reach back to the Celts: big nose, flat cheeks, long chin, lips both thin and generous, eyes both wise and innocent), of his showbiz colleagues, and of male adolescents on the Tangier beach. The daily concerns are: the shifting routine of creative work; ambition; impresarios and rehearsals; daily spats with Halliwell, who as Orton grew more self-sufficient turned more ingrown and mean; and cruising, cruising. Little gossip about the famous, little rumination on esthetics, nothing on politics or classical music, or on painting or literature other than the theater. Despite the narrow palette, intelligence radiates and the pages tremble. He could charm the birds from the trees; certainly he beguiled *me* from beyond his tomb. Precisely this personal enchantment, and the ability to transfer the enchantment to the stage and thence to an audience (an audience that embraced him in private as in public), only inflamed Kenneth Halliwell's bitterness. Orton's least quotidian routine was theatrical. Even his diary is "dialogue," especially the final, totally erotic entries from North Africa with the queeny sex-talk reportage, brittle and fine-tuned.

The nonchalance with which Orton details his sexuality is unique, and not just for the sixties. Has any other diarist, gay or straight—Casanova? Paul Goodman?—discussed cures for horniness with the same airiness as a recipe for pancakes? Orton felt homosexuality (he doesn't use the word) to be as natural as any outlet and doesn't belabor the point. And yes, this book *was* meant for outside eyes: the title he planned was *Diary of a Somebody* and the tonality throughout, even in shopping lists, echoes the clarity of a quiz kid with perfect pitch. "It's extraordinary," writes he, with his usual contempt for decorum, "how, as people grow older and they have less to hide by telling the truth, they grow more discreet, not less . . . The whole trouble with Western Society these days is the lack of anything worth concealing."

The very nonchalance, however, viewed from our AIDS-conscious vantage, is scary. Orton's visits to the public toilets of London are almost daily and most unselective ("The little pissoir under the bridge had become a scene of frenzied saturnalia [while] no more than two feet away the citizens of Holloway moved about their ordinary business"), while his liaisons in Tangier are more than daily, equally unselective, and garnished with alarming doses of Valium and hash. The author makes little distinction between his various boys named Mohamet beyond identifying them with nicknames; there is no interest in what makes them tick, or, for that matter, what the mysterious African continent may offer an Englishman beyond easy sex. *The Tatler* has quipped, in a review of this book, that if Joe Orton were alive today he'd be dead of AIDS. Well, today he would be fifty-four and possibly chastened.

Still, the diary contains annunciatory entries that now look too good to be true, as though some canny editor had inserted them with a fatal sense of symmetry. "[Kenneth and I] sat talking of how happy we both felt," he confides on May 25, 1967, "and of how it surely couldn't last. We'd have to pay for it. To be young, good-looking, healthy, famous, comparatively rich *and* happy is surely going against nature." Two weeks later: "I got back at 2:30. Very exhausting day. Took two of Kenneth's secret 'suicide pills', Nembutal. Fell into a deep sleep." July 14: "Took a walk. Nobody around to pick up. Only a lot of disgusting old men. I shall be a disgusting old man myself one day, I thought. Only I have high hopes of dying in my prime." July 30: "He showed me his cock. I let him feel mine. 'Oo!' he gasped, not noticing the sinister sore that had developed on the end over the last week or so." On August 9 Halliwell smashed Orton's cranium with nine hammer blows, then killed himself with twenty-two Nembutals.

Orton's will was made out to Halliwell, who obviously couldn't collect. The money thus went to Orton's father, whom the playwright had ridiculed in his plays. Years earlier Orton wrote: "All classes are criminal today. We live in an age of equality."

The material mentioned here represents Orton's entire output: a handful of plays, the short novel and diary, a few TV and movie scripts. The Collected Works can be perused in a couple of evenings. Is Orton worth it? Is he in fact famous anymore? Do his rambling diary and ghastly death detract from what's more urgent? What is more urgent? We are what we eat. We are what we die. John Lahr, who as son of America's greatest comic knows a thing or two about the tragic side of comedy (or, put more neatly, the comic side of tragedy), has come to be the young author's premier chronicler and editor, and he gives Orton high marks for "his ability to corrupt an audience with pleasure." So do I.

To call Orton one of our first-rate minor playwrights is not to condescend, since the twentieth century has no others, with the possible exception of Genet (or maybe the humorless O'Neill who, if only by dint of his aspirations, might be termed a second-rate major playwright). Our playwrights are minor because of their scope. Those who, like Tennesee Williams, bring tears to our eyes through their "character development" haven't much to say about the ways of the world, while those who, like Beckett, caustically portray an evil planet do so through their Everyman types who do not move us. Joe Orton falls in the second category, with the bonus of wit.

Nothing is riskier than wit in art, and when it falls flat the discomfort is more withering than the embarrassment of failed drama. Is there wit in American theater? Not in Neil Simon certainly, nor yet in the cherished Marx Brothers who, true, are comics, but witless. Wit stems from irony, not situation. Orton stems from the white irony of Wilde no less than from the black irony of Ionesco, and presages the gay irony of Ludlam. Yet except for Charles Ludlam, there is no theater that I like—that I *believe* in— today except Orton's. How I would love to have had an opera libretto from him. For me to say that is to say all.

Britten Recalled

1991

Letters," said Madame de Sévigné, who wrote the best ones of her day, "are the wings of friendship." "Keep a diary," said Mae West, whose career was based on innuendo, "and someday it'll keep you." These truths are confirmed in the gigantic new *Selected Letters and Diaries of Benjamin Britten*, amassed under the overall title of *Letters from a Life* by the late musician's keepers-of-the-flame, Donald Mitchell and Philip Reed, with the scrupulosity of Chinese scribes annotating the least gesture of their emperor. Wonderful idea. Nothing is inconsequential in the realm of genius; yet the concept of serious music, not to mention epistolary craft, is fading with the millennium as the fax and the video zoom over our globe.

Benjamin Britten, England's first great composer since the death of Purcell in 1695, and his longtime companion, tenor Peter Pears, represent the apex of high art—creative and interpretive, respectively—in our century. They are also national stars, so much so that a generation ago (like Jean Cocteau and Jean Marais in Paris) they were the brunt of knowing quips in working-class music halls. Times have changed. Today a living "classical" composer is neither hailed for his art nor mocked for his love life, because in the ken of even the intelligentsia he simply doesn't exist. "Good" music is no longer required in schools.

In earlier decades creative artists, at least in Europe, were their country's pride. The average Frenchman may never have actually read Verlaine or Balzac, heard Berlioz or Debussy, but he was still proud to have streets named after them. Benjamin Britten, born in

1913, was raised in such a period—thoughtful music was taken seriously, and letter-writing was a fixed mode of communication. His specialized schooling started soon and was first-rate (his mentors were not academics but successful practitioners), and with it began his correspondence and journals which were as prolific and continual as his composer's quill. What's more, he kept everything—first drafts and fair copies of the music, carbons and replies of the letters, and all his date-books. The documenting of this material is described by Donald Mitchell, the composer's Boswell and coordinator of the archives, in the probing preface to this two-volume book. Weighing in at ten pounds, 1403 pages, and 125 dollars, it nevertheless covers but the first half of the composer's life, up to and including the launching in 1945 of *Peter Grimes*, the second of Britten's sixteen operas, and his masterpiece.

If Peter Pears, who would become the premier performer (again like Cocteau's Marais) for the bulk of male roles created by Britten, including *Grimes*—if Pears was the second, and final, "darling" of Britten's life, the first was his mother, whose devastating death occurred only weeks before the two men met in 1937. She is the adored recipient of most of his early missiles. "My Darling Mums and Daddy—I have had a most lovely time . . . With love your loveing son BENJAMIN xxxxx." So starts and closes the opening letter when Ben was nine, establishing the juvenile tone, complete with misspelling, that resounds throughout the collection, even in business letters to strangers. He was forever verbose in his letters, but without flair, as though aware that, like Cellini with rubies and gold, since he was the world's subtlest setter of other people's words, he needn't therefore be a stylist in his own prose. His letters proffer affection, mild envy, intelligent enthusiasms for certain books and pieces (never for pictures or plays), a sense of professional savvy even as a teenager, but virtually no eroticism, and are ninety percent about music.

The diaries, in the same chatty tone, are an on-the-spot defense against memory's tendency to improve on things. (Primo Levi: "The further events fade into the past, the more the construction of convenient truth grows and is perfected.") We learn of Britten's depressions; of his perennially fragile health; of his unwavering veneration of Alban Berg who (to my surprise) seems to have influenced *Peter Grimes;* of his cooling interest in Richard Strauss, whose *Rosenkavalier* — especially the boisterous overture and the Trio—marked *Grimes* far more than did Berg. And we learn of the continual self-doubt ("My bloody opera stinks") shared by all great men.

His impulse for self-documentation, albeit without much gossip or lurid detail, was unquenchable, as distinct from his sometime collaborator, Wystan Auden, who thrived on gossip and was frank about country matters, but who destroyed personal documents, including the letters from Britten. Britten, however, kept Auden's letters. Here is an admonishment from the poet—so much more lucid an explicator than the musician—in 1942:

> Goodness and beauty are the result of a perfect balance between Order and Chaos, Bohemianism and Bourgeois Convention. Bohemian chaos alone ends in a mad jumble of beautiful scraps; Bourgeois convention alone ends in large unfeeling corpses. Every artist except the supreme masters has a bias one way or the other . . . For middle-class Englishmen like you and me, the danger is of course the second. Your attraction to thin-as-board juveniles, i.e., to the sexless and the innocent, is a symptom of this . . . You [will] probably always be surrounded by people who adore you, nurse you . . . but beware . . . If you are to develop to your full stature, you will have, I think, to suffer, and make others suffer, in ways that are totally strange to you at present.

Such un-Puritan generalizing could have been the basis for Britten's eventual distancing from Auden. Yet Britten was hardly beyond commitment. A letter to Pears (not included here) after nearly forty years of intimacy begins:

> My darling heart (perhaps an unfortunate phrase—but I can't use any other) I do feel I must write a squiggle which I couldn't say on the telephone without bursting into those silly tears—I do love you so terribly, not only glorious *you,* but your singing . . .

And Pears's reply:

> My dearest darling, No one has ever had a lovelier letter
> ... You say things which turn my heart over with love
> and pride, and I love you for every single word you
> write. But you know, Love is blind—and what your dear
> eyes do not see is that it is *you* who have given *me* every-
> thing ...

Despite a chronic circumspection, at the end of his life Britten
said to Donald Mitchell, "I want you to tell the truth about Peter
and me." Pears meanwhile, after Britten's death, had a *volte-face*.
"Is one really interested in the sex life of great musicians?" he
asked. The answer, of course, is yes. Mitchell then learned that
Pears was planning his own memoir; but when the singer died in
his turn, Mitchell, the executor presumably of both men, took it
upon himself to publish the present tomes.

Who will buy them? Britten is history now. Forty years ago, when
he was a celebrity, and when the interpretive artist was still peripheral to the creative artist, the book might have had some takers,
even at this price. (Today, when singer has become more crucial
than song, the letters, if there were any, of a Madonna or a Domingo
would far outsell those of a Sondheim or a Menotti, without whom
the performers are nonetheless nothing.) Yet forty years ago certain
of the contents would have been unprintable, and it is partly these
"contents" that are being ill-advisedly pushed in the book's pro-
motion. Both an advance brochure and the jacket copy of Volume
One quote scholar Philip Brett: "This is the composer who
turned his paranoia as homosexual and pacifist into the classic
20th-century opera, *Peter Grimes*." Isn't paranoia rather a strong
noun for a man who was, on the one hand, monogamously
tactful about his fully satisfied love life, and had on the other
hand, after years of courageous pondering, correctly concluded
that war is no alternative to peace? Maybe because I too am a
homosexual pacifist, I take these qualities as they come, finding
them neither giggly nor touristy when they arise (so rarely) in
these diaries and letters which are mainly preoccupied with one
man's work and its dissemination. Yet all the reviewers I've read

thus far come stealing back to the qualities, with various Freudian justifications.

"Britten's sister and boyhood friend agree in a startling revelation," whispers one Norman Lebrecht in the Los Angeles *Times*, "that Pears voice was identical to [Britten's] mother's." Just when we thought the Oedipus complex was dead!

Donal Henehan in the *New York Times* tells of the 1940s and Britten's "connections with Auden, Christopher Isherwood, Aaron Copland and other inhabitants of the trans-Atlantic homosexual and artistic world," as though there were a conscious consolidation of gay "inhabitants" at work. Were that the case, how explain Virgil Thomson's sniping from that period at a fellow "inhabitant," as quoted in a footnote, page 1011? As with Gershwin—whose *Porgy and Bess* with its 1935 all-black cast was more successful than Thomson's earlier all-black *Four Saints in Three Acts*—whom Thomson dismissed with "I do not like fake folklore nor gefiltefish orchestration," so with Britten. Thomson as critic prided himself, with some justice, on being America's sole explicator of Gallic culture, but grew jealous when another anglophone presumed to set French to music. Here he is in 1941 on the New York premier of Britten's *Les Illuminations:*

> The French declamation and vocal line are exaggerated without being always very expressive; their instrumental accompaniment is little more than a series of bromidic and facile "effects". I found the work pretentious, banal, and utterly disappointing, coming from so gifted a composer. Mr. Pears, who sang it, [had] neither correct French diction, nor a properly trained voice.

Britten's reaction in a letter was merely: "Peter sang Les Illuminations with really *rounds* of success the other day in Town Hall—and apart from that old stinker Virgil Thompson [*sic*] in the Tribune, had wonderful notices . . . "(Fact: The only three operas I can think of in which the curtain rises upon a chorus mending fishnets, are *Porgy and Bess, Four Saints in Three Acts,* and *Peter Grimes.)*

Another Britisher, Bayan Northcott, writes more wisely about the new book's revelations: "Yet while Britten's fixations on early adolescence or his aggressive pacifism may help to explain his choice of subject matter or the tensions behind the music, they cannot account for the quality of the music itself." He feels, too, that "while the everyday persona Britten presented to the world could be less than sympathetic, the true personality went wholly into the music. Britten himself suggests something of the sort in a letter of 1941 to his younger sister: "I can't live wildly *and* work.' "

But Paul Griffiths, London's chief music critic, reviewing the book at length in the *Times Literary Supplement*, filled most of his space with psychoanalytic speculation: "What he sought in a lover was, in part, a mother (some of the letters to Pears sound more childish than those he was writing at the age of nine)." "Britten himself reveals so little . . . he was very far from being a writer . . . lack of interest in verbal expression . . . The occasional letter by Pears comes as a beam of sunlight, his writing being so much more relaxed and competent." "Cautiousness about what was being revealed, left the music lamed."

On this last point Griffiths rashly propounds the origin for the so-called Creative Process. Can anyone know what is "revealed" in music? or if "cautiousness" figures in the revelation? or, if it does, can it indeed leave the music "lamed"? What is music's meaning? Do we compose about what we feel now, or about what we know about what we feel now? I can write happy music when sad, sad music when happy, and so can any professional.

Griffiths concludes with the idle game of might-have-been (idle, because it's always about another person—the one who "might have been"): "What might have happened if Britten had succeeded in his plan to study with Berg? [Or] if there had not been the interruption—perhaps the escape—of the period in America? But most tantalizing of all: . . . if he had maintained the alertness and curiosity . . . of his music of the 1930s?" Griffiths laments that were it not for "the lost possibility of a father figure," Britten might have "revolutionized British music in the 1940s and 1950s" the way Olivier Messiaen, "who also around 1940 was caught up in a forbidden love (in his case because he was a married Catholic)," changed the music of France. Farfetched analogy, and the speculation is vain, because Britten *did* revolutionize British music. (Not that greatness has anything to do with revolution, or even originality, so much as excellence and personal expressivity.) Britten, what's more, is the only composer ever to devote a whole opera to "forbidden love" when he musicalized Thomas Mann's *Death in Venice*.

Strauss could have done it, but didn't, at the time of the novella's appearance in 1912. The tale of an old man suffering from the love that dare not speak its name took fifty years' incubation before it could be retold in music; the matter seemed to need the British understatement, not because homosexuality was the bizarre vice of yore, but because in 1970, when the opera was composed, it finally seemed so normal.

Postscript for the record:

My only meeting with Benjamin Britten occurred in 1946 at Tanglewood for the US premier of *Peter Grimes*, which bowled us all over. Britten came to Aaron Copland's class and told us students how he'd put the opera together—not esthetically, which never means much, but technically. He was less verbal than tactile. For example, he explained, by crisscrossing his fingers in the air, how the solo flutes intermesh in their continual recurrences during the Trio in Act Two, the Trio that is so influenced by *Der Rosenkavalier*'s famous Trio. And he explained by stating, "I suppose it represents the borough at night," when Copland asked what the fifth orchestral Interlude "meant." We chatted for some minutes after class, then said good-bye and never met again.

Soon thereafter, however, I sent him a fan letter, and, since, at twenty-two I looked pretty good, enclosed a snapshot of myself stripped to the waist. He didn't reply. (Years later, when I mentioned this episode in a published book, readers began sending me unsolicited pictures. How people *do* see themselves!) But in the 1950s and until he died, we corresponded on "objective" matters, pacifism mainly, and also *Death in Venice* which I had reviewed at length in *The New Republic*, praising Peter Pears. Every letter I have from him speaks mostly of Pears. And every letter I have from Pears (who was three years the composer's senior, but outlived him by a decade, during which time we wrote) speaks mostly of Britten.

Pears I knew rather better, having spent evenings with him in Munich in 1954, and again in London and New York. As a tenor he was one of a kind, or I should say there's only one like him to every country—Hugues Cuenod in Switzerland, Pierre Bernac in France, perhaps Charles Bressler in America: tenors without an innate loveliness of voice, but with such literary métier, diction, and controlled sensitivity that they emit an illusion of beauty, even of perfection;

and, since nothing daunts them, have unlimited repertory. How Pears's reputation would have grown without the cachet of Britten is anyone's guess, though he did have something of an independent career. How Britten might have designed phrases for the human voice, or whether indeed he would have focused so much on the high pinched timbre, without the model of Pears is also anyone's guess.

But there—I too am playing the What-if game. Well, what if some young composer today wrote a new *Tristan and Isolde*, and based it on the life of these two admirable men?

PART TWO

Conversations

The Real John Simon

1985

A s our sometime Media Watch columnist, Tom Paine, reported in a news item in *Native* 112, "Just a few days after *Daily News* columnist Liz Smith reported that 30 people had overheard John Simon, theater critic for *New York* magazine, say, 'Homosexuals in the theater! My God, I can't wait until AIDS gets all of them!' at one play, Simon called another play 'faggot nonsense,' in his March 18 review of *The Octette Bridge Club.*" Simon's review resulted in numerous subscription cancellations and protest letters, including one signed by Peter G. Davis, David Denby, Rhoda Koenig, Kay Larson, John Leonard, and Tobi Tobias, Simon's critical colleagues at *New York*. In its April 1 issue, *New York* magazine printed several of these letters (the *Native* printed a larger, unedited selection, in our Carbon Copies section in issue 113), along with an apology from the Editor and a long response from Simon in which he apologized for giving offense but took back nothing he had said (instead, he attempted to justify his use of the term "faggot nonsense").

The transcript of the following exclusive interview was gone over by both Ned Rorem and John Simon and remains substantially unaltered, except for deletions approved by both.

—Thomas Steele, Associate Publisher,
the *New York Native*

The taping took place in my Manhattan living room on the hot afternoon of April 19. There were interruptions: John Simon had to make two calls; the photographer came with paraphernalia; we had lunch (croissants with Smuckers preserves, California strawberries, Gruyère, decaffeinated espresso); the phone rang incessantly; I had trouble manipulating the tape machine; Jim Holmes arrived exhausted from Nantucket with our dog Sonny who promptly lifted a leg against John's jacket. But my guest was magnanimous about all that, as he was about the cats' dander which brought on an alarming asthma seizure. Then there was a thunderstorm, and the room grew dark. Through all, we persevered to our seemingly mutual profit.

—NR

NED ROREM: *It occurred to me this morning that we first met already fifteen years ago, almost to the day, in an airplane terminal. We were both bound for the same roundtable in Columbia, South Carolina. In the years since then, we've had a staunch acquaintanceship. I certainly have admired your tenacity. You're among the best-informed critics in the world. You know what you're talking about, as well as being concerned with what you're talking about, and you're terse, lucid, and sometimes wise. You know about European, especially French, literature. Like me, you're a Francophile. Also quite exceptionally, as a literary person, you know and care about serious music, at least as an amateur.*

JOHN SIMON: As an amateur, yes.

ROREM: *Since I'm a musician, that makes a difference. We're roughly the same age (I'm older by a year). And last night, as prelude to our meeting today, we went to Larry Kramer's new play together. Although we usually meet only about every year and a half, suddenly we have a date two days in a row.*

SIMON: Yes.

ROREM: *We could have been construed as an unholy couple last evening. In fact, we're almost opposite sides of the same coin. Our tastes and modes of expression are quite similar except in one very crucial way: You are allegedly heterosexual and I am not. The main reason we're talking today, specifically for the* Native, *is the recent debacle which every* Native *reader is aware of. Let me state right off: I have never been a flag-waving gay activist; that's of a newer generation. Still, I was not amused, any more than many another reader, by your — what can only be construed as — homophobic remarks in* New York *magazine. Looking back through your books, one finds them peppered with similar remarks that seem gratuitously sneering; it came to a crux in this affair, in the vociferous reaction to your review of* The Octette Bridge Club. *What do you feel about the reaction?*

SIMON: Well, several things. First, that it is very unforgiving and fanatical. Second—and that's really the same thing put in a different way—that it's very humorless, in which sense, I think, it ties in with a general American problem, and that is that Americans are unsophisticated by and large, that they do not understand irony, that certain sophisticated forms of utterance—whether they be in a work of art, or in conversation, or in an article, or wherever—are always taken very, very literally. That, much to my surprise, some quite cultivated and civilized and literate homosexuals took great umbrage at these remarks—and I'll explain later, perhaps, why I find that surprising. What I did *not* find surprising was that illiterates of various kinds—and their letters, believe me, were as illiterate as they come, in terms of everything, grammar, syntax, pseudologic, which was totally incongruous, and so on—that such people carried on as they did, I *don't* find surprising, but perhaps even *that* was more than I would have surmised.

Another interesting aspect was that when I wrote a—what *I* consider an apology—that this was not taken as an apology; it was taken as an even worse outrage than the initial whatever-it-was. And I say, "whatever it was," because it's a confusing issue. I mean there are two things here: there is something I said essentially in private, except in a public place, but that to my mind still leaves it in the "private" category—

ROREM: *Let's stick to the* The Octette Bridge Club. *You referred in print to "faggot nonsense." You now mention, first of all, a lack of sophistication, a lack of irony, and a lack of humor in your readers. Do you feel that your remark is humorous, sophisticated, and ironic? Do you know what the origin of the word "faggot" is?*

NED ROREM

SIMON: I don't think anybody knows for sure.

ROREM: *The origin is the English for "kindling." In the era of witch burning, the only flame deemed "foul enough" to consume a witch was of homosexuals who were tied together like kindling and then set afire beneath the scaffold.*

SIMON: That I've never heard before.

ROREM: *There's a pretty good case for it.*

SIMON: Is that in etymological dictionaries?

ROREM: *Kenneth Pitchford gave me that, and I have no reason to disbelieve him. I'm saying that, for what it's worth, "faggot" is a word that you have no right to use or at least to use lightly. I feel, although I have humor, that in times of revolution humor does get thrown out the window, and it's your business to realize that. For example, the notion of camp in homosexuality (and camp is a strictly homosexual phenomenon, which is simply get-them-before-they-get-you) is now somewhat outmoded. Similarly, black people who use a word like "nigger" amongst themselves so as to inure themselves, do so less and less. For you to say "faggot" is to use an inside word which, in your mouth, becomes a pejorative term.*

Let me define that: A year or so ago, Eric Bentley tried unconvincingly to prove that "Wasp" was pejorative. Now, the term "Wasp" has no sting. Who is wounded by "Wasp," a word used generally by Wasps themselves? You showed me yesterday an article by William Buckley (who, if you have him for a friend, you don't need any enemies) taking your side, in this "faggot" business, using the freedom-of-speech defense. He gave examples, all specious, because they were not words that demolished a persecuted minority. "Usurer," for instance. A wounding or pejorative word is one used by a person in power to demean a person not in power, who has no weapon against it. Thus "nigger" is wounding because a black has no recourse against it. "Faggot" is a word that keeps faggots in their place. For you to assume that readers of any sort should find this humorous or ironic, especially in the light of your history of obsession with homosexuality, is asking too much.

SIMON: Well, "obsession" I will deny. "Frequent use" I will accept, but, I think, always relevant use. I was also amused by your initial remarks about my *alleged* heterosexuality—we will go into that, if you like, later—

ROREM: *Are you heterosexual?*

SIMON: As far as I know, I am.

ROREM: *Do you subscribe to the notion—I don't subscribe to it necessarily—that a person who is as—and I use again the word "obsessive," although you deny it—who is as concerned with homosexuality, and whose remarks about it are as often negative as they are positive, do you subscribe to the notion that that person might have subconscious yearning that, in his frustration—*

SIMON: It's certainly possible, but it is also totally possibly *not* so.

ROREM: *I've never found you, tête-à-tête, to be homophobic. Of course, I don't know what you say about me behind my back. But I've found you to be—to put it in proper perspective—in society, at least in my society, that you don't get alarmed about it. I've only seen you alarmed once in my life, and that was on the subject of Robert Wilson, where you really changed colors and had a fit.*

SIMON: Yes, but that had to do with what I think is very bad pseudo-art—posturing as art and being taken seriously by idiots, which perhaps doesn't matter except when the idiots become too numerous. Then it does begin to matter, and also when it's espoused by people who ought to know better, and *that*, to me, does matter. If I were to meet Wilson personally, which I never have—I understand he has no conversation whatsoever, and that might be a barrier—I wouldn't hold his bad art against him as a person. But I *am* interested in what is good and what is bad and what is in-between in works of art, and in works of non-art, that I have to review (I'd be much happier if I were reviewing more serious things but there are few of those), and one of the things that I feel can make something very bad indeed is dishonesty, dissembling, pseudo-this or pseudo-that, when handled by someone mediocre or worse; which is to say that, when, for example, a man of Tennessee Williams's talent, or even of the early Edward Albee's talent, writes, let us say, a play which is really about men, and he changes some of the characters into women—because such a writer is extremely talented (in some cases perhaps a genius), it doesn't really matter because the level at which he perceives humanity is so sophisticated, is so deep, is so poetic, that transpositions are possible and do make sense.

ROREM: *I'm terribly surprised to hear you invoke that old Stanley Kauffmann ploy.*

SIMON: If you want to ascribe it to him, fine; but I wouldn't call it a ploy. It's really what Stanley Edgar Hyman, with reference to Proust, dubbed "the Albertine strategy."

ROREM: *I happened to know Edward Albee quite well at the time he was writing his play, and I knew Tennessee Williams. It never occurred to me, not only as their friend, which is irrelevant, but as an aware reader, that male roles had been transposed into female roles, and they never said so. The reason that Blanche DuBois, or the female half of* Who's Afraid of Virginia Woolf?, *seems to communicate internationally to people of every sex is precisely that they depict true women, not men as women. The canard about homosexuals being trapped in men's bodies simply doesn't hold. It's a heterosexual delusion.*

SIMON: Yeah, I would agree with you there.

ROREM: *That you are privileged to know that Albee and Williams may, in private, be homosexuals should be unrelated to your reviews.*

SIMON: Well, it is and it isn't because, first of all, in the case of Williams, he admitted to many people (not, to be sure, at that time in public print, but to many people whom one knew) that Blanche DuBois was really himself, and that has now even become a critical commonplace.

ROREM: *And who isn't their leading characters? I mean, there was a lot of Stanley Kowalski in Tennessee also.*

SIMON: Oh, of course.

ROREM: *And we are what we eat, and we are what we produce. But to make an issue of that, is to, by extension, say that Flaubert was queer too, or Dostoievsky, or even Faulkner, or virtually anybody who writes about the opposite sex with perception.*

SIMON: But, as I say, it doesn't matter whether Blanche is Williams or whether Blanche is somebody else. What matters is what comes out, and that it is a poetic, artistic, believable, universal construct. And it works. However, in many cases, when some inferior writer attempts to do this, and tries, for whatever reason, to create a female role—either because he hasn't any real understanding of women, or because he doesn't *care* about women, or because he positively dislikes women, or he fears them, or whatever—very often, I think these female characters don't ring true. And sometimes this is true of heterosexual writers too, obviously, but it is *quite* often true of homosexual writers.

ROREM: *Once, in our presence, Virgil Thomson said, "Most works of art are lousy, and it's a critic's duty to say so, but he should say so with regret and not with relish." I agree with Virgil.*

SIMON: Well, I don't.

ROREM: *I'm not asking you to be compassionate (heaven forbid), I know that's beside the point. But I don't think name-calling is particularly humorous.*

SIMON: Well, name-calling certainly isn't—if that's what it is.

ROREM: *"Faggot nonsense" is name-calling.*

SIMON: In the context of that review, together with all I said, I would call it pinpointing, or defining. And now we're coming to what *I* think is the crux of the issue: I think there are odious heterosexuals, and there are, in my opinion, fine heterosexuals, and the same distinction exists for homosexuals.

ROREM: *But you have never said anything was "heterosexual nonsense."*

SIMON: Well, because that doesn't conjure up any image.

ROREM: *Because nobody sits around, ever, talking about heterosexuality. Homosexuality in itself is not an interesting subject, except insofar as it's a problem, and it's only made a problem by heterosexuals who make it one. Otherwise — live and let live — it's a small part of anybody's life.*

SIMON: I don't think so; I mean, maybe I'm a Freudian without knowing it, but I do think sex is a very important thing in human lives. And it is a principle that motivates us in many ways, regardless of what kind of sexuality it is. And I think there are differences, very substantial differences, in both sexual and nonsexual behavior, according to lots of things, according to nationality, according to social class, and also according to heterosexual or homosexual preference, thought, feeling, attitude, modus vivendi.

ROREM: *But even as you are repelled by the image of certain homosexual acts — because you've written as much, at least eleven years ago in* The New Leader—

SIMON: Well, we'll have to look at that more closely, but—

ROREM: *I have it here under my hand. In* The New Leader, *you referred, after due consideration and very circumspectly, to homosexuality as a sickness. In the new light of Larry Kramer's play, which I for one was very taken with in many ways — so strongly honed, yet economical; so didactic in hitting the nail on the head, yet so touching — the author spoke about the "sickness of homosexuality," which is imaginary to him at least, as opposed to the real sickness of AIDS. In the light of that play (and I think that I could see that you too were moved) —*

SIMON: As I was by *As Is.*

ROREM: —*the remark you're supposed to have made, according to Liz Smith, is not especially a tasteful one: "I wish all homosexuals in the theater would die of AIDS," or something of that sort.*

SIMON: That isn't quite it, but I don't know exactly what I said because when I'm really angry I don't know what I say. In a general way I do, but I can't remember the exact wording. It followed on *Octette Bridge Club,* which was the night before and which I thought was a distortion, a very serious distortion, of what women are about. I don't know the author, but he is described as the father of three children, so I imagine he is of the male sex. But you see, it's a very interesting thing about that play. I've talked to people who have seen the Louisville, Kentucky, production of it, and who say that it was very different, that, actually, what I observed they agreed with (and, incidentally, one of the principal people reporting on this is a homosexual actor)—they said that the Louisville production was very different, and it did not have this aura about it. The actor says the New York production, however, did, and that I was perfectly right to describe it so. He didn't say this to me; he said it to a colleague of mine. I felt that there was something very dishonest about this play, or production, or both. And then the next day, I saw Schnitzler's *Anatol,* which happens to be a favorite play of mine, and which I'd just seen a very good production of in Hartford, for which I even wrote the program notes. And this production was supposed to come to New York, but now it couldn't because of the Ellis Rabb version, and *this* I thought was a bastardization of the play in any number of ways, though what it mostly came down to was that it was camped up. It was camped up by people who didn't understand the play, didn't care to understand the play, didn't feel they needed to understand the play. And they turned it into something totally different, and it struck me—not so much as a homosexualization of a heterosexual play, although you could say that too—as a kind of vengeance on heterosexuality by people who have a grudge against it. I don't know whether that vengeance is conscious or unconscious, but that's how I perceive it. So having seen these two plays, one on top of the other (and both of them were so badly done, too, which of course adds fuel to the fire), I noticed Carrie Nye there, as I was leaving *Anatol,* and I said something to her, in real anger—it was not in wit, this has nothing to do with irony now—something I wouldn't have said an hour later, and something I certainly wouldn't have said in a lecture, or in a civilized discussion with civilized people, or in a review. It was something said in anger. I said, "Don't you sometimes wish that all the faggots in the theater"—or "fags" or "homosexuals," I don't know which, and it does make a difference, incidentally, to me, which of those three words I might have used—"would get AIDS and die, and we'd be rid of them, and we could go on from there." Now, obviously, this is not something I *believe*. It is not something I'm proud of having said; it's not something that in a rational moment I would have come anywhere close to saying, and it's not something I have written.

ROREM: *But you said it. In other words, your mind allowed you to say it. I don't want to belabor the matter; you've already said you're not proud of it.*

SIMON: No, in fact, I'm sorry, but the point is everybody says things in private, in moments of anger, moments of joking, moments of—

ROREM: *But you're a public figure. And, as such, you're going to be listened to and quoted, and you can't help but know that.*

SIMON: Well, yes and no. I feel that there was certainly a great deal of personal vendetta in Liz Smith's making a big thing out of that remark. I mean, I feel that a lot of people in the theater resent me, dislike me, fear me, execrate me for entirely different reasons, and they're using this now as a convenient club to hit me over the head with. In the case of Liz Smith, I have said on many occasions that I consider her vulgar, inaccurate, inept, unable to write; that I hate gossip columnists to begin with; but even on that level she's not very good. And she knows that. So she had a chance to exploit this and get back at me.

ROREM: *Has* The Normal Heart, *in any sense, heightened your perception of homosexuality?*

SIMON: Well, I don't know what you mean by "heightened."

ROREM: *Just take it for what it said, or "changed," or "enlight-ened" —*

SIMON: I have never considered that a homosexual is a worse person than a heterosexual, in any sense of the word. I may have considered—thought—two things: I do think homosexuality is a form of sickness, but I have no great love of normality; I have some respect for it, but I don't think that someone who might walk into this room, and who could prove, by fifty medical, sixty philosophi-cal, and thirty political authorities, signed on paper in triplicate, that he's normal, would therefore make a big impression on me. By the same token, the fact that someone is "sick" does not make him less interesting, less human, less worthy, less lovable, less entitled to all his civic rights, less *brilliant*, in many cases; I think the contri-butions of talented homosexuals to the arts is paramount, neces-sary, and magnificent.

ROREM: *Do you think that — when you say "sick" — do you think that aspects of yourself, corners of yourself, could be equally sick?*

SIMON: Yes, though *equally* is hard to judge. I would say that I have, for example, an excessive obsession with physical and other kinds of beauty. The only problem is that if you are obsessed with beauty in painting or architecture, nobody minds; but if you're obsessed with beauty in people, people do mind, that is to say, people who are not themselves beautiful. I have never been able to explain to a woman journalist, especially if she was plain, why it makes a big difference to me whether I see a beautiful woman or an ugly woman on the stage.

ROREM: *I've heard you say, in front of women, things about women that I don't think are very elegant.*

SIMON: Oh, I'm sure, because I am an irascible person.

ROREM: *Have you ever had a homosexual experience?*

SIMON: No.

ROREM: *Not even as an adolescent?*

SIMON: No. The only experience that had an interesting aspect to it from a homosexual point of view occurred once, in Seattle, when I was teaching at the University of Washington, and I once got—"involved" isn't the word because we never had sex, but we might have had—with a stewardess who noticed that I was reading Lucretius, and she was impressed because she was Catholic and had gone to a Catholic school, and knew who Lucretius was, etcetera—and I was reading it in Latin. So she talked to me about it, and she seemed like an intelligent person, and so I invited her, when she came to Seattle, to attend one of my classes at the university, which she did. And at some point we were walking down the streets of Seattle, and we stopped in front of a store window, and a man came up to me and made some sort of discreet pass at me. I was perfectly nice about it, and brushed him off in a polite way, not to hurt his feelings. And the girl was absolutely shocked. "You should have socked him!" she said. I responded, "Why? In the first place, the fact that he finds me attractive is certainly not an insult. In the second place, he didn't assault me in any way; he made some kind of a very mild pass." So that's the nearest I ever got to a "homosexual experience."

ROREM: *Really the nearest?*

SIMON: Yeah. I mean, I don't know why that is so surprising, though a lot of people do think it is. Maybe not living in an Anglo-Saxon culture, as I didn't in my first fifteen years, had something to do with it. I don't know.

ROREM: *On a conscious level it doesn't attract you.*

SIMON: No, and I doubt that it attracts me on an unconscious level, either.

ROREM: *If it's unconscious, of course, you don't know.*

SIMON: Except to the extent that when I see a very handsome man, I say, "This man is handsome," and if I see a very ugly man, it bothers me, as it bothers me to see a very ugly woman. I don't like ugliness, I'm sorry to say.

ROREM: *Everyone has different concepts of ugliness—*

SIMON: Oh, of course.

ROREM: *—and there are many very handsome men, for example, who repel me.*

SIMON: Yes, there's such a thing as overcosmeticized good looks.

ROREM: *Well, there's this or that, or homeliness that appeals, and there can be faces that repel me, like Willie Nelson's, for example. And there are women who, to me, are incredibly voluptuous. I like women in every way—to touch, to smell, to talk to—every way but sexual. Insofar as I'm sexual at all anymore, in these mysterious AIDS-ridden times.*

But to come back to "faggot"—for a heterosexual who makes a passing remark that slights a homosexual, and who doesn't understand that he is slighting the homosexual, it's a very small thing for him to concede. "Paris is worth a mass," said Henri IV, and turned Catholic. The word "faggot" offends homosexuals, take my word for it, and don't use it, Buckley's freedom of speech notwithstanding. In this day and age, use your freedom of speech instead to back up the solidarity of the few enough people who want to do something about AIDS research.

SIMON: First of all, those are totally incommensurate things: to help AIDS research has nothing to do with dramatic criticism, and has certainly nothing to do with rejecting bad plays.

ROREM: *No, but rejecting a group of people—*

SIMON: But I'm not rejecting—well, is it a group or is it not? Maybe it is a group. I do not like—I don't know what the proper word would be, but whatever the word is it will be found offensive because it is *meant* to be offensive—"screaming queens," would that be any better? I could say "faggots," I could say "pillow biters," as the Australians do.

ROREM: *Yeah, but insofar as you say those things, they are antihomosexual because the general public is only too willing to take them as that.*

SIMON: Well, the general public is foolish, no matter what we do.

ROREM: *They're people who are reading you.*

SIMON: Well, yes, some, but I do not write principally for them. I write mostly for those who understand what I am about, and those are few and far between.

ROREM: *But I am intelligent, and I understand what you're about, and I am offended by them.*

SIMON: Well, I think you're wrong, unless, well, let's see now. Here's what I mean: I am against extreme behavior in all its forms, which is not to say that I am always innocent of having done something in bad taste, or having been extreme in some way myself; but there are certain forms of collective behavior, whether it be redneck, whether it be macho, whether it be yahoo (which is certainly more heterosexual than not), or whether it be what I here call "faggot," and might have called by some other name. Although *all* synonyms are offensive, and there's no way of getting around that because they are *meant* to be offensive, but not to all homosexuals; they're meant to be offensive to a certain small, or maybe not so small, subgroup of homosexuals who behave in what I would call an outlandish, tasteless, vulgar, needlessly loud, obstreperous—

ROREM: *Probably a great many people would agree with you, including some homosexuals, but is it worth it when other people will use your put-down as a justification for being bigots themselves?*

SIMON: Well, you know, that is a tremendous question that goes back to at least Paul Bourget's novel *Le Disciple* [1889], which created a huge debate along these lines. Can a writer, or thinker, or, in this case, a critic, be held responsible because other people will misunderstand his "teachings," or ideas, or opinions? (In a sense, the issue goes all the way back to the trial of Socrates.) I think if you genuinely and sincerely and honestly dislike something (no matter what it is) and say so, and if you play with your cards on the table, you may be considered undesirable, you may be considered hostile, you may be considered just plain wrong—but as long as you're honest and forthright . . . In other words, everything can be misunderstood and abused. Every strong position, every highly articulate position can be misinterpreted, vulgarized, exaggerated, used for shabby purposes that the person who initially expressed it in a different form didn't intend. And there's no way you can be safe from this, unless you're totally mediocre and have no opinions of any kind of force, or shape, or individuality—in which case, you can probably still be misquoted in some ways, but with greater difficulty and it wouldn't matter—but anybody else is always open to being misinterpreted. And if people are vicious, or stupid, or intolerant, there's no helping it, and there's no way of legislating it away. I think human nature is what it is, and I think the notion that, for example, someday there won't be *any* antihomosexual feelings in the world seems utopian to me. The thing to do is to contain such a feeling. First of all, to be honest about it, to be up-front about it, and if you don't like someone or something, to say it, so that people can argue against it, and prove you wrong if you are capable of admitting it.

ROREM: *Would you concede that you enjoy these wrangles? I've seen you, with great glee, show hate letters that had been written to you — you pulled them out of your pocket. Do you like being hated?*

SIMON: Well, no, but I like feeling superior to human stupidity. And since many of these hate letters (and, I'm sorry to say, some of them are fan letters, too) are splendid examples of human stupidity in the funny sort of absurdities they spout—I must say I find that amusing. And I do like to irritate fools. I think fools are really the enemy of all people: homosexuals, heterosexuals, bisexuals, nonsexuals, asexuals. Fools are the enemy, any kind of fool: sometimes learned fools, sometimes illiterate fools.

Another form of human folly is that people never remember the things you say that do not prove some sort of a priori point they're trying to make about you.

ROREM: *Yes, but this doesn't happen with other critics besides you, or it happens more often —*

SIMON: Well, it happens for two reasons: because most other critics are so namby-pamby in their writing that you can't feel one way or the other about it; and the complementary thing is that because I am a severe and tough critic, I have more grievously offended specific people whose plays, or acting, or directing, or composing, or scene design, or whatever, I've found inferior, and said so unequivocally. So many of those people are dying to get back at me, and this is one convenient way because it makes them look liberal, humanitarian, broad-minded. And they can beat me over the head with this (which my head can take, even if they think otherwise) and, you see, the amazing thing is that they all want me fired. I mean, I could understand letters of ordinary protest, which one gets all the time, but it is this vindictiveness I find most unusual, that almost none of them will accept apologies, almost none of them will accept retractions, that they all want to have me fired, that they want the magazine boycotted, they want—

ROREM: *Would you have written your letter of apology if your senior editor hadn't asked you to?*

SIMON: I don't know. I don't know. But I didn't mind writing it. I was very happy to write it because I felt it might clarify things. As it turned out, it created more ire than the initial statement, and that again shows what terrible, fanatical forces are at work here, you know, that even apologies are not acceptable, whereas, even in international disputes, even between enemy nations, if somebody comes out and says, "I'm sorry," the other nation says, "Fine"— but here there seems to be no forgiveness.

ROREM: *Actually, no. Other nations say, "You don't really mean it."*

SIMON: Well, but that's not the way diplomacy works. Whether anyone means it or not, you pretend the other person means it (and up to a certain point, he probably does), and then you work on from there.

ROREM: *Neither of us has used the word "gay." I think that's genera-tional.*

SIMON: Yeah, I think that's an unfortunate word. I never liked the word "queer," for example. Not only because it displeased homosexuals, but also because it displeased anyone who had a sense of language. I mean, "queer" means peculiar, strange, and I think some homosexuals are about as unpeculiar as people can be, whereas some heterosexuals are extremely queer, extremely pecu-liar.

ROREM: *I think, though, the word "gay" is in the language, and there's nothing you or I or anyone can do about it. Perhaps it's a gain for people who are gay and—*

SIMON: But is it? Is it? I mean, look, if people *think* that some-thing is good for them, I suppose that is a gain because we do live, to a great extent, in illusions. You have the *illusion* that this word is serving your cause and making you feel better about yourself; I guess then it is a gain. Nevertheless, I wonder whether some better word couldn't have been found. I think that the only thing that's wrong with the word "homosexual" is that it's long and Greco-Latin, and people are getting less and less literate and verbal.

ROREM: *You yourself said earlier that words come into the language or they don't. Nobody sat down and had a board meeting about whether or not "gay" was going to be in the official lexicon, the way they did with "Ms.," for example.*

SIMON: Yeah, which I think is dreadful, too.

ROREM: *But the word "gay" is here. There are worse burdens to bear.*

SIMON: Sure, there are worse burdens. But on the other hand, we can't be absolutely sure that that's not going to change because the blacks, at one point, wanted to be "colored," so then there were people who were polite and called them "colored"; then they wanted to be "Negro," so one called them "Negro"; then they

NED ROREM

wanted to be "black"; there's no telling whether they won't change to "Afro-American," or who knows what else.

ROREM: *Could I ask you a question which is rather Joan Rivers-ish? Have you ever been married?*

SIMON: Yes, I have.

ROREM: *How did that work out?*

SIMON: Well, not really well. She was a student of mine at the University of Washington, and we came back East, and she was very unhappy about the East, and she drank. I mean, she was what is known as a "problem drinker." And I gather that's not quite the same thing as an "alcoholic," though God knows it was, for all practical purposes.

ROREM: *The definition has to be made by the person himself.*

SIMON: Does it though? I wonder. I mean, you know, at that rate—you see this bothers me, that "faggot" is a word that "we homosexuals," you say, can use, but you people, you straights, can't. Either we're all part of the human race, which I believe we are, in which case we can all use the same word—

ROREM: *Look, I have composed songs on words by female poets, and female poets almost invariably write about the female condition. I dare to set their poetry because half my ancestors are female, and I'm not unacquainted with the female condition. However, I have never set a poem by a black poet because blacks write mostly about their black condition too, and I would not presume, even in music, to know how to portray the yoke that they have carried. Assuming it's good poetry in the first place.*

SIMON: But suppose it's not a poem about "yokes." Suppose it's a poem about—

ROREM: *Well, as I said, it almost invariably is. Name me one good black poet or poetess who writes about anything other than the black condition.*

SIMON: Well, I don't know. I'm not that *au courant* with the latest developments in any kind of poetry, black or white.

ROREM: *But I am, when it comes to setting texts to music. Therefore I feel that heterosexuals should be fairly careful about being too colloquial when they talk — homosexuals have suffered, in a way that heterosexuals can't know about. I'm not trying to one-up you, but there are sensibilities, and questions of taste, that I don't think can be infringed upon. I'm very careful when I'm with black people, or with women, or Jews. Of course, that statement implies that I have to force myself to be careful.*

SIMON: Yeah, it does.

ROREM: *Which is — but I would rather do that than offend people.*

SIMON: Well, again, one doesn't want to offend *innocent* people, but I do think there's a type of reprehensible behavior, which could be heterosexual, in which case, you attack that, or could be feminist of an extremist sort, in which case, you attack that. For example, if somebody says to me, "I wish all drama critics would get cancer and die," I would not be upset by that.

ROREM: *Of course not, because "drama critic" is, in itself, not an offensive locution.*

SIMON: But "die of cancer" is.

ROREM: *And cancer is not a disease restricted to one group of people.*

SIMON: Well, supposedly AIDS isn't either, but my point is that it was a graphic way of expressing oneself. I mean, I could have said "drop dead," and then presumably people would have thought less harshly of it, and yet that means the same thing.

ROREM: *You see, in your wanting to put the guilty in their place, you do manage to offend the innocent. And your analogy about drama critics and cancer doesn't hold water, and you know it. A critic is not a vulnerable category.*

SIMON: Yes it is; ask almost any critic.

ROREM: *It's not a despised minority.*

SIMON: Look, when I turn on the radio as, for example, happened a couple of years ago and I hear someone like Jimmy Kirkwood—with whom I chatted very amiably just the other day at the theater—and I heard him say, "John Simon ought to be killed," in public, on a radio show that is being broadcast to all and sundry—this was because I had given him a bad review for *P.S.: Your Cat Is Dead.* And I turn on the radio as I come home, and these are the first words I hear—I tend to be somewhat *amused* by that.

ROREM: *But there's a big difference between "John Simon ought to be killed" and "Drama critics ought to be killed." John Simon is a specific. A drama critic, as I repeat, is not a despised minority.*

SIMON: It is by *some* people.

ROREM: *You're speaking only metaphorically, and I'm speaking quite literally when I'm talking about homosexuals.*

SIMON: Well, homosexuals are no longer a despised minority, either.

ROREM: *Yes, they are.*

SIMON: Not in my world, they're not.

ROREM: *But that's our argument. That's the burden of our discussion.*

SIMON: All right then, let's talk about it some more.

ROREM: *The supportive letters that you showed me offended me because they said the same thing that you say—there is a big difference between "faggots" and "homosexuals." Their implication, and yours too, is that the "good" homosexuals are in complicity with you against faggots.*

SIMON: No, not in complicity; it's more like agreement.

ROREM: *Well, I would rather defend the most outrageous faggot for his right to be outrageously faggoty than for him to be put down in the way that he inevitably will because he is homosexual. It's the homosexuality, within the faggotry, that offends, rather than the faggotry itself.*

SIMON: I don't think so. Again, I can't speak for everyone. I don't know what is true of some illiterate boor in the Pentagon, perhaps, or some illiterate boor in the Ozarks.

ROREM: *It was noticeable, even in Larry Kramer's play last night, that the Brad Davis character separates himself from the transvestites trying to hog publicity on television — do you remember that line?*

SIMON: Yes, yes.

ROREM: *And I thought about that line even as I thought about the fact that there were no token blacks in the play, which is something that could offend black theatergoers.*

SIMON: Well, that's just the trouble. I mean, nowadays we've reached the point where everything is construed as an offense to somebody.

ROREM: *But, John, I'm the least flag-waving of people —*

SIMON: That may be.

ROREM: *—but in my dotage I do have a certain — I'm terribly interested in what younger homosexuals are up against, as opposed to the good old days when there were well-defined walls. It would appear that those walls are still standing, but that the people wailing at them are making much more noise. I don't think that there's that much more acceptance. What I'm asking you to do is something that is perhaps irrelevant to the —I think that along with making your little jokes, you could also make some big points —*

SIMON: Well, I've made some big points, in that I was, for

example, one of the first heterosexual critics to go to bat for *Torch Song Trilogy.*

ROREM: *A play which, by the way, I don't adore, though I'm in a minority of one. I don't despise it, and I rather respect the author. But the play's twice as long as it needs to be, and as comfortably stereotypical as* The Boys in the Band, *which I happened to like. Both plays make matinee-goers feel complacent about, and removed from, faggotry.*

SIMON: Yes, well, exactly, but that's the point, you know. I think that the play handles faggotry, if you will—

ROREM: *You're allowed.*

SIMON: —yeah—with wit, and with amusement, with self-criticism, but not with any kind of groveling self-abasement, which would be unbearable.

ROREM: *But it does stigmatize homosexuals as being of a certain kind, too distinct to be menacing.*

SIMON: Look, both you and I know, and everybody else in his right mind knows, that there are revolting people in all groups, and I think they should be called revolting regardless of which group they belong to, it doesn't matter. Or it matters in some superficial, strategic sense that maybe this group is not in a good position to defend itself, but that is not true of homosexuals any more. Homosexuals are now in an excellent position to defend themselves, at least in this—in the part of the world that reads *New York* magazine. For those readers, many of whom are homosexuals, and many of whom are closely involved with homosexuals, in business, friendship, whatever—I don't think that for those people homosexuals are a threatened species anymore, nor should they be, nor can they be, nor will they be. And if in such magazines and circles we can't pretty much speak our minds, we're in serious trouble. And I think that the strength that the homosexuals can now afford to show lies in not being oversensitive to the least slight or the least attack.

ROREM: *I never use what I call "the ungrammatical 'we,' " which younger homosexuals bend over backwards (or forwards, sometimes) to use to show that they want to stand up and be counted. But I do feel a binding solidarity. I've never particularly suffered for my sexuality, much less than I have from being a composer. Yet if as a composer I feel I'm a pariah in our philistine society, actually that society doesn't even hate me, for the simple reason that it doesn't know artists exist. You can't hate what doesn't exist for you.*

Jim thinks it's indelicate of me to say that I haven't suffered, in public gay forums, because too many people have suffered, and I would seem to evade that suffering. I do say it, though. I've been privileged, and I've had a—I've always been mainly in a society of artists, of people who don't have bosses, where I could do what I want, and could afford to thumb my nose without being fired. I don't know many people, personally, who have nine-to-five jobs, wherein they feel threatened to come out of the closet. I just don't know them—that's how things have worked out—but when more and more people seem to be in that situation, and yet are coming out of the closet, it does interest me, sociologically and humanly. I feel more strongly about these things than I did ten years ago. And I feel that you, as the mensch I know you to be, ought to feel responsible to your own integrity as a critic. Still, you overstep the bounds, in spite of your various, semiconvincing rationales that have been brought up today. And I can't help but feel that, in your heart of hearts, you agree with me, but that you are a theatrical creature, that you like to be controversial at all costs.

SIMON: Mmm. I don't know—possibly, but I doubt it. I think I like to speak my mind; if that's being theatrical, fine, then it's theatrical; if that's being controversial, which it can be, fine, then it's controversial. But as I see it, I am much less of a threat to any individual or any group than thousands of people I can think of who do not speak their minds, who are not willing to discuss any problem as we are now discussing one, in a rational way, but who nevertheless represent, secretly and therefore dangerously, all kinds of special interests, or special prejudices. The simplest way I can put it is that I respect decency in any form, I respect wit in any form. But I do not respect outrageousness for the sake of outrageousness—

ROREM: *And you sincerely don't see that your remarks carry the same tonality that you deplore in others — remarks either outrageous or hysterical?*

SIMON: I don't think so. But you see, I think a lot of people do exactly what I do, but they don't use a certain word, or they don't make a certain statement. Yet the assault against a certain play, or against a certain production, is just as strong, but without having the courage or honesty to say where the antipathy originates. At least, my way there is a chance for a better kind of dialogue.

You see, I think one of the worst things in the world is the blinkered vision, the kind of vision that sees what it wants to see, what it has predecided is there, and absolutely refuses to see other things. I wouldn't mind getting black marks where I deserve black marks for any statements I've made, or not made and should have made. But I would like to get some good marks too. For example, in this very review, in this very column in which *The Octette Bridge Club* was reviewed, I also reviewed *Virginia*, the play about Virginia Woolf and her husband and Vita Sackville-West. And I find, in this column, the following statement from me: "Still, if you read the last few letters exchanged between Virginia and Vita, about such mundane matters as procuring hay in wartime for Octavia Wilberforce's cows, you cannot fail to be moved by the affection in the lines and the greater one between them." This to me is a very sympathetic statement to lesbians, and to lesbian love. Here's a heterosexual man being moved by a homosexual relationship, by its delicacy, by the fineness of it.

ROREM: *On the other hand, one bad apple can ruin the whole barrel. One anti-gay crack, and people will reread everything you've written with a different eye, looking for the latent homophobe.*

SIMON: I know, but again, we cannot be responsible for what other fools will do.

ROREM: *They're not necessarily fools, though. They aren't fools just because you say so.*

SIMON: Well, if they're all looking for one thing only and trying to make more of it—

ROREM: *But what you've said, apparently homophobically to some people, is powerful enough to disqualify what you may say compassionately in other contexts.*

SIMON: But you say a lot of things as a person, as a human being, and as a critic, and as a critic perhaps you say them more publicly, and if people want to make more of it, or less of it, or too much of it, or not enough of it, you have no control over that. There are friendly positions towards homosexuals and homosexuality which should be taken into account before people start making a huge hue and cry over something I said, or may have said, or may have been quoted as saying, or whatever.

ROREM: *How do you account, then, for this hue and cry, because the people who have hued and cried aren't all stupid, including your five or six colleagues on the paper who signed the letter —*

SIMON: Well, I think my five or six colleagues have here proved pretty stupid, actually.

ROREM: *Well, then, who isn't stupid?*

SIMON: Well, you're not, for example, and a lot of other people are not. But I do feel that I'm probably guilty of a whole lot of things, and I'll be the first to admit it. I think I make too much of the looks of people, for example, men or women—though more so women because I'm sexually attracted to women and I'm not to men. I probably put too great an emphasis on grammar in an age which, rightly or wrongly, seems to think that's not a very important issue. This is all very possible, but I do not think that I hate any person for his color, for his religion, for his sexual preference, for his philosophical beliefs, or even for the fact that he may hate critics, or Yugoslavs, or whatever it is that I am, because it's not important. There are more important things: What is a person all about in a bigger sense? If, for example, he is a serious poet, or a serious diplomat, or a serious scientist, and he makes his contribution as a poet, or a diplomat, or a scientist, that's far more important to me than whether he says an offensive remark to me along the line that might upset me personally. I think the homosexuals are winning their fight for recognition, their fight for survival, their fight for equality.

ROREM: *Do you feel that the AIDS situation has set back that fight? You would know better than I, in the eyes of the heterosexual world.*

SIMON: I would guess that a lot of heterosexuals are going around saying, "They're getting exactly what they deserve," and that's not the way to look at it. Whether that is a setback, I don't know; I don't know whether that will in any sense prevent certain laws on the statutes against homosexuals from being revoked, laws that should not exist and that, as I've said more than once in writing, must be revoked. I don't think that's going to make it harder —or I *hope* it's not going to make it harder—for homosexuals to get civic rights, etc. Nevertheless, it is a vindictive attitude and I don't like it. However, I myself feel that promiscuity of the kind that the extreme homosexual lifestyle represents is not a good thing, and I think Larry Kramer feels that too, and that's partly or even largely what his play is about. And while I don't think anyone should be punished by death, or horrible illness, or pain for his lifestyle— because I'm not above reproach, and you are not, and nobody is— I do, nevertheless, think there is something ugly about devaluing sex. And I think that two groups have devalued sex more than anybody else; one is the macho, yahoo, male brutes who have invented prostitution, and who have allowed prostitution of the ugliest kind to thrive, and at the same time punish the prostitute but not the whoremonger, which is totally wrong; and the other group, smaller, I daresay, in numbers, but quite active and I think quite degrading to sexuality—what I would have called "faggots," and what I might still call "faggots" between you and me, even if not in *New York* magazine—include those who will have eight sexual encounters during one night.

ROREM: *Supposing I told you that I had done that, does that make me a faggot?*

SIMON: Well, if you were to say that you did that, yes, I would have to say that you were behaving, in this instance—

ROREM: *No, that's a misuse of the term, quite simply. A "faggot" is a man — I would have thought by your original statement — who devalues the dignity of what he is. You said a minute ago, you thought that Larry Kramer was against promiscuity. It's not provable that he's against promiscuity, except insofar as it may disseminate AIDS. Therefore he advocates celibacy. If the AIDS crisis hadn't arisen, it remains to be known what would have happened to promiscuity. What if I were to tell you that, in my life, I've had thousands of random encounters? And I am not compulsively sexual compared to many of my friends. Now, where does promiscuity begin? With a woman or man who has slept with thirty, as opposed to sixty, as opposed to a hundred and ninety? Who determines? Is it determined by the anxiety or smugness within the sleeper himself? Gore Vidal said in one of his essays that any heterosexual man, given the opportunity, would have as much sex, promiscuously, as a homosexual.*

SIMON: We *create* our own opportunities. The fact that heterosexuals have not created that opportunity means something, and the fact that homosexuals *have* created that opportunity also means something. The opportunities don't come from heaven. Now you can say this has to do with the Bible, and Puritanism, and religion, and marriage and children, rather than personal inclination. But whatever it has to do with, there it is. And I think, such as it is, and it's imperfect (God knows heterosexual marriages and relationships are nothing much to boast about in many cases), it is still not quite so crass, so frequent, so cynical.

ROREM: *I would say they're as frequent. There's as much divorce amongst my straight friends as amongst homosexuals, and amongst homosexuals, there is as much mutual respect in a ménage.*

SIMON: Obviously, but now we're talking about a higher type. We're talking about what I would call "homosexuals," and never would call "faggots," although it's possible for a homosexual, for a time in his life, to be a "faggot," and vice versa.

ROREM: *What is the equivalent to the word "faggot" for a heterosexual male?*

SIMON: I think it's "macho" or "yahoo" or "sexist" —

ROREM: *Those are not wounding words.*

SIMON: Well, they are to a person of sensibility. I would hate to be called that.

ROREM: *Well, I don't like being called a "faggot," which you inferred that I was during promiscuous moments. Many a macho person, on the other hand, is only too proud to be called "macho."*

SIMON: If he's a fool, yes; if he's not a fool, no.

ROREM: *A "faggot" who is a fool still doesn't want you to call him that. So it's not the equivalent.*

SIMON: Perhaps nothing is a one-hundred-percent equivalent. We have to deal with approximations in life.

ROREM: *Look. Straight males as a group are never a laughingstock, so there's literally no demeaning term for them as for women — terms like "slut," "cunt," "bitch," "gash." What's in a name? Everything. And terminology — which you so worship (you once had a column on it in Esquire), as I do — is what this is all about. But maybe the brave man does it with a sword.*

SIMON: I think that there are corresponding problems for heterosexual men, terms such as "prick" or "male chauvinist pig," or, more recently, "cunt" as applied to them. And if such a term sticks, it sticks equally to them. But this line of discussion will take us too far afield.

ROREM: *If you can put me in that faggot category, you'd have to be able to imagine yourself in a similar category, and that category doesn't exist.*

SIMON: Suppose you had ten affairs during a summer. I wouldn't consider that bad. I would consider that excessive, but I wouldn't consider that bad.

ROREM: *But if I went to the baths and had ten in one evening —*

SIMON: I would consider that bad.

ROREM: *Therefore, during that evening I was a "faggot" — not before and not afterwards.*

SIMON: No, and if it's not your predominant form of behavior, if it's something that you—

ROREM: *Then you're being pretty casual or pretty loose about the term, or else tactful because I'm a friend.*

SIMON: Well, one has to be loose about it because there is a great deal of variety and flexibility in human behavior. *[Dog pees on John Simon's jacket.]* He must be a gay liberationist!

I do want to say—and, again, I don't think I deserve any special credit for this, it's the most natural thing in the world—that I was genuinely moved by *As Is* and by *The Normal Heart*. You know, I was crying at both of those plays as I very often do at heterosexual plays when they're beautiful and moving. And I did not feel that I was seeing some kind of strange, alien, unrelated-to-me sort of world. I felt these were suffering human beings like any of us. And the plays were good, and they were honest, and they got to the roots of the problems, and they were humane. In fact, these two plays show far more humanity—if one can use that kind of a standard of comparison, and I think one can—than almost any heterosexual play I've seen in recent months.

ROREM: *Can you say what that indicates?*

SIMON: It indicates that there is a serious problem dealt with here, that AIDS is certainly a serious problem, and that dealing with it brings out the best in people. Trying to fight it, trying to find a cure for it, trying to get people to recognize its existence, is a worthy cause. And worthy causes, sometimes even from not especially worthy playwrights or poets or novelists—can strike a human chord, which enables a person who might have written a very bad play about a flight to the moon that meant very little to him, to write a good play about *this* because *this* affects him in a genuine and profound and necessary way. So these plays are about *something,* and that's part of what makes them good, that they are a real problem, a felt problem, an important problem, a human problem, a problem that concerns all of us. And I don't think it concerns heterosexuals merely because heterosexuals also can get AIDS, and I find it a bit annoying when someone like Harvey Fierstein (someone I like a lot, by the way) makes a speech at a film critics' dinner and says, "You heterosexuals will have the same problem when you start making love." You see, that's a kind of snideness against heterosexuals that's exactly the same thing as the heterosexual snideness against homosexuals. But, you know, even if I resent it, I wouldn't seriously hold it against Harvey; I wouldn't write a letter about it; I wouldn't dream of thinking that a play of his is any worse because he made that statement. But it is a hostile statement.

ROREM: *However, there is a difference in kind between your statement and his statement. He is attacking the master, and you're attacking the slave. Straights run the world. The attack bounces right off a heterosexual's back. It means nothing; it is not damaging. It only offends your pride, not your status.*

SIMON: But you see, this is I think where my basic disagreement with your position comes in: if you assume that a homosexual is the slave, then he *is* a slave—

ROREM: *"Slave" is not the correct word: "pariah."*

SIMON: I don't think he *is.* He may have *been* —

ROREM: *I don't think he is in fact, but he is treated that way —*

SIMON: Well, not anymore, not anymore.

ROREM: *You've claimed several times that gays are better off than before, while blacks are not. But only blacks and gays themselves are qualified to make that claim. Legally, gays are worse off than blacks. Well, thanks to the Kramers —*

SIMON: Yes, thanks to a lot of things; thanks for the general movement of culture; I mean, we've come a bit of a way. True, when something like the Holocaust occurs, one wonders how far we've come, but by and large we have come a way since the year one; and we are more tolerant, more flexible. There *is* progress, and I think, in this day and age, especially in New York, and in the other bigger cities of this country, a homosexual cannot, must not, need not think of himself as inferior socially, inferior morally, inferior politically. I mean, it may still seem so, in some areas, in some jobs, and in some situations, but that's changing. And I'm all for it, and everyone I know is all for it. And this is a kind of slave reaction, when an intelligent homosexual takes enormous umbrage at a casual line, whether in a review or uttered in an angry moment. I think that is not the reaction that befits a liberated, a proud, a self-respecting, an *arrived* group, such as the homosexuals now are.

ROREM: *Nevertheless, you, who dropped the casual line, are in turn a slave to your angry moments.*

SIMON: All right then, let's hope all slaves will become emancipated, and soon. In my world, there are so many homosexuals, and they're so interesting, and so successful, and so deserving, and such fun to be with, that I don't know of anyone who discriminates against them. But I don't know what would be true in the banking world, let's say, or in the medical world, you know; in any world except the arts or something vaguely related to the arts, I wouldn't know. I move very little in those worlds.

ROREM: *John, I've not been out to nail you here, really not. I've wanted to see what makes you tick. I haven't quite seen. Though probably if we learned what makes our friends tick, we'd grow less interested in them.*

A Conversation with Ned Rorem

Lawrence D. Mass

1988

*N*ed Rorem, the Pulitzer Prize– and Grammy Award–winning com-
poser and author of twelve books, including The Paris Diary *and* The
Nantucket Diary, *was one of the first and has remained the best-known
of openly homosexual figures in the world of music. His most recent book
is* Settling the Score: Essays on Music *(Harcourt Brace Jovanovich,
1988). The following conversation, which focuses on opera and homosexuality, began in Rorem's living room in New York City on February 15,
1988, and was completed by correspondence in mid-1989. Entitled "Homosexuality and Music III" (following conversations on homosexuality
and music with Philip Brett and George Heymont), it was published in my*
Homosexuality as Behavior and Identity: Dialogues of the Sexual
Revolution, *volume II. A specially abridged version appeared in* Opera
Monthly.

*My dialectic with Ned, rich and frustrating, was inevitably about
group bonding and identity. Ned had often made the point — in interviews,
in his diaries, and in conversations and correspondence with me — that
being homosexual was no more interesting or pertinent, no more worthy
of comment or analysis, than being heterosexual. In* The Nantucket
Diary, *his engagement of our debate revealed earnest struggle and courage
as well as generational differences:*

> The so likable, and to an extent intelligent, Larry Mass,
> unable to see the forest for the trees, keeps writing me
> about what he feels to be the responsibility of the gay
> composer. Yes, at this point I am indeed attracted by the

thought of a "gay libretto" (whatever that might be), but I'm more strongly drawn to a pacifist libretto. I am as much a Quaker as a gay, and man's inhumanity and identity and poetry are expressed as much through common conflict on our fatal globe as through sexual conflict. Perhaps an opera on a debarred hero? Oscar Wilde? Even Alexander the Great?

Larry Mass responds docilely to my ultimatum about discontinuing our, to me, fruitless exchange on gay music, with: "On Thursday Arnie and I are going to see [sic] the NYC Gay Men's Chorus, which will feature music by Barber, Bernstein, Copland, Gershwin, Porter, and Rorem. Nowhere, not in the program notes, certainly not in the mainstream press, but probably not even in the gay press or in Ned Rorem's diaries, however, will one read that all of these composers were/are homosexual, or any analysis of what that might mean."

Larry can't stop. Perhaps pink triangles could be placed by appropriate names in the program (although I never knew that Gershwin was homosexual). Doesn't Larry worry about Jewish composers? What has Bernstein's and Copland's (and, yes, Gershwin's) Jewishness to do with their music? . . . What would a program note say about, for example, Poulenc? "Poulenc, rumored to be gay (although he sired a daughter upon whom he doted), wrote his mass in . . ." Or Copland? "Copland, rumored to be gay, was also Jewish, but wrote goyish music all his life, being the first to celebrate cowboys." To dignify Larry's obsessions here is sadistic. Maybe I'll eat my words one day.

The answer to Ned's first question is a resounding affirmative. Stimulated by my evolving awareness of sexual identity, I naturally have pondered the issue of the Jewishness of Jewish composers. What I've discovered, moreover, is that it is almost as closeted as the sexuality of homosexual composers, and in similar ways. The greatest culpability for this, I believe, rests with Richard Wagner, the composer whom the lovers of European classical music relish finding excuses to adore. Owing to

Wagner, principally, and the racist and nationalist attitudes everyone knows he propounded—most notoriously in his anti-Semitic tract, Jewry in Music, among many other political writings, and metaphorically in his Nibelung tetralogy and Die Meistersinger, among other operas— the earnest desire was born after World War II to minimize, if not completely repress, awareness of the Wagner problem, a movement that was central to the greater process of attempting to establish nonpolitical status for music in a world of post-Holocaust chaos, wherein any significance that might be granted to the Jewishness of Jewish composers would be effaced. For an example of the internalization of the anti-Semitism resulting from this, one has only to turn to Eric Gordon's biography of Marc Blitzstein to reveal a case both combined with and paralleling internalized homophobia. "Blitzstein rarely thought about his Jewishness," Gordon observes, "and took no pains to explore Jewish themes in his work. He knew almost nothing of Jewish history." "Rather like Ned Rorem's frequent assertions," I concluded in my review of Gordon's book, "ongoing today, that homosexuality has nothing to do with art and music, Blitzstein's rare observations about Judaism and music were negative and defensive." As for Ned's second question—what would programs say about the gayness or reputed gayness of composers such as Copland and Poulenc?—if you take out the facetiousness, what he wrote isn't a bad start (though, "true to form," as my life partner Arnie Kantrowitz observed after reading these Nantucket Diary comments, "Rorem doesn't know there were Jewish cowboys"). I not only agree with Ned's (devil's advocate?) point about the pertinence of Copland's Jewishness to his art, but I suspect that, as with Blitzstein, it probably cannot be disentangled from the pertinence of this important American composer's homosexuality.

Since some degree of ambiguity is central to the nature of much, if not all, art, and because of the multiplicity and complexity of variables involved in its creation and appreciation, questions of the relationships of art to politics and identity, like those of the relationships between behavior and identity, will never be answerable absolutely. But it is important to continue the dialectic, a process that is as integral to the vitality of art as art is to vitality. In the interview that follows, Ned Rorem again demonstrates his formidable gift for insight and debate, even with regard to scores that, in a more progressive and knowledgeable era of gay liberation, we may believe are being permanently resettled.

LAWRENCE MASS: *Where do you think you stand as an opera composer today?*

NED ROREM: Can one ever know one's own standing? All I can provide is facts rather than opinions.

I've composed seven operas, each of them published and available. The first, *A Childhood Miracle,* in 1951, was based on a Nathaniel Hawthorne text and was a collaboration with my friend [*Village Voice* film critic] Elliot Stein. It runs approximately thirty-five minutes and is a virtuosic turn for thirteen instruments and six singers. It was first done in 1952 and later televised in 1956 in Philadelphia with Curtis undergraduates. An adolescent Benita Valente starred, and a boy of fifteen named Jaime Laredo was concertmaster. Another Curtis student, Plato Karayannis (now head of the Dallas Opera), directed. Then I did a second one-acter called *The Robbers,* based on a Chaucer tale and using my own libretto. Marc Blitzstein drastically revised the rather arch text. In 1965 I wrote *Miss Julie,* my only "full-length" opera. My cowriter was Kenward Elmslie, and the piece was glamorously though unsuccessfully produced by the New York City Opera. Next came *Bertha* and *Three Sisters Who Are Not Sisters* in 1968, both on commission (unpaid) from the Met Opera Studio. The librettos were by Kenneth Koch and Gertrude Stein. In those days, I was still young enough to do things because I liked to do them. Later came *Fables,* five operas in a grant total of twenty-two minutes, based on Marianne Moore's glittering translations of La Fontaine. In 1965 there was yet another opera, *Hearing,* originally a song cycle on poems of Kenneth Koch, which Jim Holmes, many years later, reworked into a scenario which I orchestrated for an unusual combination of nine instruments.

So, of my completed operas, six of the seven are brief, and they all saw the light between 1951 and 1968. It's been twenty years since I've written a new opera. There are still four that are half done—one based on *The Suicide Club* of Robert Louis Stevenson; another on *The Matron of Ephesus* from a tale in Petronius; a student work in 1946 drawn from Paul Goodman's play, *Cain and Abel;* and, in 1962, to Jascha Kessler's libretto, I all but completed and even partially orchestrated *The Anniversary* for the City Opera before we scrapped it in favor of *Miss Julie.* For completeness, let's include a pop musical called *The Ticklish Acrobat* written in 1957 with Elmslie, but never produced; and a seven-minute *scena* I composed just last spring on Cocteau's *Anna la bonne*. Which brings the wavering total to thirteen, most of them, to some extent, on books of my choice, without any coercion.

I know that you're interested in finding relationships between composers and their choice of librettos, and there have to be such relationships, but I've never really thought much about that.

As to where I stand . . . I would love to write another (and I use the term "opera" *faute de mieux*) . . . another dramatic piece for singers before I die. Not a cantata, but a staged affair. Whenever I get around opera people, as in Santa Fe or like [philanthropist and leading opera patron] Robert Tobin, who's contributed lavishly to the Met, and the conversation turns to "What shall Ned do?" I get enthusiastic, but it's dangerous to get too enthusiastic about an opera unless you're going to be commissioned. Because unasked-for operas never get done.

MASS: *Several years ago you told me that there was a possibility of a commission from the Santa Fe Opera.*

ROREM: I did talk to John Crosby [director of the Santa Fe Opera] at some length in 1985, and he said, "Write me an outline." Robert Tobin was anxious to subsidize it if he, Robert, could also have a say about the subject. If I were them, I'd want to have that say, because more than any other musical format, opera is a collaborative venture. But I'm not very good at collaborating.

MASS: *In* The Nantucket Diary *you discuss some of the subjects you've considered for a new opera. You then go on to say, "Probably I'll settle with JH [musician and writer James Holmes, who is also Rorem's life partner] on a sort of 'Life of Whitman,' or 'Aspects of Walt,' rather like* The Mother of Us All.*"*

ROREM: Jim [Holmes] and I were extremely enthusiastic, but Robert Tobin felt that Whitman was out of date. Tobin was upset by the AIDS crisis and felt we needed to do something more "timely." What does that mean? Is *Oedipus Rex* timely?

MASS: *You say that Tobin was upset by the AIDS crisis. Did he want you to do something about AIDS? Did he have a specific suggestion for a libretto?*

ROREM: What he wanted was that it *not* be about Whitman.

MASS: *As I recall, around 1985, when you first told me about the possible commission from Santa Fe, you were considering a wide range of subjects, including* Oedipus. *In fact, you asked me if I had any ideas for operas with gay themes. I suggested two possibilities: Mishima's* Confessions of a Mask *and the story of Ganymede. You read* Confessions, *but decided it wasn't right because, among other reasons, it wasn't sufficiently "mythic." Obviously, that was not the reason for rejecting Ganymede, but I don't remember what the reason was. In* The Nantucket Diary *you imply that you also considered* Kiss of the Spider Woman *and an unspecified collaboration with William M. Hoffman. Clearly, the possibility of doing an opera with a gay theme has been an issue you've grappled with.*

Has anyone ever written an opera about Walt Whitman?

ROREM: I don't think so. [Theater producer, director, and designer] John Wulp wanted me to do an opera on the life of Henry James. I read all five of the Leon Edel books, with mixed feelings. I worship James, but operas on the lives of great men are flirting with danger. Like that movie on the life of Billie Holiday using another singer. The greatness was in the oeuvre, not in the life.

MASS: *You say that you and Jim were extremely enthusiastic about the idea of doing an opera about Whitman. Have you and/or Jim done any work yet on such a project?*

ROREM: No, for the simple reason that I haven't pushed it. If I really wanted to do this opera, if I were ready, I could probably arrange to get a commission. Maybe there's something in me that refrains. Most opera composers always have a new opera up their sleeve. I don't. But I do have enough other work contracted for during the next few years to keep me from brooding too much about an opera.

MASS: *In your essay on Joe Orton (from the* Advocate, *June 9, 1987), you say that you would love to have had an opera libretto from him. In the absence of a specially conceived libretto, would you, if you had the time, consider setting one of his farces, such as* Entertaining Mr. Sloane *or* What the Butler Saw?

ROREM: Orton's plays are already very musical, like Edward Albee's, oozing with echoes, rhythms, and colors that are so exact in themselves, and with wit so pungent and dependent on time, music could only slow them down. As opposed, say, to Tennessee Williams. The difference between Albee and Williams is that Albee's theater is music already. [Scored] music cannot add to it. It would only detract from the icy aptness of his clipped phrases; whereas Tennessee's writing is all rhapsodic. It's about music, but it is not music in itself, which is why Tennessee's plays lend themselves so much more gracefully to opera. I worked with Tennessee on two occasions (providing incidental background music to *Suddenly Last Summer* and to *The Milk Train*). But I wouldn't consider turning any of his plays into an opera now. They don't hold up with the passing of time. They embarrass me.

I read everything that has been published of Joe Orton's in preparation for that essay, but song didn't come into it. When I reread Jane Bowles's *In a Summer House* every five years, I think maybe I should do that. But the last act deteriorates. It's a noble failure. I've also considered Colette's *Chéri*, which would have been ideal for Poulenc. But whenever I reconsider it for myself, it becomes more and more remote.

It's easy to know what you don't want to do. In the abstract, I know what I do want to do. Something about myself. I'd need to be inside of the main male or female character if I'm going to live two years with those damn people. Something of Mishima, yes, might work, but not Ganymede, since I'm not interested in children. There's a lot of me in Chéri, and in Leah, his mistress, but the story is dated. Of course, all art dates from the moment it's penned. Beethoven and Stravinsky date well. Tennessee Williams doesn't. Colette dates wonderfully, but *Chéri* isn't apropos any longer.

MASS: *We were talking about Orton. Charles Ludlam is an artist whose work you've said you believe in as much as Orton's. Did any of his works present themselves to you as possibilities for opera?*

ROREM: I haven't seen much of his work. I seldom go to the theater anymore because it's dull and expensive. I go to movies. Ludlam's plays aren't all that suitable for singing for the same reasons that Orton's aren't. They're ironic and crisp and extremely dependent on words and on timing. Wit in opera is not the same as wit in plays. Nobody's going to understand the words anyway.

There's more potential with film. Like every self-respecting American, I was raised on movies. *The Umbrellas of Cherbourg* bowled me over. That was twenty-five years ago, but it's still the sole opera originally conceived for the movies. In all of its corny glory it truly works. Since then nobody has tried anything else new with opera and film. It's an open field. There are, of course, the television and screen adaptations of the standard repertoire, and many of these come off well. I got a lot more out of the TV presentation of *Lulu*, for example, than I ever did from seeing it on the stage. Interestingly, George Perle, the world's foremost Berg scholar, told me he really understood *Lulu* when he saw it on the tube, and he adored the subtitles.

MASS: *Are you saying that if you were to do a new opera you'd like to conceive it for the cinema?*

ROREM: Yes. If I had an idea. I'd want to work with a director like Antonioni, for example, not a director who knows about music so much as one who knows about film.

MASS: *Is Antonioni still doing films? (Is he still alive?) In* The Nantucket Diary *you discuss your work with such famous directors as Zeffirelli. But there are a number of leading directors you don't mention, like Visconti, Ponnelle, Caldwell, Felsenstein, Wieland Wagner, or Chéreau. Any comments?*

ROREM: In 1962 Zeffirelli had never directed anything in America. That's when the Strasbergs reigned supreme. Zeffirelli thought he'd like to begin big, so he hired Susan Strasberg, the world's least talented actress, to take the role of Marguerite Gautier in *The Lady of the Camelias,* adapted by, among others, Terrence McNally. I wrote the score, working every day for a month with Zeffirelli. They put it on as a Broadway play. I wrote about forty minutes worth of music for four or five instruments filtered through an echo chamber. Romantic, Chopinesque, Frenchish, decadent. It was a horrible experience. Collaborations always are. It lasted four performances. I didn't personally care for Zeffirelli. His vaingloriousness was oppressive.

We were all raised on Visconti's films. When I lived in Rome in 1954–55, he was sort of a god. I met him once or twice at Bill Weaver's. That's in the days when I never knew what to say to idols, so I'd get drunk. I was very impressed. Late one night we all went to a nightclub with Massimo Girotti. Remember him from *Teorema* (which, incidentally, is going to be made into an opera by Michael Torke)? Remember that last scene, when Girotti, virile head of the family, ends up sneaking in and out of a men's room in a Milan bus terminal? Very, very sad. When you recall that in *Reflections in a Golden Eye,* Brando had taken a homosexual role similar to Girotti's in *Teorema,* and then recall these two old icons in their scene together in *Last Tango in Paris,* it was something very special.

I saw the Callas-Visconti *Sonnambula* at La Scala that Lenny Bernstein conducted. Visconti, like all Italians, knew what opera was, and he knew how to cope with Callas. But I once overheard her talking to someone at the little café next to La Scala (she was toying with fresh strawberries in mid-February) about how he was on the right track but got off somehow. "Era sulla buona strada," said she in her accented Italian. I heard Callas many times. Now, I don't worship divas, but Callas represents one of the two or three greatest experiences I've ever had in any theater. The others were Mary Wigman, the dancer, when I was in third grade, about 1932; the early Martha Graham; Billie Holiday; Nazimova in Ibsen; Edith Piaf. All female, needless to say. There are no male equivalents, Whitman notwithstanding. Theater is artifice and artifice is feminine.

I've never seen a Felsenstein production, but I've seen many of Caldwell's things, and so many of my friends have worked with her and just adore her. Let's see. I saw the *Lulu* at BAM [Brooklyn Academy of Music]. She may be a bit on the gimmicky side. Ponnelle?

MASS: *I don't think gay men are more involved with divas than divos because "artifice is feminine." I think the reason gay men's stage and screen idols have been predominantly female has mostly to do with our stronger identification with women. (We identify more with Judy Garland and Maria Callas than with Frank Sinatra or Elvis Presley.) For gay men in our time, this identification is a lot more easily expressed than sexual attraction, whereas the opposite is grossly true of heterosexual women. If there were no homophobia, maybe gay men would be more prominent among the fans of the Sinatras and Presleys. Conversely, if our operas, movies, and songs were less patriarchal (conceived, written, and directed by men), maybe women would be more prominent among the most ardent fans of the likes of Garland and Callas. [These issues are explored in Catherine Clément's* Opera, or the Undoing of Women. —*LM*]

Ponnelle's the one who did the recent Manon *at the Met. You know, the one where Manon ends up in a pile of garbage.*

ROREM: The trouble with all of those directors: they're trying to breathe life into dead horses. Why doesn't Chéreau coerce his friend Boulez into writing an opera instead of doing the Ring? They spend their energies on masterpieces that have long since proved themselves. They're not taking any real chances. The important thing is new music. It always was until our century. Now all we do is these eternal revivals. The so-called "alternative versions" of the Ring or *Manon* or whatever, say, Frank Corsaro touches, all deal with updating, so that today's public will find it relevant. They update the costumes, sets, direction, viewpoint—everything except the music. But why not the music too? Why not add a "beat," as someone once did to Bach, adding tom-toms to *The Well-Tempered Clavier?* Because then it would be a truly new opera. Well then, just commission new operas instead of sprinkling bitter sugar— expensive sugar!—on old chestnuts?

MASS: *On this extremely important point, I've heard you say that concert music and opera, as we present and appreciate them here in the US, are the only major art forms whose art is almost exclusively of the past. Would you care to say more about this?*

ROREM: Movies didn't exist before our century, so they're by definition new. At the theater, nine out of ten plays are by living playwrights. Such plays of the recent past as those of Inge or William or O'Neill are called revivals. (Imagine calling a Beethoven symphony a revival, since Beethoven is the rule, not the exception.) The book reviews we read in the *New York Times* are virtually all about vital, breathing authors. The exhibitions in the galleries are nearly all by vital, breathing painters. (Only in the museums is there emphasis on the past.) This is true of every art except music, where the present is anachronistic and the past is sovereign. For most people, the serious living composer isn't even a despised minority. He doesn't exist enough to be despised. The vitality of contemporary music is something that even cultured nonintellectuals mostly aren't aware of. And I'm afraid that's true of people like Ponnelle and Chéreau too.

MASS: *But it's not just the directors. Who shares the responsibility for the mortuarial state of opera today? Is it our critics? Our audiences?*

ROREM: It's our managers. There are more gifted young composers around today than there ever were, but there's no outlet for them. No big orchestra will touch them. No opera company or recording company or publisher cares about them. So they are going to have to find their own way as creative artists, just as they will be forced to concoct new sexual rules since the advent of AIDS. They're going to have to do what Britten did in Aldeburgh or Peter Maxwell Davies in Scotland—start their own little groups. Management has a lot to do with it. Impresarios are in it for the dough and they lie when they say they're not.

MASS: *Herbert Breslin is in it more for the money than the art? I don't believe it!*

ROREM: To think that the great Jennie Tourel was required by her manager to go out on those tours in the sticks and sing "My Hero" from *The Chocolate Soldier,* in the face of her nuanced repertoire in eleven languages! And the condescension that her managers forced her into, of singing music that she didn't sing very well simply to pay the bills. Money shouldn't be what dictates. Beverly Sills shouldn't have to say, "I can't afford to take the chance." In every era but ours, one could afford to take the chance. Now, it's difficult if Pavarotti can make $100,000 for one concert—three times the amount a composer gets to write a whole opera. Conversely, it's difficult for a manager to ask a Pavarotti to sing a recital of contemporary American songs, or even one such song.

The legitimization of pop music with its huge public has thrown a monkey wrench into the situation. With that kind of potential for making money, why would managers want to do anything else? William Parker, for example, the best recitalist in America, has exactly zero recitals lined up for the next year. His singing engagements are mainly for foreign-language operas. There isn't one singer in America today who can earn a living fundamentally as a recitalist. In Europe, the few who can, like Ameling, Souzay, and Fischer-Dieskau, are all over the hill. As a result, the whole sense of how to shape a song is fading. There's no public for it, and that's management's fault. I don't know many managers personally. I don't have much to do with them because they have so little to do with living composers. I sometimes meet them at parties and never fail to say what I think. What have I to lose? With rare exceptions, they are unconcerned with contemporary American music. Yes, Matthew Epstein says he is. Tommy Thompson (who was Donald Gramm's manager) has been terrific. On the whole, though, they don't want their string quartets even playing Bartók, much less Elliott Carter, if it's going to scare away the women's club in Podunk. The dishonesty lies in their saying, "I want such and such singer to sing this, but the audience doesn't." Now, audiences will take what they get, if it's given to them right.

American singers are the only singers who don't sing first and foremost in their native language. They learn to sing badly in every language except their own, and on the rare occasions that they approach their own, it's by rolling their r's and doing all kinds of Europeanistic things that have nothing to do with English. Imagine a young French singer specializing in every repertoire except French! When American singers understand what they're singing about, they're terribly embarrassed. The great poetry in English is not really part of the tradition of American song. If you do get a small audience of 300 in a small theater for a recital of songs based on poems by Emily Dickinson or Elizabeth Bishop or John Ashbery, that can be a very heady experience. Managers would like to discourage this, because they don't want audiences of 300. They want 300 million. They're size queens.

MASS: *Hmmm ... I never thought of Cynthia Robbins as a size queen before. And what about our critics? Do you think they could have more influence on this situation?*

ROREM: Most of them have their hearts in the right place. But take Andrew Porter, who is arguably the most read critic in the country. He just doesn't have that much influence, judging from all the suggestions he makes that are never taken.

MASS: *Somewhere in the new* Diary *you note that John Rockwell wrote his annual piece urging the New York City Opera or the Met to do* The Mother of Us All *or* Four Saints in Three Acts. *And you ask, why doesn't he ask the managers directly?*

ROREM: Critics write these things, but nobody listens. Occasionally, a performer might become interested in a piece the critic has mentioned, but that's about it. Critics can stifle or even break a performer's career if it hasn't already gotten off the ground. But they can't really launch a young composer, or do much damage to an old one.

MASS: *One more thought about management. Any observations about Terry McEwen? [McEwen had just announced his retirement, for reasons of health, from the position of director of the San Francisco Opera.]*

ROREM: None, except that he's an old friend. His tastes are specific. He once said to me, "I'm not a music lover, I'm an opera lover." [As director of the San Francisco Opera], he couldn't have been more reactionary.

MASS: *Yes. During his tenure there was no emphasis on new works.*

ROREM: Yet he did commission, of all people, Hugo Weisgall, who writes very knotty music. When people like Terry finally decide to do their good deed, they'll be damned if they'll call on someone "accessible," like Carlyle Floyd or Tom Pasatieri.

Mass: *Terry McEwen is widely known in the gay community to be gay, though he has never been openly so in interviews. Respecting that opera was McEwen's business and that he was a professional, I think it says something about the minority status of gay people in the music world that he was the officially closeted homosexual director of the opera company of the city with the world's largest (proportionately) and most politically progressive gay community and audience during the era of gay liberation and the AIDS crisis. For New York, I think similar observations could be made about such leading musical figures as Stephen Sondheim.*

We touched on McEwen's tenure as director of the SFO and the issue of new commissions. To some extent, we've been exploring the status of opera in America. How would you contrast the place of opera in America with that in Europe? [The reason for the abrupt transition from discussion of McEwen and Sondheim to the question about contrasting the place of opera in America with that in Europe is that Rorem refused to comment on the homosexuality of living, closeted figures in the music world. As he says later in this interview, "I will not, and neither will Lou Harrison, compromise my friends." On this account, I was obliged to make a statement out of what had been a question ("How do you feel about . . . ?"), and move on to the next topic. In a recent telephone conversation, incidentally, Lou Harrison, with whom I've been in contact in efforts to set up an interview, tentatively confirmed Rorem's statement that he (Harrison) would not out someone who wasn't overtly involved in homophobic or fascistic endeavors and who didn't wish to be publicly identified as gay or lesbian — LM]

Rorem: Almost without exception, opera in Europe has been written by what we call experimental composers, from Monteverdi through Wagner to Nono and Berg, by chromatic composers, composers breaking or inventing the mold, starting new musical as well as theatrical systems. One of the reasons this has been so is the subject matter, which in Europe has always been rather short on humor and high on horror. Murder, incest, rape, you name it, from *Poppea* to *Lulu*. Except for Mozart—and Mozart was not necessarily, fundamentally an opera composer—I think this obtains. The Europeans were fundamentally opera composers—experimental, nondiatonic.

The reverse obtains in America. We don't have much of a history of opera, but what we do have is by plain diatonic composers. The operas that have lasted are the two operas by Virgil Thomson, which are possibly the best by an American, maybe Deems Taylor's two operas, Aaron Copland's one, Barber's two, the several by Douglas Moore, Blitzstein, Menotti. All of this is music with no accidentals. White-key music, as we say.

Look at the operas in this country that work. They aren't by Elliott Carter or John Cage. They're by Philip Glass and John Adams, and it's all nonmodulatory, super-simple music.

Doesn't this reflect a difference in the psychology of Europe and America? Is that why jazz is an American rather than a European thing and why a lot of our opera, like Gershwin's *Porgy and Bess*, stems from that kind of music? It's something to think about. Our opera themes aren't psychotic themes.

MASS: *What about* Lizzie Borden?

ROREM: But *Lizzie Borden* was never a hit. I'm talking about our most successful operas. We don't even have a failed opera by, say, Milton Babbitt. We do have madness, however, in the tradition of Martha Graham. There is no new music being written for so-called modern dance today, but there used to be. For every new score that's used, now, fifty are based on preexisting music. Except for Martha Graham, who's deliciously psychotic. She once commissioned a hundred different composers. But them days is gone forever.

MASS: *On the subject of utilizing preexisting music, I want to ask you something about your hypothetical Whitman opera. You've set a lot of Whitman to music already. How would those compositions that you've already created figure in with the new one?*

ROREM: It's always tempting in a case of this sort to want to cheat, to reuse something you've already composed. Yes, I have set a lot of Whitman to music. I've found, though, that when you cheat in that way, it never works. I might be able to use a tune or two, but I doubt that I could take intact a song written thirty years ago and put it into the opera. Unless the opera were a mere garland of songs and were in a sense my biography as well as Whitman's. But there's a difference in kind between a song and an aria, between something that's sung in a theater and on a recital stage. There's a difference in scope and intimacy.

For example, Whitman wrote the following:

> Stranger, if you passing meet me and desire to speak to me,
>   why should you not speak to me?
> And why should I not speak to you?

(The answer to the poem's questions, by the way, is: because you might get a sock in the jaw.)

I set that to music for piano and voice. It takes the same time to sing it as to say it. Now if I were to rethink that and put it into an opera, it would need some sort of introduction and postlude, something to get the piece onstage and off. Would I use the same music? Maybe not.

MASS: *Are there many examples of composers who take the text and rework it with lots of different versions?*

ROREM: Usually opera composers are not song composers. For example, Verdi and Menotti aren't known for their songs, and Schubert and Fauré aren't known for their operas. There are exceptions, like Virgil Thomson and Britten and Poulenc.

MASS: *And Richard Strauss.*

ROREM: Yes, but for every exception . . . People always use to say, "Ned, you write such great songs, you were born to write an opera." It doesn't necessarily follow. Song is a self-contained experience of two or three minutes. It's a distillation. A song is conceived on preexisting poetry that is unaltered, or should be unaltered. Operas are based on prose that often can't stand alone. When they try to write operas, song composers write visual song cycles and then cross their fingers. Opera composers are more involved with dramatic thrust. It must be worth watching as well as hearing. Arguably, Wagner fails. But Menotti, who is no Wagner, does not write boring operas . . . at his best.

MASS: *Did you see* La loca *or* Goya?

Rorem: Before I saw *Goya*, I read the frightful reviews and sent a letter of condolence to Menotti, who is an old acquaintance and who was my teacher when I was a nineteen-year-old at Curtis. About ten or twelve years ago I wrote an essay in his defense, against Henahan who had given him short shrift in a way that seemed undeserved. Henahan smirked about Menotti's moving to Scotland, more or less saying good riddance and isn't it silly that Menotti should take himself seriously. Well, I don't think that's very nice or right since Menotti, whatever he may be "worth" in retrospect, single-handedly put opera on the map in America.

Anyway, when he got my letter about the reviews of *Goya*, he phoned in tears, saying, "Oh, Ned, you're the only one who understands!" in that Italian way, and, "Let's get together soon," etc. Then I saw *Goya* on the television, and, well, I should never have sent that letter. The Menotti situation is a sad one. *The Medium* and *The Consul* are unflawed in their own way. His music is corn, but it's inspired corn. Like Tennessee Williams. After those early plays, everything went downhill. *Goya* missed the boat at every turn. Domingo was valiant to learn that thing by heart.

Years ago, around 1946, Menotti said in my presence that he would like to write a homosexual opera. One didn't say "gay" in those days. He wanted to do something on Proust, which, God knows, would certainly tempt me. But it can't be done. Like Kafka. It's too personal.

Mass: *If you were to write a new opera, would you write it with a specific singer in mind (e.g., the way Menotti wrote* La loca *for Sills and* Goya *for Domingo, or as Barber wrote* Antony and Cleopatra *for Price)?*

Rorem: It's hard to explain why the least difficult aspect of writing an opera is the music and the most difficult is finding a proper book and honing it into singable shape. What you're asking about is really one of the last considerations. To come up with a good idea about Whitman is simply the tip of the iceberg. You get the idea but *then* what? Sometimes a perfect preexisting text falls in a composer's lap. Lee Hoiby took *Summer and Smoke* and used it intact, after Lanford Wilson dolled it up a little. Barber did the same with *Antony and Cleopatra.* These operas are literally the play.

Dialogues des Carmélites is exactly the Bernanos film script plus a few set numbers from Catholic liturgy. If the right property existed now and didn't need to have much done to it, and it were in public domain, I'd grab it, whether it was old or new.

In the case of Walt Whitman, the work would need a point of view, which I still don't have. Once you get the point of view, the work should let him speak for himself through his own words, while trying also to be a biography.

As for a specific singer, I would coldly decide the role's going to be this or that kind of voice. Sometimes it's interesting to go against typecasting. It'd be interesting to do Whitman as a black countertenor.

MASS: *My first thought was that this would have been the perfect vehicle for the late Donald Gramm.*

ROREM: But Donald's dead now. He was the most intelligent and persuasive male singer we've ever known. I would have entrusted the role to him, but that's now idle conjecture.

MASS: *In* The Nantucket Diary, *you repeat a question someone asked you about which singers do you admire. You then go on to list a number of wonderful American singers, many underappreciated, about whom you say wonderful and interesting things. There were several prominent ones you didn't mention. Teresa Stratas, for instance.*

ROREM: Don't forget that a lot of the diary entries you're talking about were written years ago. Well-known singers change quickly.

Fifteen years ago I was a different person and the singing situation was different. I was the sole composer in the USA one thought about when American song was mentioned. That's not the case today. I'm not complaining, simply stating a statistic. They sing songs by Bolcom now and they still sing Barber a lot, but they don't sing my songs much, which makes me wistful.

Stratas? I've seen her in *Lulu,* in *Mahagonny,* and in the movie of *Traviata.* I don't care for her record of Kurt Weill; it's too slick and Slavic, but she's otherwise pretty interesting, though no more so than Migenes-Johnson.

MASS: *Did you see/hear her Mélisande?*

ROREM: Yes, years ago, and I liked it. It was too slow, but that was Levine's fault. I heard Von Stade do it on the radio the other day and I like her, too. Cool and mature. *Pelléas et Mélisande* is my favorite opera. Of course, Pelléas and Mélisande are really silly children. Bruce-Michael Gelbert recently quoted me for having once used that naughty word "gay" to describe Pelléas on the grounds of the text. There *was* something up between him and Marcéllus, whom he never gets to see again. But it's another one of those cryptic, dangling themes that's introduced by Maeterlinck, dropped, and never resumed. So Pelléas decides he's in love with Mélisande, but I think he's telling the truth when he says they've never sinned together. They were just pals.

Von Stade lent an unusual dimension to Mélisande, probably because of the darker sound of her mezzo, but also because of her less babyish (babyish the way Bidu Sayão used to do it) point of view . . . Mélisande is the escaped last wife of Bluebeard, or so Mary Garden used to contend, justifying her crazed performance.

MASS: *I remember when I read Mary Garden's biography I got the very strong impression that Garden had fallen in love with Lily Debussy.*

ROREM: Why not?

MASS: *In* The Nantucket Diary *you say that "the most valuable composers are apolitical and aristocratic (Wagner, Ravel, Stravinsky), or bourgeois and bearish and pseudopolitcal (Bach, Beethoven, Debussy), or just straightforwardly religious members of the status quo, like all those before the Industrial Revolution." Please elaborate.*

ROREM: Art can make political statements, but it cannot have political effect. Art is not moral, it is something else. It cannot change us, but it *can* reinforce our convictions and help us get through life. If I were able to make a political statement as an artist, I would. If I were able to write a song that could make people march away from war, I would. The way to stop wars is not to fight them. Art is created in leisure, not in the heat of battle. Art won't make a Democrat out of a Republican and it won't make a peacenik out of a warmonger, as the Nazis, who were very sensitive to music, have proved. And it won't make a nice person out of a bad person, as Wagner, who was a great genius and misguided rascal, has also proved.

I've written only one "political" piece, which is "War Scenes," drawn from Whitman's Civil War diary, but that could just as easily have been about the Trojan or the Vietnam war. It's about the horror of war in general. I'm moved by Britten's *War Requiem*. Who isn't? It's political yet enduring; but, again, he's using timeless words rather than timely ones.

MASS: *You're acknowledging that something timely can be just as timeless as something ancient or mythic, but you're skeptical about the prospects for anything very topical enduring as art. "Imagine* As Is *as an opera!" you once quipped. Hence your skepticism about doing a "gay" opera. Perhaps that's why, up until your current setting of one of Paul Monette's* Elegies for Rog *for the New York City Gay Men's Chorus, you had never scored anything with explicitly gay or other "political" content. I think it's sad that the only conceivable contribution of the Santa Fe Opera (the management of which has always had gay people in its highest ranks) to the AIDS crisis ended up being Penderecki's* The Black Mask *(based on Nazi collaborationist Gerhart Hauptmann's racist 1929 soap opera about the second wave of the black death in seventeenth-century Europe). Why couldn't a new opera about real people of our time (but no more than the extent to which* Figaro *and* Lulu *are explicitly of their times) have made just as strong a bid for artistic propriety?*

Did you see Malcolm X?

ROREM: Yes. In a Philadelphia tryout. I certainly wasn't against it in principle. Malcolm X was a powerful figure, a hero, but also an abstraction. You can humanize a hero, but not until enough time has passed for the hero to become a symbol, an invention, like Julius Caesar or Henry VIII. Real live heroes don't go into the street singing.

MASS: *Had enough time elapsed, according to your criteria, for this to work? That is, was* Malcolm X *a success, and, if not, was it because it was "too political" or "too timely"?*

177   *NED ROREM*

ROREM: No. The main problem was that it was unbalanced. The whole first section was completely improvisatory and fell flat. But as a tragedy it worked.

MASS: *What about* Mahagonny?

ROREM: Brecht was a political man and a less important artist than Kurt Weill. Weill succeeds in spite of his propaganda content rather than because of it. Music, insofar as it's propagandistic, can never persuade. Insofar as it veers from propaganda, it can work. *Malcolm X* became a tragedy about a hero, but Malcolm X himself is too remote now for even me to quite remember. A speech *by* Malcolm X is far more jarring than an aria *about* him.

MASS: *But in addition to the general human interest in Malcolm X as a tragic human being, the hero's main concern, racism, is timely, just as the fate of capitalism, the principal subject of* Mahagonny, *remains timely. So* Malcolm X *and* Mahagonny *are political rather the way* Figaro *was.* Figaro *was literally revolutionary in its views of contemporary class relations, and it dealt with everyday people and everyday life in contemporary Europe and was based on a play by a living playwright. It incited people to riots. What you're saying is that the long-range value of, say,* Figaro *transcends the class struggle in France that stimulated and permeates it. Everyone can agree with that. What I'm emphasizing, though, is that some great, timeless works like* Figaro *were originally as topical as some of the contemporary works — operas about Vietnam, racism, sexism, homophobia, and AIDS — you're so certain would be too propagandist, too timely, to endure.*
But even when an artist's themes are ancient and mythic and don't appear to be political, they often are, as in the case of Wagner. I was thus intrigued by your generalization that Wagner was apolitical.

ROREM: The Wagner case is a healthy example, like that of Rock Hudson dying of AIDS. Hudson showed that even a national idol can have AIDS. Wagner showed that a great artist can also be a son of a bitch, even wicked. It's necessary to demythologize the Hollywoodian notion of artists as "good people." I'm always moved when strangers tell me what a good person I must be, because I'm not. If they knew the real me!

MASS: *Some writers characterize* Lulu *as a "feminist opera." Are they bad?*

ROREM: Bad? The use of words like "homosexual," "Negro," "black," "gay," depends on how old you are, what part of the country you're from, and to the class of people you hang out with. The word "feminist" didn't exist during the 1930s when Berg wrote *Lulu,* at least not with the same resonance as today. Negro was a noble word when I was a kid, in an extremely radical milieu. Now that word is banned and we're supposed to say "black," which used to be a "wrong" word. Well, Paris is worth a mass, so I say "gay" now and "black" too, though I never used to. Like friends who change their names when they become famous. Sooner or later you get the hang of it.

MASS: *Do you think gay liberationists like myself are misguided in regarding the Countess of Geschwitz, the first explicitly lesbian and homosexual and feminist character to enter the international repertoire, as a source of gay and feminist pride? Or is she no more interesting or pertinent to gay or feminist history or to the so-called heritage I'm claiming of gay people and women in music and opera than, say, Mohammed, "Der Kleine Neger" in* Der Rosenkavalier, *is to the musical heritage of black people?*

ROREM: You've criticized me for talking about groups of people, like Jews, as though they weren't individuals. But you are inclined to talk about gay people as a group. I'm willing to talk about gay people as a group if it helps the situation. I don't think that homosexuality is a very interesting subject, *except* politically, just as heterosexuality is not a very interesting subject. As you well know, homosexuals are just as boring as heterosexuals. Homosexuality is interesting only insofar as homosexuals are a persecuted minority. (Of course, that's pretty interesting.)

We can make the past what we want to make of it. We can put motivations into Berg's works, and we might even be correct on one level, although he may have been quite unaware of what we think he was thinking. One can write doctorates about *Lulu* until the cows come home. The Countess can be interpreted in many different ways, unsympathetically as well as sympathetically. Finally, she is only what the music tells us she is.

MASS: *You must think, then, that I am likewise misguided in expecting our music critics to have said something about why the Countess might be especially interesting to today's opera-going public, with its large numbers of gay and lesbian persons, during this era of gay liberation struggles and AIDS. Incidentally, George Perle, who has characterized lesbian sex as "naughty," wrote me that he knows of no criticism, neither at the time of the writing and premiere of* Lulu *nor today, that engaged this question, period. I don't think he sees the pertinence of the Countess to today's audience and to our time as any more worthy of comment than you or Peter G. Davis do.*

ROREM: George was being naughty himself to have used such a characterization. Of course, all sex is naughty, which is why it's fun. Now, when you say critics, you're talking about nongay as well as gay critics. I recently read Ed Sikov's comments about [Christopher] Lehmann-Haupt's review of the Oscar Wilde book [by Richard Ellman] in the *Native*. Sometimes people point out homophobia where I don't see it, but in this case I did.

I was interviewed recently by somebody in Philadelphia for a straight magazine. In the galleys, the interviewer said something about "cheery" homosexuals. I wrote him back that I thought it was homophobic to stereotype a bunch of people as "cheery." He changed the reference, but reluctantly. By the same token, I'm not looking for homophobia all the time. Lehmann-Haupt would doubtless deny that he's homophobic, while being more careful in the future.

MASS: *Like your good friend John Simon, who graduated from his interview with you, in which his homophobia is the principal subject addressed, to become the film critic for William F. Buckley's* National Review? *Lehmann-Haupt has been homophobic many times in the past, and there have been repeated complaints in the gay press. I myself have written him letters.*

ROREM: Did he ever respond?

MASS: *No.*

ROREM: The disappointing thing is that someone like Norman Mailer, who's smart and, I gather, rather well read, is homophobic. It would be so much more interesting if he weren't. Most of our star heterosexual writers are inadvertently homophobic—Styron, Updike, Mary McCarthy . . . But going back to the question of critics, I think you're asking them to discuss something that's not pertinent in a review. It might be in a Sunday article.

MASS: *In a little review in the* New York Times *of Albert Herring, Donal Henahan, of all people, suggested that perhaps Britten identified with the character as a homosexual and that it's possible to see the opera as a kind of "coming out" story. That's the kind of timely, pertinent observation about something of interest to lesbian and gay persons that we almost never get in mainstream music writing, even when the critic is gay.*

ROREM: But Henahan's point had to do directly with Britten and the opera. With *Lulu,* you're asking critics to talk about social issues in their performance reviews.

MASS: *When the social issues are pertinent and interesting, yes, that's precisely what I'm asking them to do!*
When the Waldheim affair broke, the New York Times *published several op-ed pieces (by Anthony Lewis and others) urging James Levine to cancel his performances in Vienna and Salzburg, the way Toscanini did in protests to the Nazis and Fascists. Not only didn't Levine cancel his performances, he never publicly responded to these challenges. Was he wrong?*

ROREM: During the Second World War, I was almost a conscientious objector because my mother wanted me to be. But at the army exam, I arranged to get rejected not as a CO, but as a 4E, on the basis of nearsightedness and flat feet. A year later I again had to go through that same sordid business of the induction exam, so I got a letter from my psychoanalyst, who explained that I was "not sufficiently mature" to be in the army. (The army, as we know, is made up only of mature people!) I felt, and my parents agreed, that since the army is immoral, why be "moral" about staying out of it? I didn't want to be a conscientious objector. My sister's husband was a conscientious objector, and it was hideous. I'm not of that fiber. I have music to write. I don't like to throw stones . . . During the 1950s when I was living in Europe, and people talked about the cold war and collaborationists—did you know that so-and-so went to bed with German soldiers during the occupation?—I kept my mouth shut and listened. Who am I to say what they should or should not have done, since I was not in their place? Nobody has asked me to go to Austria. If I had been asked to go to Austria and my friends had asked me not to, I would certainly have thought about it. If I were Jewish, I don't know what I would do. I know people who have gone to South Africa. Will Parker, for example, gave recitals there but told his friends to keep quiet about it. Edward Albee, meanwhile, refused to allow his plays to be done there, which is sort of pretentious. It doesn't accomplish anything, unless it gets a lot of publicity. I can't presume to speak for James Levine. But Lenny Bernstein conducts in Vienna, and he's not exactly a fascist.

MASS: *In* The Nantucket Diary *you quip that you are a "gay pacifist," as opposed to being a gay activist. Actually, you're not the only prominent composer who is known to be both homosexual and pacifist. Britten and Tippett are two others. Do you know of any straight composers who are similarly, outspokenly pacifist?*

ROREM: Sexual orientation and pacifism are not related, certainly not in my case. I was born a pacifist and raised by convinced Quaker parents, both of them ardent heterosexuals. Britten, on the other hand, came to his pacifism by conviction. Probably, the same ten percent of pacifists are homosexual as the ten percent of taxidermists or horse racers are. I don't think there are any real generalities that can be made here. It has never occurred to me that homosexuality and pacifism have anything to do with each other. Pacifism is far rarer than homosexuality and, unlike homosexuality, pacifism has to do with intelligence. Pacifism used to be a dirty word. It's become less so since the 1960s. Also, with regard to your quoting of me, the opposite of pacifist is not activist. Pacifist has to do with peace, not with passivity. So it's a false play on words.

MASS: *In your essay on "Women in Music" in* Setting the Tone, *you ask the question, "Why have there been so few women composers?" If you've given the answer somewhere, I've missed it. Beyond your belief that art is ineffable and follows no rules, do you have a theory?*

ROREM: They've all been discriminated against. It's that simple. There are more women poets because there's less "manual" labor, less dirty work, involved in being a poet than in being a composer. It's hard to raise children and still spend twelve hours a day orchestrating.

But all composers are discriminated against. I don't think female composers today are any worse off than male. If I had to name twelve living composers who interest me, four or five would be women: Thea Musgrave, Betsy Jolas, Barbara Kolb, Louise Talma, Miriam Gideon, Ellen Zwilich . . .

MASS: *You've pointed out that I speak about gay people as a group. I do, to some extent, even though that group, like all groups, is unquestionably made up of a wide diversity of individuals. But as you've also acknowledged, most of my generalizations about gay people are affirmatively defensive of gay people as a minority. Your observations about Jews, by contrast, are often negative stereotypes about the entirety of a people. You once asked me if I thought you were anti-Semitic. I said then that I didn't think you were. I'd like to continue to believe that you're not anti-Jewish, Ned—and I know that many of your best friends and at least one of your principal patrons are Jewish—but a number of entries in* The Nantucket Diary *challenge that belief.*

For example, the last entry of 1973 concludes as follows: "I've never read The Diary of Anne Frank *([Meyer] Levin's book* [The Obsession] *concerns her rape by those presumed monsters who denied him use of his own theater adaptation), but while hearing him kvetch one wonders if [Otto] Frank did not himself author that diary. Could such a document— an intact work of art—have just been left like that? And many a broken-hearted poet has keen financial instincts."*

Now, how is this different from the sick jokes that were circulating about Marilyn Klinghoffer conspiring with the terrorists aboard the Achille Lauro *to murder her husband so she could collect the insurance money? In any case, hasn't the authenticity of* The Diary of Anne Frank *already been proved beyond a reasonable doubt?*

183   *NED ROREM*

ROREM: You're making a comparison that I didn't make. I don't know the *Achille Lauro* details. Nor do I see anti-Semitism in what I wrote. I *do* believe there's too much objective distancing in the Anne Frank book to convince me that she wrote it, such as after-the-fact generalities about the Holocaust that she couldn't have known both because of her age and when she lived. In any case, why is it anti-Semitic to believe this? Or am I obtuse?

MASS: *In transcribing your remarks here, I've capitalized Holocaust, mindful of your observation in* The Nantucket Diary *that you're tired of hearing about the 6 million. From now on, you want to hear about the 20 million or not at all.*

We touched on the subject of sick jokes. On page 407 you state categorically that "Jews did invent the sick joke." Certainly, it's legitimate to talk about Jewish humor, as you do in several places, but Ned, is there any real basis for this allegation? I mean, is it something you could prove, or even develop a consensus on?

ROREM: I was quoting Paul Goodman, who was Jewish. I should have credited him. By "sick joke" he meant the joke of despair—when all is so hopeless there's nothing left but laughter. He even wrote a play about it, *Jonah*, which Jack Beeson (a gentile) made into an opera.

MASS: *That's what seems so fascinating and contradictory about you, Ned—your willingness, habitual and often zealous, to generalize about every group one could think of except homosexuals.*

ROREM: That's mostly because when they themselves generalize, they get ungrammatical [*laughter*]. Every time I pick up the *Native,* I read something like "gay people don't like lavender but we do like gin." It should always be "We gay people don't like lavender, but . . ." etc. In their zeal not to be thought of as standing apart from their brothers and sisters, they forget to scan their written phrases. Even Ed White should know better.

MASS: *Let me ask you about one more of these statements. On page 412 of* The Nantucket Diary *you say, "Jews, more than Catholics or American WASPS, seem to feel a loathing for homosexuality." In view of the exhaustive history of Catholic and Puritanical tortures, witch burnings, and other Inquisitional persecutions of homosexuals (which has no counterpart in Jewish history, whatever the Old Testament prejudices and whatever the prejudices of Jewish fundamentalists and neoconservatives), and especially with regard to the current positions and statements of the Catholic church, is this statement really tenable?*

ROREM: My understanding of Jewish upbringing is that the notion of homosexuality is offensive biblically to Jews, whereas it doesn't even arise in the New Testament, much less in the Koran.

MASS: *I often wish you would tell us more about the gay lives of many of the important people you discuss, especially those who are still officially in the closet. The reason I wish you would do so is that it's in the interests of clarity as well as truth. Here's an example of what I mean. On page 196 of* The Nantucket Diary, *you note that you attended a recital by Eleanor Steber at the Waldorf Hotel, where you ran into socialite musicologist Joseph Machlis, who whispered to you: "It's like running into your best friend at a whorehouse." Now, that's very funny. But it's a lot funnier knowing that both of you are gay. Since Joe is still in the closet, however, this part of the humor (and the psychology it exposes) is lost on the vast majority of readers. By the way, in* The Nantucket Diary, *you mention a documentary for television about gay composer Charles Griffes. It was to be produced or directed by Roger Englander and hosted by you. Do you know if it dealt with (or was to have dealt with) the composer's homosexuality?*

ROREM: As narrator, I wrote my own script for this documentary. Naturally, I mentioned Griffes's policeman boyfriend, but CBS cut the reference.

MASS: *Generally speaking, do you think your being gay has had any impact on your progress as a musician and writer?*

ROREM: I don't know. You've pointed out that I've written pieces on Sappho and Whitman and Stein, but Whitman is the most used poet, internationally, by composers. In Japan his words are set to music, and by heterosexuals—Kurt Weill and Hindemith and Roger Sessions—right and left. It's not his homosexuality but his universality that has made him beloved throughout the globe. The first Whitman I used was in 1946, a pacifist poem, but also quite homophilic. I used Sappho the same year for choruses, but Sappho and Gertrude Stein are not exactly unknown and their publics are not queer publics, except for the classical ten percent. Also you overlook the fact that if I've done these three, I've done approximately 150 other poets, ninety percent of whom are, or were, straight, though some were drunks. Roethke for example. These issues don't arise when I'm composing—except, maybe, with the *Calamus* poems and *The Whitman Cantata,* which were made for special occasions. I will sometimes, because of the commissioner, use something that's a bit gayer than something else, most recently the setting of Paul Monette's agonizing AIDS elegy for the Gay Men's Chorus. But on the whole, I set whatever speaks to my condition, of love or hate or hunger. Too many nongay American bards have uttered universal feelings that strike home—Wallace Stevens, William Carlos Williams, Robert Frost, and so on—for me to restrict myself. Music cannot be defined as having any sexuality, although words, especially the prose of a libretto, can.

MASS: *Ned, with all due respect, may I suggest that what you can't see is how negatively defensive you are, like most homosexual artists of earlier generations, but in striking contrast to your colleague Lou Harrison. You're saying, yes, such and such person may be homosexual, but that has no meaning or importance, except for the fact that we are a persecuted minority. Bill Hoffman is similarly defensive about being called a gay writer. By contrast, Toni Morrison is proud to be thought of as a black writer, just as Isaac Bashevis Singer is glad to be called a Jewish writer. Morrison sees clearly that being a black writer does not mean that she's not also a woman writer and an American writer and a great writer. It's the same with Lou Harrison. Being gay is something affirmative. He's proud to be a gay composer and interested in talking about what that might mean. He doesn't feel threatened that this means he won't be thought of as an American composer who is also great and timeless and universal. Am I being bad again?*

ROREM: You say I'm defensively negative, but how can I win when you're making the rules? I'm not defensive. I'm simply defending myself. I will not, and neither will Lou Harrison, compromise my friends, especially those of an older generation (those happy few!) who have their own set of perfectly decent standards. If I've done so in the past, I regret it.

MASS: *The standards of older generations of closeted gay composers may have been decent and sympathetic twenty, even ten, years ago, but they're not now. They obscure the truth and abet homophobia. You keep saying that artists and composers are more discriminated against in our society than gay people. Ned, are artists routinely, daily, mugged, maimed, and murdered for being artists the way homosexuals are for being homosexual?*

ROREM: Jim has told me I must stop going around saying that. What I should say is that I have suffered less for being homosexual than for being an artist. I did suffer to some extent during childhood, when I was called a sissy, but my primary identity is as a musician. I do what I do best. I could never do what you and Larry Kramer and Andrew Humm are so nobly doing.

MASS: *But that's what's so funny about you. You do! As Bruce-Michael Gelbert recently suggested, you're like Katharine Hepburn, a living champion of women and feminist goals who vigorously denies having anything to do with women's liberation.*

ROREM: I think Gelbert's constant chiropractic bending of anything toward gaiety is at once touching and burlesque. It distracts from the business at hand: his often perceptive, often caring, criticism of music.

MASS: *I have the opposite reaction to Bruce-Michael. I think he communicates gay perspectives that are legitimate for the audience he's writing for (and often for a more general readership), and that he does so naturally, richly, and professionally, without eschewing the caring, objective criticism of music that may or may not be of overriding interest.*
You refer to Parker Tyler in your writing. Tyler wrote about homosexuality and movies. Did it ever occur to you, in the course of your friendship with him, that someone might write about homosexuality and music?

ROREM: Parker didn't write about gay people in movies. He

wrote about gay movies. Yes, somebody could write about gay music, but they'd have to be able to define it first. A movie is definable. Music is not. You're comparing genres that aren't comparable. Still, I'm not saying it can't or shouldn't be done.

MASS: *I think the following statement by another very outspoken gay American artist might well apply to you: "Do I contradict myself? Very well then I contradict myself. I am large. I contain multitudes." Am I wrong?*

ROREM: Of all the silly statements Whitman ever made, that's the most irresponsible. Even poets should not give themselves a loophole by saying they are so complicated that they think all sorts of different things. Of course, they do . . . But the contradictions need to be organized and then frozen into art. For people to use their complexity as an excuse for laxity is too easy an out. I don't approve of it, not for Walt Whitman, not for me nor anyone else. In the guise of being contradictory, evil things can happen.

Talking with Cole Gagne
1990

*N*ed Rorem currently teaches at the Curtis Institute, and divides his time between his house in Nantucket and a New York City apartment. I spoke with him at his Manhattan home on December 8, 1990, and again on February 24, 1991. Although he has published several volumes of diaries and had at that time just begun writing his autobiography, he has intentionally written very little about his own music. In speaking with him, I sought to learn more about his earlier, less well known compositions, as well as his more celebrated scores, vocal and instrumental.

COLE GAGNE: *You've called your* Four Madrigals *of 1947, on texts by Sappho, your "opus one," but I'd like to start a little before then. I read that you did music for two puppet shows earlier that year:* At Noon upon Two *and* Fire Boy.

NED ROREM: *At Noon upon Two* was on a text of Charles Henri Ford, who's still very much kicking, with puppets designed by the late Kurt Seligmann, a Belgian surrealist. All that came about through John Myers, one of the three editors of *View* magazine. *View* was the American artery of Surrealism published during World War II by Ford, Myers, and Parker Tyler. The European branch of Surrealism, as founded by Breton, was, of course, notoriously unmusical as well as homophobic, so the *View* contingent was something of an offshoot, certainly an antidote. (Those Europeans, incidentally, hadn't much humor, except perhaps for the filmmaker

Buñuel. I remember with amusement his announcement that, having just made out his will, he had decided to bequeath everything to Nelson Rockefeller. That news rings a cogent bell today when the Guggenheim Foundation is soliciting money from those still-living composers who once held fellowships. What cruel irony, when composers are, by definition, poor, and whose music should be more than enough recompense to the Guggenheim empire!)

Anyway, I got involved with them and wrote background music for a weird playlet about a puppet-man looking through a keyhole at two other puppets doing odd things to each other. The score was for flute and piano, with a bit of percussion which I played myself. *Fire Boy* was on a text of Charles Boultenhouse, Parker Tyler's friend. I wrote three songs for it. I've since recycled material from both of these works.

GAGNE: *Have you recycled a lot of your music from that time?*

ROREM: Not a lot. It might look that way, but that's not really the case. I'm quite prolific, but occasionally I do go back and pillage goodies from second-rate or unrealized things of my youth. Why not? Bach and Handel and Vivaldi and everybody else did. Or I'll take a song out of an unpublished cycle of yore, discard the words, and rearrange it. The Violin Concerto, for example, has a movement that's simply a song without a text.

GAGNE: *I was also curious about* That We May Live *from 1946, which is described in your catalog simply as a "pageant."*

ROREM: David Diamond was one of the first grown-up composers I befriended when I came to New York. He had been approached to collaborate on a grandiose affair about Israel, of which every aspect was completed except the music. David couldn't do it, so he threw it my way. I got all of $500, which was a lot in 1946 —certainly for me, when I was whatever, twenty-two or twenty-three. I'm very not-Jewish, except by association; I'm a Midwestern Quaker with a WASP background. But that made no difference to the producers. So I got together with writer Milton Robertson and his wife Marie Machovsky, a Martha Graham dancer. (At that same time I was working as rehearsal pianist for Martha Graham, so it was all part of the family.) They showed me a lot of horas and other Palestiniana. Robertson provided the script and Bob Schneider produced the thing. I've never seen them since. But I wrote a lot of Hebraic music.

GAGNE: *You were actually composing in that style?*

ROREM: I tried more then than I would today, for example, because I just sort of did what I was told. Have I salvaged anything? No. But it was a good exercise in orchestration. I hadn't heard any of my own orchestra music before 1946.

GAGNE: *That music was for full orchestra?*

ROREM: For full orchestra, dancers, speakers, mimes, singers— the whole damned thing. It was a pageant and was first done in Madison Square Garden. Then it was done later in Philadelphia. I remember having to hire a lawyer because they'd promised me another hundred dollars, and I couldn't get it. She got it for me, then charged a hundred-dollar fee.

GAGNE: *Regarding your studies at Juilliard,* People *magazine quoted you as saying you "learned nothing."*

ROREM: It's unfair to say I learned nothing at Juilliard. After high school, I went to Northwestern for two and a half years. My father, who was an angel, and my mother too, were both very decent about my wanting to be a composer. When I was very young, Father asked me, "Well, how do you expect to make a living?" A very American question. I gave a very un-American answer: "I don't care how I make a living as long as I have enough to eat and can write what I want." He was impressed. Today, even more than then, a child is gauged by how much money he hopes to make, and parents are proud of "my son the doctor." But Father and Mother, although cultured, intelligent, middle-class Chicagoans, were not specifically musically directed; now suddenly they were confronted by a *composer* in the family! That doesn't happen every day. When I quit Northwestern in 1943 to go to the Curtis

Institute, that was because Father himself had, in his many travels, presented some of my juvenilia at Curtis and they accepted me right away, which made my parents feel good. But I left Curtis after one year.

GAGNE: *I've read that it wasn't a very pleasant time for you.*

ROREM: I loved it in many ways—I made dear friends at Curtis. But I didn't see eye to eye with my teacher, Rosario Scalero. He was an unsuccessful composer, though he'd successfully guided both Barber and Menotti, his two prize pupils. He was their sole teacher. But they were a lot younger when they first went to the maestro in the '30s, whereas I was already nineteen and had ideas of my own. I strongly feel that young people need to study with, not great teachers necessarily, but someone experienced enough at hearing his own music well played that he needn't be jealous of the student. I left Curtis having learned a lot about the performing world. Some of my best friends today were colleagues at Curtis. Last night I dined with pianist Gary Graffman, who currently runs the school—he was just a little kid at school in those days, four years younger than me. Ironically, now I teach at Curtis, and am writing a left-hand concerto for him.

Father was very annoyed that I went to New York to work as Virgil Thomson's copyist. He cut off my allowance. But Virgil gave me twenty bucks a week for twenty hours copying. I put five dollars in the bank, paid ten dollars rent to my friend Morris Golde, with whom I lived, and had another five left over to get drunk on. A year later, for Father's sake, I went back to school and got a Master's Degree at Juilliard. To get a degree there, as distinct from a diploma, you must take a lot of extra-musical stuff. I passed the musical entrance exams and so didn't take music courses, except piano minor. I took English literature, sociology, a course called hygiene, phys ed, stuff like that. The English teacher was Elbert Lenrow, who gave a pretty good course which included the Greek tragedies in English and the Bible. I'm a literary person, always was, but had never formally studied the classics. Thanks to that I composed my first choruses on Sappho madrigals, and have never done better.

GAGNE: *Were you composing all that time at Juilliard even though you were taking so few music classes?*

ROREM: My teacher was Bernard Wagenaar. I liked him as a man but didn't learn much from him, really. I did write my Master's Degree piece, called Overture in C, which won the Gershwin Memorial award. I deserved the prize but it didn't. Michel Piastro conducted it in Carnegie Hall, and I got a thousand dollars to boot.

GAGNE: *When you won that prize, the* New York Times *reported, "With the money, Mr. Rorem will continue his musical studies in Europe, and it is his intention to devote himself to writing popular music."*

ROREM: What does that mean? What month was that?

GAGNE: *December of 1948.*

ROREM: The Gershwin event was in May of the following year. The Philharmonic played the Overture on May 19. I had planned to go to Europe in '48, because Eugene Istomin and others were already there, and I was going to meet them. But I got chicken pox. At twenty-three! I convalesced at Mother's and Father's in Philadelphia, and wrote the First Piano Sonata—the "Chicken Pox Sonata." But it was never my intention to write what would then be called popular music. The *Times* could have been misled by just the name Gershwin Award.

I took the thousand dollars and went to France, like everyone else for a few months. In those days, all good American went to Paris, as they had after the First World War. Nobody went to Germany, it was too close to the Holocaust, nor to England because it was full of English people. But France was there and everyone, black and white, went to France. I had planned to spend only the summer, but I met somebody, a doctor, who lived in Morocco. By a fluke I stayed on for eight years. The doctor, Guy Ferrand, invited me to spend a month in Morocco. This was in June, and I still had my boat ticket back to New York in September. But when September rolled around, I didn't want to go back. I cashed in the ticket and never returned.

GAGNE: *Was Morocco something of a retreat or withdrawal for you, or were you involved in its musical life at that time?*

ROREM: Morocco was a perfect spot for two years because I was out of the rat race: There was no competition, no pressure. In Fez, then later in Marrakech, I sort of composed my first everything: I sat down and categorically declared, "I shall now write a symphony"—it was not commissioned—"I shall now write a string quartet." And I wrote things that are just part of the repertory: my Symphony No. 1, my String Quarter No. 1, Piano Sonata No. 2, a violin sonata, choral works, piano suites, etcetera. I never wrote "Moroccan music." Well, yes, on two occasions, I did take Moroccan tunes heard on the radio and wove them in an American fabric just for the trick of it. But you'd never guess it. Morocco was the right place at that time. I got a Fulbright around then and went back to Paris to study with Honegger—whom I loved; he was a gentle, intelligent, dying man, and I was the star of his class. But I missed Africa and Guy Ferrand. I told Honegger about my ties in Morocco. He said, "Go on, there's nothing much I can give you now. I'll simply sign your monthly voucher and see that the Fulbright check is sent down there." What a mensch!

So I went back to Morocco. The tension was off there. All I did was compose and live with my friend. I did have an interesting "social" life because every week or two Guy would go off to inoculate tribes full of people who had never seen a city like Fez, where we were living, let alone Paris. I had a new education, learning French thoroughly by going to American movies dubbed in French with Arabic subtitles, reading the papers, and having a lover— lovers are more patient than real people. The best way to learn a language is in bed.

Still, I would go back to Paris every few months to get into trouble, hear concerts, go to parties, sleep around, do things young people do. But I did it with more violence than most. Then I met a woman, la Vicomtesse de Noialles, known to all as Marie-Laure, who was rich, famous, powerful, talented, opinionated, with the most beautiful house in Paris. She and I became very close. So I went back and forth over the Mediterranean, then finally settled in Paris for good. But I had come back to France with a backlog of works, most of which were then played in France, mainly because I was there to shepherd the performances. France is the least musical country in the world, and certainly ignores Americans, unless the Americans are there in the flesh.

GAGNE: *You've become well known for what you've called your "innate Francophilia." Yet you've written that Paris in particular is "the least musical of cities," and France "the most heterosexual of European countries." Either one would take some of the philia out of anyone's Franco; together, they seem positively damning.*

ROREM: Did I write that? Well, such generalities are themselves quite French.

The music part first. France has produced great musicians, great composers, and great performers, but not a listening public. Now Italians, for example, have a bigger whistling knowledge of their own opera literature than I do or than you do, and they rise in their seats and sing along. Any Roman barber knows his Rossini or Verdi inside out. Germans pridefully know their lieder, as the Spanish know their zarzuelas. But the French, who coined the word "chauvinism," will say, "Isn't it beautiful," even as the music is playing. They like to talk about music, more than they like to listen to it. The French are visual, culinary, sartorial; they know about food, about dressmaking, about painting. I love the French and have perhaps earned the right to say all this, though I don't necessarily like it when other people do. Boulez, for example, had to leave France in order to become a prophet in his own land. They intellectualize about music. France of course is going downhill now, culturally. They've got money, or seem to have, but they no longer have creative urgency in any of the arts. Boulez has got France in a stranglehold, with all that dough from the government and that hole in the ground called IRCAM. With hindsight, his own music seems now to be quite accessibly Impressionistic, in the style of the land, but he might not like to hear that.

As for homosexuality, that's a quaint thing to say. Does it mean anything? What I must have meant is that any country that's filled with expatriates is inclined to cater to the sexual needs of those expatriates. France used to be more broadminded than the USA, and probably still is. But the expatriate milieu is actually quite small, while the artists' milieu is even smaller. Painters are not on the whole very gay (likewise musicians). Certainly not in the France of the 1950s. And the French are a lot more bourgeois than one realizes: They get married, have children, gain weight, look at television. Italians get married, have children, but they don't gain weight; they'll spend their last lire not on a bottle of *vin rouge* but on a necktie. Again, I'm speaking of the old days. I don't know about today. Germany was always far more decadent, in the delicious sense of the word, than France, and overt homosexuality comes with decadence, at least in the eyes of the right wing. These quips are Gallic generalities. If I once believed them, they no longer seem very clever.

There are only two mystiques, or aesthetics, in the whole universe, French and German. French is superficial in the deepest sense of the word, whereas German is profound in the shallowest sense of the word. The French are interested in surface: Impressionism. Debussy shows us the glint on a wave during one split-second, and captures the glint forever. Monet shows us the peach-colored tint on a water lily which will never, never, never come again. The French are also very economical. They don't use too many notes, don't double in their orchestration, avoid thickening with schmalz. Germans are the reverse. They dig deep but in one small hole. The four-note motive (on but two pitches) of Beethoven's Fifth Symphony repeats itself until the cows come home. That's neither good nor bad, it's simply a way of thinking.

My attraction toward French culture was instilled long before I ever went to France, and comes partly from being raised in a Quaker Meeting where we didn't have much high camp. No incense, no saints, no gold, no choirs, no *tralala* at the French say. I was fiendishly attracted toward the Catholic church, which made my parents uneasy; they were wary of Catholics and they were probably right.

GAGNE: *But they'd let you visit those churches and their services on occasion, as part of your education.*

ROREM: Oh sure. But when I came home and started drawing pictures of crucifixes and things, they took a dimmer view. They didn't realize that I wasn't interested in the lore of the religion or the holy water per se, so much as in the balletic mystery of it all. In fact, Quakerism has as much mystery, but less veneer.

GAGNE: *And today, in pieces of yours such as* Gloria, *it's not the religious idea of the words that's important to you but the poetry and the imagery of the texts.*

ROREM: Exactly. Because I am an atheist. There is no God. Yet it's a philosophical necessity for people to have a God. I wish I could believe in Him, but I don't. I do, however, believe in the Belief that has caused great works of art to come about. Of course, there's also a lot of lousy art in the name of the Lord. Just as when I take a bow, thinking myself glamorous on the stage, and am surprised when people say, "Why are you timid and childish when you come out on the stage?," so with my music: I think of it as sensual and heart-on-sleeve, but Poulenc once said, "Be more like us, *mon cher* Ned. Be more French instead of such a Norwegian Quaker." We never "see oursels as ithers see us."

GAGNE: *How reciprocated is your Francophilia? Your books haven't been translated into French, have they?*

ROREM: No, they haven't. Which miffs me. Nobody knows me in France anymore.

GAGNE: *Do they play much of your music there?*

ROREM: If they don't, at least I am in good company: The French don't perform anybody's music. They know Cage and Carter. That's all. The last time I was there, in '84, I saw a lot of young people. I didn't like Paris then, but it was still the most unbearably beautiful city in the world. You need to be in love to live there.

GAGNE: *The idea of your composing a ballet on* The Picture of Dorian Gray *for a production supervised by Jean Marais sounds like the perfect convergence of talents. Yet I understand you've buried the score in a trunk somewhere.*

ROREM: That's an example of something occurring because I

was an American in France. Henri Sauguet, who died just last year at ninety, a dear friend of Virgil's, was a friend of mine, too—the wittiest man in the world. He was a disciple of Satie, and on the edge of Les Six. Jean Marais, whom I'd never met, said to him, "We need some music for a ballet we've got in mind," and Sauguet thought that I would be ideal. He was one of those who used to call me "Dorian Gray" when I was in France. Typecasting. So I met with Marais, who didn't really know much about music but was a direct and simple guy, considering that he was as famous then as Frank Sinatra. He came to the Hôtel des Saints-Pères where I had a sixth-floor walkup. The telephone man downstairs was all a-twitter when he announced, *"La marée monte."* Anyway, up came Jean Marais. I was in a room half the size of this, with an adjoining bathroom. On the sofa were pictures that Jean Cocteau had done for me (those on the wall over there). And of course Marais was Cocteau's principle protégé, and he said, "I feel right at home." But he wasn't at home, he seemed nervous. His friend, the American George Reich, danced at the Opéra Comique, whose chief choreographer, Paul Goubé, dreamed up the idea of doing *Dorian Gray* with Jean Marais as the painting and George as the living, ageless Dorian. So they got me for the music.

I'd written for modern dance, but never for ballet, and certainly not in France. It was about forty minutes, and scheduled to be premiered in Barcelona. The man who commissioned it, Alberto Puig, paid for the whole mess of people, orchestra and all, to come to Barcelona and do a one-night stand in May of '52. What a bomb! Julius Katchen had previously played my Second Sonata in Barcelona without my being there, so the Spanish knew my name, thank God. I went back to Barcelona in 1964, when Steinberg did my Third Symphony there. By then the *Dorian* fiasco was forgotten. But I recall Marais with pleasure, and still see him occasionally.

GAGNE: *Had you stayed in France, could you have carved out more of a career for yourself in terms of commissions and performances?*

ROREM: Probably not. I wouldn't have stayed if it hadn't been for Marie-Laure. My life was hardly a typical American life: I lived with the richest woman in France. Private patronage is a thing of the past, yet for me then there was still a touch of Proust's *avant guerre* dribbling in. Every day for lunch she would have worthwhile people, Cocteau, Balthus, Poulenc, the Aurics, Dora Maar. Well, not *every* day. I did not lead an idle life; I worked hard. I thought of the physical ease as, in a way, a scholarship. I'm alcoholic, though it's no longer a problem because I now just don't drink—it's been twenty-two years. But I would play as hard as I worked, and I would go from Hyères in the south of France, where she lived, to Cannes to get drunk and screw around. Well, I'm still alive to tell the story. Anyone today living the life I lived then would not survive, for various reasons, not just health: You'd get killed. Life in bars and streets was less dangerous in those days. Partly because of her—not to mention lovers—I stayed in France. But finally I told myself, I'm American, my problems were born in America and can only be solved in America.

GAGNE: *Musical problems?*

ROREM: The whole concept of what it means to be a composer in our world.

I had a relationship that ended badly in 1957, which is when I returned to residence in New York. Here, I started earning my living as a composer, and have been doing so ever since—knock wood.

GAGNE: *Back in the '70s, John Gruen wrote that you were one of the few people who supports himself as a composer.*

ROREM: I support myself, yes, but humbly. I've never been a whore though I sometimes wish I could be. I'm too lazy to write the kind of music I don't want to write, music that's in style, serial one year, minimal the next. To write a musical and make big money —or even to have a flop—you have to know people that I'm not interested in knowing, like producers, backers, collaborators, cash-minded Broadway types. If I do live off commissions, it's not a grand life, and with no guarantee for what will happen after two years from now. But I do exactly what I want.

GAGNE: *I had thought that it was the money from writing prose which made the difference for you financially.*

ROREM: No. When I published my first book I was already forty and had lived as a professional musician twenty years before that. Since then I've led a schizophrenic life, or rather two parallel lives. People who read my books often don't realize I write music, and people who invite me to music schools to do a stint often don't realize I write books. What I earn from prose is less steady than from music. I'm a composer who also writes, not a writer who also composes.

What a composer gets, even the best-known composers—and there aren't that many—to write a symphony is a tenth of what, say, Philip Roth gets to write a novel. And I'm still talking about high art, not about Harold Robbins, much less Mick Jagger or that whole world of pop, where they make billions.

Money is always a concern, just to pay the bills. What I get from teaching is negligible; what I get from prose and royalties and so forth is negligible. I have an advance for an autobiography from Simon & Schuster, but it's not all that much. It'll keep me alive for a year and a half.

GAGNE: *You've gotten money in the past from the NEA, both as a composer and as a writer. Have you had any dealings with them since they've started policing the work they partially support?*

ROREM: I've signed various petitions that are against the dumbness of it all.

GAGNE: *Does that put you on an NEA shit list?*

ROREM: I don't care at this point. I've had two or three (or four or five, I forget) grants, both as composer and author, directly from the NEA, and I appreciate these grants. But now, and not just because of Helms, the bottom seems to be falling out of the NEA.

I'm not a pornographer, though I'm not against it. It's amusing to hear people talk about their "tax dollars," because it's not dollars but pennies that go to the arts in the USA. In Australia, which hardly has the money that America has, citizens pay the equivalent of eight tax dollars a year for the arts. The NEA has done a lot of good, yes. But they're inclined to push populist art without making a definition, and there is a difference in kind between me or Wuorinen and school children or street mimes. That doesn't mean I'm any better. Also, pop music can look elsewhere for money, because it's inherently a more lucrative thing.

It's rather healthy, all the flap. The Mapplethorpe pictures are perfectly beautiful. How embarrassing—what the French must be thinking of all this about fundamentalist fuss! But for all I know, they're doing it now too. The French can be evil and mindless, but in different ways. They have people like Le Pen, a real fascist, anti-Semitic, and who has fifteen percent of the vote or something like that in France. But I doubt that he's concerned with cultural pollution.

GAGNE: *In* The New York Diary *you commented on the difficulty of writing your Flute Trio.*

ROREM: It's hard to write music, period. Writing anything is hard. The last movement of the Flute Trio, I remember, was hard because it's fast. It's easier to write slow music. You can sometimes improvise or even compose at the speed it takes to hear it; whereas with fast music, it can take a month to set down thirty pages that last one minute. This has to do with gauging and perspective and distancing and so forth, and not just mooning around and being inspired. You can't be inspired for much more than an hour at a time anyway, and some pieces take weeks, months, years.

Also, as I remember, there's only a small amount of information in that last movement. Which meant using that information upside down and backwards with the age-old devices of elongation and diminution, then trying to make it all theatrical, make it have contrast, and still hold together.

GAGNE: *You wrote almost no chamber music for a long stretch after the Flute Trio. There's* Lovers *and several scores of incidental music for the theater, but it's only in the last twenty years that you've produced a real body of chamber pieces.*

ROREM: Chamber pieces without voice.

GAGNE: *Yes, precisely.*

ROREM: Because there are a lot of chamber pieces with voice: trios, quintets, quartets. *Lovers* is ten movements and lasts the same amount of time as the Flute Trio, which has only four. The Trio was a question of development; *Lovers* was a question of using one inspiration and shutting up after it had been expressed—there's a movement in *Lovers* that's only eight measures long.

GAGNE: *That form of a series of images is a congenial way for you to work.*

ROREM: It was. I'd like to get out of that rut. I'm writing a piece now, the Piano Concerto for the Left Hand, which I think will have only eight movements! But the piano trio *Spring Music* has only five, and the String Quartet which I've just finished has five.

GAGNE: *I'm very interested about that piece, because it's been forty years since your Second String Quartet.*

ROREM: Will I ever write another one? The First Quartet doesn't count; there are only two quartets, but the Second Quartet was printed so quickly, and with that title, that I couldn't change it to "First Quartet."

When dealing with the human voice, I have a text and so I know where I'm going before I start. Without a text, I flounder more. I have to decide where I'm going according to some sort of imagined scenario. I'm a bit at a loss if I don't have a voice, which means in a way that I have to work harder. Maybe, as a result, the piece will be a better piece or at least better crafted. Then again, it's not for me to say.

GAGNE: *Did it seem a bit much to be working on both a piano trio and then a string quartet, after not having done either for so long?*

ROREM: And the Trio was written right after *The Auden Poems*, which is for trio plus voice. However, that's a radically different thing. With a trio plus voice, you think orchestrally. And the voice is the star—even if you don't want it to be, it has to be. That's the nature of the beast.

I didn't want to write a quartet. But then, when it was the Guarneri that would play it, I decided I should.

GAGNE: *You felt reservations just about the genre itself?*

ROREM: Well, about getting ideas for this abstract combination —until I put aside the worn-out notion that the string quartet is the most profound and intimate of combinations. Why can't a person write silly music for quartet? Why can't they write French music or light music or gorgeous music? Why must it always be so bela-bored? So I composed what I wanted to, and think it's a pretty good piece as far as structure is concerned. I don't know yet if it comes to life (it won't be played till next June), but I'm not ashamed of it. Yes, it is more complex perhaps than other pieces of mine, but certainly Milton Babbitt wouldn't hear it that way. One of the five movements already existed in the multisectioned *Remembering Tommy*, which is not as a whole an entirely successful work. I re-arranged the movement for string quartet, which meant a fifth of my work was done! It's exquisitely tonal, and the rest of the music is less so. In the Piano Trio, the next-to-the-last movement was written two years ago as a four-hand piece for the birthday of a friend, but the rest of it is all original.

GAGNE: *Did writing chamber music pick up for you in the '70s mostly because of commissions? They can run in cycles for a composer.*

ROREM: I usually get commissioned to write what I want to write anyway, because people know what they want from me. But some time ago, I would get more commissions than I wanted to write pieces for voice and orchestra. Once pieces of that genre get premiered they're seldom heard again, so I didn't want to write yet another piece for voice and orchestra.

I got commissioned to write *Night Music* for violin and piano right after finishing *Day Music* for violin and piano. I didn't want to accept because I now had other things in mind.

GAGNE: *Yet you went ahead and made it a companion piece to* Day Music.

ROREM: They nourish each other. In one way, it was difficult because I was stale on the idea; in another way it was easy because I wasn't stale—the idea still churned.

I also wrote two concertos, the Organ Concerto and the Violin Concerto, at the same time, and used the same device in each of them. Things come in pairs. Just like I wrote the saxophone suite, *Picnic on the Marne,* and the cello suite called *Dances* at the same time. I tend to have any piece I write feed off the previous piece. But the third piece doesn't feed off the first: They go one-two, two-three, three-four, four-five, five-six, like that. And then sometimes six-one: I'll steal something from before.

GAGNE: *You've produced a good deal of orchestral music, but the last time you wrote a symphony for full orchestra was in the late '50s. Do you think symphony writing per se is old hat?*

ROREM: I called pieces symphonies to impress my mother and father—"symphony" means you're grown up. I now have a student from Scotland, David Horne is his name, who wrote a two-movement orchestra piece and wondered what to name it. I said to call it "Symphony." Instead of those currently "in" titles like "And the River Flows Through the Jade Nightmare" or "The Easter Eggs of Fate," just call it "Symphony." Symphony applies to anything now. It always did. Between a Tchaikovsky symphony and a Haydn symphony, there is a gulf. And *Francesca da Rimini* could as easily be called a symphony.

Of the four symphonies I've written, none is a symphony in the sense that their first movement is in sonata-allegro form. But they all deserve the title because they're all big-scale, multimovemented affairs with cyclic use of material. Including the String Symphony. But I don't know if I'll ever write another one. I try not to disqualify any species per se; just about whether the species is done well or isn't done well.

GAGNE: *Was the String Symphony commissioned as a symphony?*

ROREM: The orchestra in Georgia wanted me to write a piece for voice and orchestra, and I said no way. (That's the first time I've ever used that phrase!) I had just written *After Long Silence,* a very pretty suite for voice, strings, and oboe. I wanted to write a straight, big orchestra piece, and then thought that just strings, which I've never done for that size, would be fun. I also definitely had Robert Shaw and his orchestra in mind, and tried to write a piece that would impress Shaw because I worshipped him when I was a postadolescent.

GAGNE: *And part of the way to impress him was to do the piece as a symphony?*

ROREM: I wanted to write what I wanted to write, but I didn't want to lose him by being huffy about not writing what he wanted. I said, "Please, I've just finished that. Can't I write something not with voice?" I might have done it if he'd wanted a choral piece; but I don't remember that he did.

The two big choral pieces, the *American Oratorio* and *Good-bye My Fancy*, are both symphonies. Especially the second one because it's a three-movement structure. I might do another piece like that and call it a symphony.

GAGNE: *Your projected orchestral piece* Whales *I understand was intended to form a triptych with* Eagles *and* Lions.

ROREM: Actually, I wrote three big gorgeous pages and orchestrated them and copied them. That's a long, long time ago, in the early '60s. After I wrote *Lions* and *Eagles* and thought about *Whales*, both Crumb and Hovhaness came up with whale pieces, so I lost interest. Which is understandable: We were all three barking up the same tree. An underwater tree, of course.

GAGNE: *Were you at all interested in the actual whale's sound? That's a common thread in both the Crumb and Hovhaness works.*

ROREM: No, I wouldn't have done that. I did it once, with the music for the original stage production of *Suddenly Last Summer*. When Sebastian's mother is talking about the gulls that swoop down and eat baby turtles, I wrote some long, quivering, ominous phrases to back her up, and in the studio we superimposed the screeches of real gulls, which was effective enough, I suppose.

GAGNE: *Would* Whales *have had a dream as its basis, as* Lions *did?*

ROREM: No, I was going to base it—as I'd based *Eagles*—quite literally on a preexisting poem, D. H. Lawrence's *Whales Weep Not*. In fact, the only time I've ever written illustrative program music has been in the tone poem based on Whitman's "The Dalliance of the Eagles." Every one of those ten long lines I parsed ahead of time and said, "I will represent this first line in music this way; the second line that way; the third line; the fourth line; and so on." If you read the poem, the music inevitably—dare I say literally?—reflects each verse. The verse became an excuse to write music, the way another person would use sonata form. I don't really believe that nonvocal music represents anything beyond itself; or if it does, we can't pinpoint it. But such is music's flexible power, that whatever its composer says, in words, about it, is likely to be visually conjured up by the listener. This was true with *Lions*—I'd based that on a dream. But *Sunday Morning* isn't really based on Wallace Stevens's poem. The titles were tacked on after the fact. Thanks to program notes, listeners "see" the sea when they hear *La Mer*. But if Debussy had named his tone poem *Abbatoirs*, listeners would "see" slaughterhouses while hearing the identical score.

The solo cello suite *After Reading Shakespeare* is in nine movements, each with an epigraph from the bard. I had those pretty much in mind while working. But those are intellectual statements made by man on the state of man, whereas *Eagles* is about animals. It's easier to think up musical reflections of animal behavior than a musical reflection of King Lear at his own death. It's easier at least for me to get a musical idea from a depiction of nature than from a human outcry.

GAGNE: *Is* A Quaker Reader *something of an exception to that?*

ROREM: Yes. The epigraphs for those eleven pieces stood before the fact. Certainly in "Mary Dyer did hang as a flag . . .": There's a trill at the beginning on the pedals, like the jiggling feet of a person just hanged. In a scene from Sartre's filmed version of *The Crucible*, they hang a bunch of witches: The camera goes to their feet. We don't see their necks cracking or eyes bulging, we see their feet

shuddering. Hence the pedal point at the opening of my music—
an image I would never have gotten if I hadn't seen that movie.

I don't like to intellectualize music. But the older I get the more
useful it seems. I would have turned up my nose twenty years ago
at thus describing music visually to a performer.

GAGNE: *Do you find there are common misconceptions among per-*
formers when they first approach your music?

ROREM: Since I compose mostly on commission, I usually
know who I'm going to get before I get them. Nor is my music
problematical in the sense that, say, Elliott Carter's music is. You
can pretty much get the point of what I'm after just reading through
it. So when I show up at a final rehearsal, all I'll say is: faster or
slower or louder or softer. I seldom say, "More something else."
When a group like the Beaux Arts Trio, who are used to playing
standard repertory, play a new piece, they approach it as though it
were real music rather than "something contemporary." They practice and then we talk. They'll sometimes put in interpretive things,
a tinge of vibrato or a twist of rubato, which I might not have
thought of. I'm always vaguely flattered when people "interpret"
my music. But of course, I've lived among singers for so long, and
as performers they have the broadest gamut of approach. With a
female as opposed to a male interpreting the same song, the approach is by definition wider than two oboists or two pianists
playing the same thing. When I teach a class of singers, I am more
lenient about even the speed of a given song if a bass sings it or if
a soprano sings it. With your eyes closed, there's a big difference
between a bass and a soprano, but none between a male and female
drummer. Sopranos can demand and get equal pay, which women
instrumentalists cannot.

GAGNE: *I was wondering if perhaps, precisely because your music*
isn't like Elliott Carter's, musicians might assume it's simpler than it
really is, or that what's happening is more on the surface than it really is.

ROREM: I've nothing to add—I mean, you've said it.

A good musician gets the point, so that nothing you say is
really necessary, while a bad musician never gets the point, so

nothing you say can help. Sometimes you'll hear a piece played so wrong, usually by people who don't have much métier. All I can do as a composer is try to spark enthusiasm—especially if I'm enthusiastic. That helps. People like to be flattered. If I'm not enthusiastic, they can't help but know.

GAGNE: *I'm familiar with your comments about Billie Holiday's phrasing and nuance in your own development as a songwriter. What I'm curious about is your remark that Count Basie's piano playing still shapes the way you approach composing for piano. Was that a bit of an overstatement, in retrospect?*

ROREM: It's certainly true of Billie. I loved her. Still do. Her name is sacred to me.

GAGNE: *You knew her, didn't you?*

ROREM: Well, sort of. In Chicago, when "Strange Fruit" first came out in 1938, we all went to see her at the Panther Room. It was magical, it was theater, it was grown up. She smelled good, she looked good, with that gardenia in her hair, she drank mintlike drinks and wore satin clothes and long red earrings, and sang those unbelievably sad songs—almost always by white people, standard repertory, as distinct from Bessie Smith, who did the blues. It wasn't the tune but her way with the tune that influenced me.

I'm American and no American of my generation was unaffected by jazz, even Elliott Carter—or so he claims.

GAGNE: *Could you describe how the way in which you notate or even conceive the piano writing for your songs has been affected by your work as an accompanist—I mean, as a pianist?*

ROREM: "Accompanist" is a good word.

GAGNE: *Is it? It makes me a little bit nervous.*

ROREM: It's a good word if you clarify that the singer too is an accompanist—accompanying the piano. The two accompany each other through the adventure of the song.

I've always been a pianist—it's my only instrument, my sole point of reference. The fact that sometimes I do and sometimes I don't play my own music in public might affect some pieces. If I'm composing, say, a chamber music piece that includes piano, for somebody else, I don't conceive for my hands. Last summer I wrote a piece for trio plus voice—*The Auden Poems*—knowing I was going to play it myself. I fashioned the patterns according to my performing ease. When I've had to learn certain pieces by myself but not written for myself, I learn them as though I were learning somebody else's music.

GAGNE: *You mentioned the element of theater in Billie Holiday's singing. You've written that Marc Blitzstein helped show you how the theater was integral even to what you called "remote forms like recital songs."*

ROREM: All art is theater. Any art that exists in time—like drama, or music—is theater. People pay to sit still and experience something. That is theater. Song is theater. Last night, while coaching a baritone, I said to him, "This is not real life, it's a concentration of life. You are a singer, you have to look at the audience, from you to them. You can't hide behind your instrument as a violinist does, or a pianist. Your face will be scrutinized, it's part of the show. If you lift your eyebrow ever so slightly, it must mean something." If Billie Holiday closed her eyes, it's because she had to. It was the tiny gesture that made mountains crumble. A song is a miniature opera. A song that lasts for one minute is still an event that goes from A to Z.

GAGNE: *I'm curious about your 1965 opera* Miss Julie *and its revision in 1979. Was that mostly a matter of cutting and tightening, or did it involve some real rewriting?*

ROREM: It was originally a two-act opera, two hours long. The librettist, Kenward Elmslie, and I did the sensible thing and went back to Strindberg's version, which was one act. Intermissions are always dangerous. We cut the chorus, and squeezed the opera into an hour and thirty-five minutes, which was also much less expensive.

GAGNE: *The* Painted Smiles *LP of highlights from the '79 performance made a big impression on me, not the least reason being I could understand almost everything that was sung. That isn't true of a lot of recordings of your songs — with the exception of most of Donald Gramm's performances.*

ROREM: He's irreplaceable. I miss him.

GAGNE: *He comes right through — it's just amazing. And it makes me wonder to what extent intelligibility and the communication of words contribute to the theatrical sense you've been describing.*

ROREM: It's maximal. All singers should forget about their voice ninety-nine percent and think about the words ninety-nine percent. The great ones, like Donald Gramm, when teaching classes for singers, don't talk about diphthongs, they talk about verse. Phyllis Curtin says, "I think about what the poem means. It's got to mean something to me. Whether I like the poem or not, I have to pretend that I do, because I impart the poem to the audience through the music." Donald said, "I know I have the greatest voice in the world, so I forget about that and think mostly about the text. But I don't psychoanalyze it." A man inherently has better diction than a woman because he sings in the spoken range more than a woman does.

GAGNE: *In your notes to* Pippa's Song, *you said that because the coloratura register was so high, for once it was your fault, not the singer's, that the words couldn't be readily understood.*

ROREM: I wouldn't perhaps set it that way today. When I take a liberty with prosody, I have a reason. I don't repeat words which the poet has not repeated, but I will do a melismatic thing, as in *Pippa's Song.* Or I'll decide the words don't make much difference since everybody knows them anyway, or at this particular point the tune's more important than the text, and so forth. I don't do this out of inspiration, but out of calculation.

In *The Schuyler Songs,* "It—the war—goes on" is said twice because Jimmy Schuyler repeated the words. I'm always amazed when somebody like Benjamin Britten, who's no fool and knew a thing or two about word setting, would not only repeat words but functionless words, like "the." In his operas, that's OK, because the character might be someone who stutters. But on poems of Michelangelo or Thomas Hardy, I don't know why he does it. There's always an alternative whereby a composer can keep his notes and eat them too.

GAGNE: *You've set texts in other languages than English. Is it true that you've promised yourself not to set French anymore?*

ROREM: America has for generations been the leading country in the world, so far as prosperity and business and munitions are concerned. Nevertheless, we've always had a vague inferiority complex about the arts, which is why we still hire European conductors; which is why most of the opera that is done is still done in the language it was written in, with or without supertitles; which is why composers of vocal music (I mean just songs, not opera), of whom there are fewer and fewer, will as often as not write music in languages not their own. And why singers learn to sing (usually badly) in every language except their own. If I and my brothers and sisters don't create an American song literature, no one's going to do it for us. Certainly there's no Frenchman setting only words in American to music, the way George Crumb so madly sets Lorca rather than letting the Spanish do it. We've got a huge literature of first-rate poetry in the American language, from both the 20th and 19th centuries, just as legitimate as any other language, and it's a waste not to use it. I'm still surprised when song composers of all persuasions in America will still write in mostly other languages.

Yes, I too have written in other languages, mainly on commission. In a way I've earned the right to do it because I've set hundreds of different poets and prosifiers in English. I did two poems of Plato in old Greek because a young person in the early '60s wrote me a letter and said he would give me a hundred dollars apiece if I would do so—as a birthday gift for his lover. The idea touched me. I did a mass in Latin, as a phonetic experiment, because nobody knows how Latin goes anyway. I did many songs in French in the '50s, but I was after all living in France, and it was a second language. And I've set some Italian poems that have never been published or even sung, during the winter that I lived in Rome. The trouble with all that is, if a Frenchman is going to stoop to singing something by an American, he's at least going to try to sing something in English; and if an American singer's going to stoop to singing something by an American, he's not going to want to sing French songs by that American. So the songs never get performed.

It's important to stress the evil of Americans writing in foreign languages. I feel even moralistic about it, as I feel moralistic about repeating words that the poet hasn't repeated. Song in English should come from pride in our own tongue, the way the Germans and French have pride, the way the Italians have it, the way even the English have it, but which we don't. Not repeating words: that has to do with respect for the poem.

GAGNE: *I was very interested to read that you'd received some flak for writing* Ariel, *your piece for voice, clarinet, and piano, on the basis that a man shouldn't be setting poems by Sylvia Plath.*

ROREM: That was at the beginning of the women's movement. Robin Morgan was more hyperthyroid in 1971 than she is now, twenty years later. I recall being shocked when she, a close friend, told me, "Keep your hands off Plath, she belongs to our sisters," because poetry doesn't belong to anyone, including the poet, once it's written. When I composed *Women's Voices* for Joyce Mathis, a black soprano who commissiond me, I set to music all women's poems. But I didn't take any black women, for the simple reason that there's no black in me.

GAGNE: *In the Plath poems you set, the persona is female but there's nothing she describes which is so unique to being female that those images couldn't be appreciated by a man or used by a man.*

ROREM: However, time has passed and I don't know whether I would use them today. The interesting thing is not whether I have the right, but whether Robin Morgan or her clan can tell whether a woman or a man had done the settings, if they didn't know beforehand. Women composers are not as worried as they used to be. "No one's going to call me a woman composer," they would seem to declare, and write music that was far more butch than any man's.

All that's changed today. There's a wider space between a good and a bad composer than between a male and a female composer.

GAGNE: *Has* Ariel *been performed as much as your other cycles?*

ROREM: Well, things go in . . . cycles. One teacher, say, will get ahold of the piece and assign it to a lot of students; or one singer will hear it and then decide to perform it on tour; or the shove will come from a clarinetist, because it's a showy piece. If I go to a college or something like that, they might get a soprano and a clarinetist on the faculty to do it with the pianist. And I've heard it done very well indeed by lots of different kinds of people. I would just as soon hear a man sing it if he wanted to.

GAGNE: *I wanted to ask you about that.*

ROREM: Music is above sex. It can be about sex, but it isn't sex; it represents sex. Therefore, a woman playing a man's role in the Strauss or Mozart operas, once you get used to it, you don't question it. When black Leontyne does white Tosca, you get used to it in about a minute. When men do women's roles, we're not used to it, so it strikes us as either funny or macabre (as when *The Maids* of Genet, which was written to be performed by men in drag, was done that way as a ballet by Herbert Ross—it's frightening). A lot of people don't agree, but I think that a man can sing a woman's songs and vice versa—providing that the voice can adapt itself without too much transposition. A woman once asked me if she could do *War Scenes*, and I said, why not? It's her world too; the war effects her just as much.

GAGNE: *There's a wonderful observation you made about William Flanagan's music: "In refusing to conform to the nonconformists, he presents himself as the most avant of the avant-garde."*

ROREM: He was still alive when I wrote that. I wouldn't say it now.

GAGNE: *Would you write that about your music?*

ROREM: I don't write about my own music.

GAGNE: *I've noticed!*

ROREM: I'm not interested in what composers say about their own music. Composers can't really know anything about their own music from the outside in. I may be astute about other people's music, and say things that need saying, and I love writing about music that I love, rather than music I hate. But my own music must sing for its supper all alone.

GAGNE: *I'm interested in this idea of conservatism as a form of rebellion. Were you thinking also of your own music when you wrote that about his?*

ROREM: I might have been sympathetic to Bill because musically we were two of a kind. I was more publicly successful than Bill and a lot more prolific. He didn't resent that, although he did try to imitate my devices. But he wasn't me so it didn't work. I don't mean imitate the music, but the life I led. His metabolism was different from mine.

I write what I write. I survived a long, long period when my music was not in fashion. As I said before, I'd like to be a whore but can't. I'm too lazy. Never during that period from 1955 until 1980 did I write a piece of the kind everyone else was writing, willfully ugly, which nobody liked anyway. Copland did it, but I knew his heart wasn't in it. Plus, all the other younger people. It's easy to hide behind such music, because you can't tell the good from the bad. When the revolution came and my music became fashionable again, I felt like the Prodigal Son's brother who had always been a good boy.

Probably I'm a contradictory type, as I try to see the outside world seeing me. On the one hand, I'm a conservative because I write tonal music, and *au fond* I feel that all music is tonal. Yet I'm radical by being a gay atheist. Then again I'm a monarchist in a way, an aristocrat—I don't think everyone's equal. I despise William Buckley politically, but concur with much that he believes in artistically. And I am many things that he detests.

GAGNE: *You've made a very interesting distinction between what you've called conservative and reactionary music, that reactionary music uses traditional devices unchanged, whereas conservative music uses traditional devices freshly. Have you ever written reactionary music, do you think, looking back?*

ROREM: Not on purpose. I might have. But first of all, that's my definition. Nor can freshness be willed into being.

Originality per se is not a very important virtue. Anyone can be original. Anyone can do something nobody else has done, but that's not necessarily going to make what you do any good. Nothing comes from nothing, everybody is influenced. People who don't know what their influences are are the innocent reactionaries, because they go blithely along with their postcard pieces unaware that they've stolen them intact from somebody who does it better. A true musician knows that he is stealing, and tries to cover his traces. The act of covering the traces is the act of creation.

GAGNE: *You've commented many times about the distinction between the art of composition and the craft of orchestration.*

ROREM: Now I wouldn't even say the art of composition. It too is a craft. When talking to lay people or to the National Endowment for the Arts, I may talk about the "artist," the "creator," and all of that nonsense, because they should think the artist is somebody special. And he is! He should be offered barrels of rubies and not have to give anything in return—except his own gifts. He should be allowed to be a bastard, and most people are—not bastards, really, but yet no better than they should be, since the beginning of time. I can teach anyone to write a perfect song. Because it's a craft. But whether the song bleeds and breathes is up to God—the God I don't believe in. It's up to whatever art is.

Now, I wouldn't say that to everybody. I'm of two minds. I do think that before the Industrial Revolution, music was considered a craft. Would that it could be taken seriously as a craft today! It's only taken seriously by people who put composers on a pedestal but starve them to death. In fact, composers don't exist at all today —as opposed to painters or authors. A composer does not exist in the ken of cultured intellectuals who know Kafka and Kierkegaard and painting of the past and present; when it comes to the music of the present, it's pop music. What I'm doing, and the other people in your book, is very, very peripheral to the general consciousness —with a few exceptions. Philip Glass is an exception, but his audience is not essentially a musical audience; it's a yuppie audience. Steve Reich's the same: Fred Waring without the tunes.

GAGNE: *I'm interested in your attitude about writing orchestral music. How separate are the two things, composing for orchestra and then orchestrating what you've composed?*

ROREM: When a composer is writing an orchestra piece, he has the orchestra constantly in mind. When he gets an idea for an instrumental piece, he's not just "getting an idea," but an idea for English horn or four horns or strings or guitar or whatever. Most of my orchestra music was originally conceived for the orchestra. One can tell, in the final analysis, what was originally conceived for the orchestra. (Chopin's and Schumann's symphonic music reeks of the keyboard.) But sometimes I've taken pieces from the past— inevitably small ones—and out of perversity revamped them for a different medium.

Does this inhibit inspiration? Inspiration's an outsider word. All composers are inspired: Their main problem is how to hone the impulse into something communicable. The greatest artists have no more than about five inspirations in their whole life. These come like flashes in the night: The sky is aflame and suddenly you see, as through mescaline, some sort of truth for a few seconds—you couldn't live longer with such brightness without going mad. You spend the next few years trying to recover that flash in various sizes and shapes and mediums. Then along comes another inspiration— or not. But even without these flashes, I don't think composers necessarily get "better." Is the late Beethoven or late Ravel or late Chopin any better than the early? But in Beethoven's case (not Ravel's or Chopin's) there *is* a change in grammar. People don't see themselves, which is why I don't write about my own music—at least not inspirationally. I do know that after I started publishing books, and realizing that total strangers were going to be reading such madness, I got a new sense of responsibility about my prose. I've tried to make it less self-centered. My music got tougher as the prose got sharper. Maybe. In any case the two crafts are unrelated —I'm schizoid.

GAGNE: *The image of your work is that the music expresses your sense of order, control, and balance, whereas the writing, particularly the* Diaries, *is wild and uninhibited and expresses the appetites. Yet your writing, whatever the subject matter, is always disciplined, controlled, and discreet, never sensual or erotic, whereas the music, especially for orchestra, is filled with sensuality and the visceral, and is extremely volatile and changeable.*

ROREM: That's you talking.

GAGNE: *You don't see those qualities?*

ROREM: It doesn't make any difference whether I see them or not. The important thing is that you see them. I'm making them for you. To say I agree with you, that's sheer vanity. I should say only that I'm very interested in what you're saying. Which I am.

GAGNE: *This impression makes me think of what Poulenc had said to you, that the orchestra was your true nature.*

ROREM: When I told Virgil Thomson that Poulenc had said that out of jealousy, so I wouldn't write songs, Virgil was shocked by such arrogance. But I was probably right.

GAGNE: *Perhaps Poulenc was implying that the texts of the songs provide a mask or persona, whereas the natural expressiveness that's at the heart of your music functions more on its own when you write for orchestra, regardless of any programmatic ideas the composition may have.*

ROREM: But that's involuntary. Even with prose, when I'm writing about something beyond my navel—an obituary, a précis of an opera, a historic souvenir—I hope it comes across that way. When writing about someone I never knew, like Ravel, I don't know how other people read it, but I try to include intelligent and original information. I don't know if I put information in my music, because I don't now what information means in music. Do I give the impression of being conceited? I'm not. I think I know my worth, and that there are certain things, however small, I can do that nobody else can do. If I didn't believe that I would stop. But I don't know how important these things are. Then again, I don't know how important anything is. I don't know how important George Bush is, and he runs the world; or how important Michael Jackson or John Cage are, who are disproportionately famous. No one knows the future, but I persevere, mainly because I need to keep living. I do love my work, though the driving urge is not what it was in adolescence. Self-doubt looms always. Is it for everybody? Even if it were, does that mean it's going to be any good?

PART THREE

Opera

Eight Looks at
American Opera

1991

• 1 •

"It's very easy to write American music. All you need to be is American, and then write any kind of music you wish." Virgil Thomson's quip holds true only if you're bred to the American tongue.

We are what we speak. Even the nonvocal music of a country reflects that country's language. Beethoven's symphonies emit the gutturals of German, and differ from, say, Dutch and Danish symphonies as German differs from Dutch and Danish. De Falla's *Nights in the Gardens of Spain*, without benefit of human voice, seethes with vowels and tildes, yet seems severely Iberian when contrasted with, say, Respighi's *Fountains of Rome* with its liquid Italianisms. Arabic instrumental music differs from Hebrew instrumental music as Arabic differs from Hebrew, and both differ from themselves according to their ports of call. The ballets of Bartók and Prokofiev, though arguably similar in psychological impact, are as far apart in sonorous tang and metrical ictus as Hungarian is from Russian. Since French is the only Indo-European language with no tonic accent, any metricalization of a French phrase in music can be construed as correct. Lacking natural pulse, all French music becomes impressionist. French composers when they opt for rhythm exploit it squarely, like children. (Only a Frenchman could have composed *Boléro*, as though to prove "I too got rhythm.") And thus American music differs from English music as American speech, with its jazzily extroverted monotony, differs from English speech, with its tight-lipped modal tact. If this is true for nonsung music, how much more so for song and opera.

We are what we sing. Only an American with his mainline Philadelphia accent like Samuel Barber could have written *Anthony and Cleopatra* drawn from that quintessential Englishman, Shakespeare; and only an Englishman with his special pronunciation like Benjamin Britten could have composed *Billy Budd* drawn from that quintessential American, Melville.

"American," of course, depends on perspective and opinion. The country is, or was, the world's melting pot; yet despite the mixed origins there has been for a century a sonic prosody that distinguishes our speech from that of the British Isles. Still, if foreign-born movie directors decreed how we see our heartland, sculpting to our satisfaction a Myrna Loy into the "perfect wife" such as is never found abroad, do we suspend disbelief when, say, Marlene Dietrich, an unsettling presence such as could only have matured in Europe, defines the Wild West by belting "The Boys in the Backroom"? Is Kafka's *Amerika* American? Is Britten's *Turn of the Screw* (the only durable opera ever made on a Henry James story) American? Is Lukas Foss—who arrived full-blown from Germany at fifteen, and by twenty was setting texts of Twain and Sandburg with those lean, Coplandesque flourishes that symbolize the prairie, yet still with a wisp of Nordic accent which he retains to this day—is he American? Is Gian Carlo Menotti—who arrived full-blown from Italy at nineteen and by twenty-five was already famous for composing, to his own texts, Puccinian airs more Catholic than the Pope, and retaining to this day more than a wisp of Latin accent—is he American?

Unlike Foss, Menotti never attempted to localize his music. Yet Menotti single-handedly revitalized the concept of living opera in the United States. (An adolescent Stephen Sondheim, seeing *The Medium* on Broadway, assumed, because it was in English and not at the Met, that this was musical comedy.) Thanks solely to the vision of Menotti's success in the forties, dozens of operas spouted forth by other composers hoping to hit the jackpot. The efforts persists after five decades, and it's safe to state that Menotti, whatever his own final worth, violently altered the nature of lyric theater here, and by extension throughout the globe.

Before him, who was there? People I knew didn't think much about opera, let alone American opera, not even as my fellow students in Menotti's Dramatic Forms class at Curtis in 1943 (I was nineteen). Yes, I was curious about Damrosch's *Scarlet Letter* penned in 1896, precisely because it seemed anachronistic, and by Deems Taylor's *King's Henchmen*, penned a generation later, because it was based on Edna Millay, whom I adored. But I never actually heard these. Less interesting were the patriotic "Pocahontas" affairs with tom-toms, rife during World War I. American music meant, at best, MacDowell, at worst the German-educated pap by Cadman et alia. My instincts were French; Griffes came close, but he hadn't done opera. (Is it funny or sad that, as late as 1957, I agreed to complete, anonymously, two scenes of an "Indian" opera in the style of its ungifted composer, a wealthy dilettante whose funding of the San Antonio company depended upon the mounting of his work, but who died before he could finish?) It was a sterile generation. Perhaps the burgeoning of movies in the teens and twenties, with their indigenous Americanality, precluded a parallel growth in music. Piano backgrounds for "silents" about Texas cowboys were inevitably rehashes of Rossini.

The first American opera worthy of the name is Virgil Thomson's *Four Saints in Three Acts*, finished in 1928 on Gertrude Stein's text and Maurice Grosser's scenario, but not produced until 1933. The decision for an all-black cast (predating *Porgy and Bess* by four years) was fortuity ex post facto. "The Negroes proved in every way rewarding," wrote Virgil. "Not only could they enunciate and sing; they seemed to understand because they sang. They resisted not at all Stein's obscure language, adopted it for theirs, conversed in quotations from it."

Why is *Four Saints* so American? Because Stein spent her life (as Henry James did) perceiving herself as American, *being* American and exemplifying this on her terms with the clarity that only the distance of expatriatism could provide; because her word sequences, with their redundant nursery slang, possessed a colloquial diction that could only have sprung from the United States; because Virgil took this declamation and musicalized it intact with no Romantic elongations and no melisma; and because the tunes he used —his privately concocted folksong, if you wish—sprang from the plain unsensual churchly ditties of his Midwestern youth.

Around this time Marc Blitzstein, like Barber a Philadelphia intellectual, was constructing his proletarian operas *The Cradle Will Rock* and *No for an Answer,* in the style of Kurt Weill (a weird case of an American influenced by a German influenced by America), while Aaron Copland was about to shed his "difficult" stance and write his first "accessible" piece, the schoolchildren opera, *The Second Hurricane.* These three composers had all studied with Nadia Boulanger and were the first strong non-German-trained utterances we heard. Indeed, Boulanger, herself French to the bone, single-handedly inspired what has come to be the American Sound by, on the one hand, stressing *dépouillement*—the shedding of extraneous Teutonic flab—and on the other, admonishing her Yankee flock to exploit homegrown products.

Virgil and Aaron remained the father and mother of American music until around 1950. Aaron may survive as the more beautifully necessary of the two, but credit Virgil for having inseminated the raw matter that was later nurtured by Aaron into a sophisticated expression. (Will I be forgiven for presuming to use first names? Since I'm not a scholarly historian, and these people were friends, it could seem arch, even un-American, to use last names.)

• 3 •

Opera in Europe has come mostly from experimental composers. Monteverdi and Purcell, Wagner and Mussorgsky, Berg and Henze: they invented roles that are often psychotic, or at least tragic in the grand manner—Poppea, Dido, Wotan, Boris, Wozzeck, the Prince of Homburg. Diverted by visual tales, audiences accept without flinching chromatic dissonances which, partaken of in concert, would send them off screaming.

Opera in America—at least such opera as has been viable for a time—has come mostly from nonexperimental composers. Our Babbitts and Cages, with their dramatic flare, have never flirted with the form, while our Blitzsteins and Moores concentrated on the form exclusively, with a terseness that resembles the revue.

Significantly, *The Rake's Progress,* Stravinsky's only opera composed during his United States residency, and his only extended work in English, represents, in its obsessive diatonicism, the most conservative piece in his catalogue. Copland too opted for accessibility in his two forays into the genre, *The Tender Land,* like *The Second Hurricane,* being almost a folk opera. Indeed, unlike his instrumental music, none of his vocal works is complex or devious.

I mustn't press my luck with sweeping statements. Britten, after all, as a buffer twixt the USA and the Continent, wrote lasting operas in a nonchromatic mode (and Peter Grimes is probably psychotic). So did Orff in Germany and Poulenc in France. Italy meanwhile becomes a law unto itself: Verdi and Puccini are hardly experimenters. Still, American operas that hold up appear to use tamer rhetoric, indeed a *reverse* rhetoric, in verse and in song, than European operas.

• 4 •

Is it subject matter alone, or treatment of subject matter, that makes an opera national? To hear *Don Giovanni* in Paris is to hear music by an Austrian about Spaniards composed in Italian but sung in French for Swedish tourists. Still, Mozart's national frontiers are apparent in the waltzes, slow and fast, teeming everywhere. (Did waltzes connote then what they did fifty years later?) Is it inapt to cite work from two centuries ago when composers from all countries used similar languages—or seemed to from our vantage, now that the radical edges are blurred? Well, Schoenberg too was Austrian, and his *Moses and Aaron* too teems with waltzes, yet it is hardly ballroom music, and was mostly composed in America. The text, of course, is nothing if not Jewish, and one cannot imagine a gentile being urged, as Schoenberg so desperately was, to use it. Still, generalities backfire. If Darius Milhaud, Schoenberg's sole Jewish contemporary in France, was also drawn to an Old Testament story, *David,* for a major opera, so was the anti-Semite Florent Schmitt with his *Salomé,* and the Huguenot Honegger—who was actually Swiss—with his *Judith,* a subject used again by the current gentile German, Siegfried Matthus. Mostly, though, the French stuck to Greek tragedy as updated by Cocteau, or kept safely within their borders, like Poulenc in all three of his operas, which are the best to come from modern France. Meanwhile, of the twenty-eight operas by Verdi, the ultimate Italian, only one is on an originally Italian text.

The game on our shores requires three considerations: the composer's style, his nationality, his subject. The subject of the "Indian" operas of yore was American with a vengeance as were the composers, but their language was European. The librettos to Copland's two operas are by and about Americans (Edward Denby wrote *The Second Hurricane*, dealing with high school kids lost on a picnic, and Eric Johns wrote *The Tender Land*, dealing with small-town romance), while of Thomson's three operas only one, *The Mother of Us All* (also on a Stein text), deals in Americana. *Four Saints* is Spanish, and the third opera, *Lord Byron*, libretto by Jack Larson of California, takes place in London. Raffaello de Banfield, the Triestine musician, also wrote, in English, a Lord Byron opera based on a Tennessee Williams playlet set in the New Orleans French Quarter around 1900; the tale is genteel-Southern but the soaring score is in the Cilea dialect. Will the real American please stand up!

Is *Our Town* the most American play ever written? Copland thought so, and since he'd scored the movie in 1940 he hoped Thornton Wilder would grant him opera rights. Wilder said no; but sixteen years later said yes to Louise Talma with whom he collaborated on *The Alcestiad*, of all things. Is *The Glass Menagerie* the second most American play ever written? Then why has no composer ever used it? Paul Bowles thought about it, and since he'd composed the background music for the first production in 1945, it seemed a natural. But except for Banfield and Lee Hoiby, whose *Summer and Smoke* is something of a staple, no other composer used this most singable of playwrights, because the rights are impossible to obtain. Is Eugene O'Neill the third most logical contender for music? Except for Gruenberg's *The Emperor Jones* (1933) and Marvin Levy's spacious version of *Mourning Becomes Electra*—the last opera (before Corigliano's upcoming fantasy) to be commissioned by the Met, back in 1967—almost no one has done much about O'Neill.

What about Edward Albee who, on the face of it, would seem ideal opera bait for his composer friends? Well, parallel arts do not always evolve at the same speed. Albee is hard to musicalize because, like virtually all American playwrights succeeding him, his recipe lacks the sweep, the bigger-than-life villains and heroes, the verbose tragedy of Greek or Renaissance or 19th-century dramas that cry out to be cried. The difference between Albee and Williams as users of language is that one is a poet, the other a "musician." Williams's prose, being poetry, is easily set to music. Albee's prose, being music, is impossible to set to music. Albee's prose is musical, not through images (which in his case are seldom flights of fancy, but pedestrian halts) but through rhythm—the use of echo, balance, pause. Like Mamet, or Pinter: Their characters are smaller than life, unconcerned with love. Nothing to sing about. So present-day composers remain mired in the past. When Michael Legrand's delicious and moving *Umbrellas of Cherbourg* was seen in 1964—the only opera ever conceived and produced as a movie with every phrase intoned—I was convinced that this was the mode of the future. It turned out to be a one-shot deal.

Opera composers nevertheless mushroomed all over, thanks to the new NEA, to subsidized school programs, and to the Fords, who sponsored the City Opera's commissioning programs. Of these composers, Dominick Argento is the most currently conspicuous and perhaps our premiere example of the breed. Yet of his ten operas, often on his own librettos or adaptations, only two are more or less American, *Postcard from Morocco* and *The Voyage of Edgar Allan Poe*. (Others are based on Dickens, Molière, Chekov.) Six of Jack Beeson's seven operas are American—very much so —being concerned with homegrown crazies like Lizzie Borden and Aimee Semple McPherson. Jack's music is also quite thorny, so there goes my theory about successful American opera being diatonic and about normal folks. (Except that these are not "successful" in being, like Argento's, repertory items.) Beeson's writers include Hawthorne, Saroyan, and Kenward Elmslie who, with Bernard Stambler, was America's most ubiquitous librettist of the period.

None of William Bergsma's twelve operas, which include *The Return of Martin Guerre*, are American in theme, nor are any of John Eaton's eight. But nine out of ten of Carlisle Floyd's are, all based on his own texts—most eminently *Susannah*—or those of Steinbeck, Robert Penn Warren, etc.

Thea Musgrave, Scots born and with a touch of burr ("But I'm married to an American and pay taxes here") scores three out of eight operas on books by and about Americans: Ambrose Bierce, Harriet Tubman (libretto by Musgrave), and Henry James. Thomas Pasatieri's score is four out of fifteen, mainly on his own texts: Henry James (*Washington Square*), O'Neill, plus stories about the Penitente and Mary Todd Lincoln; but like so many others he has elsewhere turned to Chekov and Yeats. George Rochberg's score is one out of one (Melville's *The Confidence Man*), while Robert Ward has three out of six, including Arthur Miller's *The Crucible.* Stanley Silverman also worked with Miller in one of his six (out of seven) American operas. His collaborator has otherwise been author Robert Foreman.

• 5 •

That most American of instruments, the saxophone (invented, however, by a Belgian in 1840, and employed by Bizet and Massenet before coming to the United States, eschewing New Orleans, and settling in Chicago as late as 1920 where it finally grew "vulgarized" into jazz), was paradoxically never used by that most American of composers, Aaron Copland. Yet saxophone *means* America —and by extension the blues, with their sleazy, wistful, urban sexiness evoking both poverty and wealth—to the extent that when Stephen Paulus preludes *The Postman Always Rings Twice* with a long sax solo we know just where we are, and when I rashly introduced the instrument into the Swedish parlor of *Miss Julie* the audience burst out laughing. American longhair composers can sound as hickish—sometimes more so—as their European cousins when being jazzy. Listen and squirm at Virgil's square hot-stuff licks in *Filling Station* or at Giannini's conga-chain sequences in *Rehearsal Call.* This is old-fogy stuff, undigested and remote. Ravel and Milhaud, meanwhile across the ocean, refined our jazz into something of their own—without realizing it was their own.

If I miscalculated with that sax in *Miss Julie,* the gaffe was merely instrumental. For what it's worth, my musical education, like everyone else's of my time, was equal parts classical and pop (or swing, as it was termed). My vocal writing was more influenced by Billie Holiday—not the tunes, but her way with the tunes—

than by any famous diva. Did I *know* any divas? Opera, insofar as it was about singing per se, never interested me. Opera buffs, by and large, are not practicing musicians, or if they are, they are not composers. I was less drawn to singing than what was being sung, less drawn to what was being sung than to what the poetry imparted. Young composers in America today, like yesterday and the day before, aren't raised in standard opera, don't listen to it except as an extension of some 20th-century composer—Britten, Berg—or as a lesson in theatricality. Bel canto is not despised, it is ignored.

As for *Miss Julie*, it is the only one of my five that's based on a foreign play. The others, all one-acters, are on words of Gertrude Stein, Kenneth Koch, Marianne Moore (after La Fontaine), Stein (after Hawthorne).

And in the 1980s? Philip Glass is something of a law unto himself. Music is not a universal language (play Mozart or Madonna for a Malayan or a moujik and see where you get), but Glass does aim for a sonic Esperanto. His plots are hardly along the line of boy-meets-girl; rather, abetted by Robert Wilson, he has made himself into an Egyptian Virgil Thomson, with triadic *faux naif* ostinatos that echo Kansas while illustrating exotica. The only other operatic "minimalist" is John Adams whose *Nixon in China* is American to the teeth and financially successful. *The Death of Klinghoffer* would appear to be less of a contrast—a political gesture —than a sequel; and while one could have hoped for an about-face (a soaper like Fanny Hurst's *Imitation of Life*, perhaps), one awaits a U.S. hearing before drawing conclusions. The third official minimalist, Steve Reich, doesn't write operas, although his interminable vamping on 1930s pop harmonies might benefit from simultaneous visuals. David Del Tredici doesn't write operas either, but has spent his career transforming the oeuvre of the 19th-century Englishman Lewis Carroll into a twenty-hour tantrum which, despite an overlay of Mahler, is in its childishness deeply (or shallowly) American, and essentially operatic.

• 6 •

It does not follow that a good song composer will automatically write—or even be interested in writing—a good opera, nor that good opera composers can write good songs. Some composers excel in both mediums (Britten, Strauss, Poulenc); but Verdi and Puccini are not known for their songs, if indeed they wrote any, and Fauré and Schubert are not admired for their operas. Song may be opera in microcosm, but opera is not song in macrocosm. The "lyric gift," as it's called by Music Lovers, is not what's primarily needed for opera. Opera is looked at, has silences, character development, is by nature theatrical; it doesn't even require obvious tunes to be great (*Wozzeck*). Still other composers excel in neither medium. Chopin wrote no opera and his songs are at best incidental.

Among Americans who are not primarily vocal composers, William Schuman and Leon Kirchner have each taken a dutiful stab at opera, and each commendably produced works as native as the Constitution: *Casey at the Bat*, and *Lily* (after Saul Bellow), refreshing after so many "American" operas on foreign texts. Oliver Knussen, in the meantime, offers the example of a foreign composer using an American text. *Where the Wild Things Are* was especially adapted for him by Maurice Sendak, with spookily thrilling sets and constumes by Sendak himself. The 1988 City Opera production, however, was not seen by the composer. Miss Sills would not raise the necessary sum to bring him from London on an economy round-trip. Composers, from whom all blessings flow in better worlds, are low men on the totem pole of opera in America. San Francisco last year bumped, without explanation, the completed *Esther* of Hugo Weisgall, one of our few proven experts in the genre. Christopher Keene talks big, but is cavalier when it comes to brass tacks. James Levine has been unavailable to John Corigliano during all the years of Corigliano's labor on the mammoth commission scheduled for the Met in December.

John played his opera for me the other night—all four hours of it—and I was not bored for one second by its troubling, odd, sumptuous, skillful, contrasting, vast, and daring noises. The fast music, often *pasticheuse,* is inherently, kinetically, rewardingly fast, and the slow music heaves and surges with a knack that can't be faked or borrowed: true melody. No other composer today, except the ghost of Britten, possesses the gift of the *grande ligne* as naturally as John. In fact, ghosts are the stars of his very singable opera, which is based, as Milhaud's last opera in 1964 was based, on

Beaumarchais's *La Mère Coupable*. Figaro, Marie Antoinette, and others are specters two centuries after the fact, observing how, for reasons of love, history might be rewritten. Or something—the story's overly complex and (to me) confused as realized by William Hoffman. Since Hoffman's play *As is* six years ago was a major statement, political and poetical, on the AIDS crisis, and since Corigliano's recent symphony is referred to by him as "an AIDS symphony," one wonders that the pair haven't written a more contemporaneous opera.

And one wonders why Tobias Picker, who has also written an expansive "AIDS symphony," should choose for his opera-in-the-works Judith *(Looking for Mr. Goodbar)* Rossner's *Emiline,* a tale of nineteenth-century incest and the social cruelty that ensures. Will no one ever compose an unapologetic romance between two men? or two women? A setting of Genet perhaps, or of Forster's *Maurice,* or of Colette's *La Seconde?* Other than Britten's *Death in Venice,* and the role of Geshwitz in *Lulu,* are there any major references in opera to the love that dare not speak its name? Rarely by Americans, certainly, excepting Lou Harrison's incomplete puppet drama, *Young Caesar,* and Leonard Bernstein's *A Quiet Place.* Pasatieri, with Elmslie, is rumored to be doing a life of Oscar Wilde: the challenge (beyond the not inconsiderable one of how to make epigrams songworthy) is immense.

What of the under-thirties? Among the 150 scores I examined at a competition recently by this age group, only two were operas, both on noncontemporary themes. Those under-thirties I talk with are all "thinking about it," but of course they need a boosting that doesn't come. Some speak of doing a rap opera "because it's new," though what is Walton's *Facade* (1922) if not rap? or Milhaud's *Les Choëphores* (1915)? Those few who *are* writing operas, as distinct from the more financially approachable mixed-media pieces, are enunciating a musical language that is almost defiantly unassuming.

If architecture is frozen music (a silly quip variously credited to Goethe or Pater), then music must be liquid architecture, and the proof may lie in twenty-eight-year-old Daron Hagen's upcoming opera about Frank Lloyd Wright, libretto by Irish poet Paul Muldoon, age forty. Of course, no art truly resembles any other: if the arts resembled each other we'd only need one. (Song, like opera, or like any choreographed music, is actually a bastard—the result of two arts that never asked to be conjoined. Like most bastards it can be healthy; but the crossing of breeds in nature, like horses with donkeys, produces mules which themselves are sterile. In the world of theater, the more senses that are simultaneously combined the more vulgar the result, as witness the circus, or the Mass, which is spoken, touched, tasted, heard, seen, and smelled.) Anyway, Daron's opera, *Shining Brow,* is vocally graceful, dramatically viable, and willfully American—and scheduled for production by the Madison Opera in 1993.

• 7 •

The sole difference between opera and musical comedy (which can be tragedy too, as *Show Boat* showed thirty years before *West Side Story*) is that one uses conservatory-trained voices while the other uses show-biz voices. (Stanley Silverman says that opera is merely musical comedy an octave higher.) It's not an esthetic but a practical difference, not a matter of art-versus-entertainment but of the kind of voice a composer had in mind. There are no crossover singers of each genre. It's not that pop singers haven't the scope of op singers (though they haven't), or that op singers can't master the glottal sob. It's that the need, hence the literature, of each genre is disparate. This need dominates the earliest training of each kind of vocalist. Thus composers are faced with separate constructional considerations for each genre.

The genres, like church and state, have run forever parallel, and in Europe—less specialized than we—have sometimes merged. But whatever the musical speech or philosophical intent of the lyric theater piece, that piece's definition rests on the composer's technical intent. Only in America could one be so concerned about the matter. If our sense of cultural inferiority, still at this late date, is salved by forever hiring Europeans for our symphonies, the same inferiority complex asks us to dignify a recent and unique commodity—musical comedy—with the name Opera, as though Opera with its long and tacky history were a serious sign of worth.

"Do you write operas?" I ask Stephen Sondheim.

"No." But immediately he defines the distinction as lying with the audience, with the venue. *Sweeny Todd* is a musical when on Broadway with Angela Lansbury, an opera when at City Opera with Rosalind Elias.

But he continues to redefine when I ask, "Would you write an opera?"

"No. Because you can't make changes." He goes on to specify that during rehearsal periods—"and this goes for Lenny too, and all the other composers who don't do their own orchestration"— songs and fillers are continually recast, transposed, and otherwise altered, according to timing, testing, and actors' limitations. These considerations would be prohibitively expensive with "real" opera, where all composition is finalized before the first rehearsal. (I don't point out that Lenny, and the others, could do the orchestration if they wanted. Sondheim, who has a quicksilver mind and has invented crossword puzzles on a professional basis, is defensive about not knowing this craft.)

He doesn't care for opera, really—doesn't "get" Mozart—and claims to have seen only twenty. (To a class on The Musical he recently made an impression by claiming to have seen none.) He feels that new operas on old texts don't seem legitimate—operas on Shakespeare, for instance. Would this disqualify Britten's *Midsummer Night's Dream*, Amram's *Twelfth Night*, Eaton's *Tempest*, and twenty dozen other settings, not to mention *Kiss Me Kate?* But his attitude is as valid as the reverse attitude: leaving Shakespeare intact but dolling it up *à la page*.

"I'm not crazy about the human voice," says Sondheim, and I empathize. He listens to the music, not to the instrument making the music. If his writing technique is very vocal, it's because "I sing along as I make it up"—which, of course, is the case of every so-called creative artist from Homer to Hovhaness.

"Do you write operas?" I ask John Kander.

"No. But I can't say quite why. You know it when you hear it. *Les Mis* is not an opera. *Sweeny* comes closer because the drama is forwarded through the music. *Porgy* is an opera. There's a far greater difference between classical and pop than between an opera and a musical."

Kander says he "wouldn't know how" to write an opera, despite being (unlike Sondheim) an avid opera buff. The biggest in-

233   *NED ROREM*

fluence on his pop songs has been Lotte Lehmann's Marchallin—
not the music itself so much as her emphases. (Which mirrors Billie
Holiday with me.) He feels that "musical theater" is going toward
opera.

"Do you write operas?" I ask André Previn.

"No." Then how should one define his piece for actors and
orchestra, *Every Good Boy Deserves Favor*, on words of Tom Stoppard? But "No" he repeats, nor will he ever write one, though he's
toyed with the idea of *The Great Gatsby*.

Nor will George Perle, now seventy-six, ever write one. "But
then again, I might," says he, "so I won't tell you my ideas, because
I don't want anyone to steal them." Yet he hints that he has a
story "by a non-American on a universal theme." Isak Dinesen?
"Maybe."

Of course, it's not ideas that are lacking, and the risk of having
the ideas stolen is negligible; five operas on the same text would
produce five different operas, all autonomous. What's lacking is
someone to whip those ideas into singable shape. Poets are too
poetic, they need drama and push. Dramatists are too dramatic,
they need poetry and repose. We need librettists. But it's a job
without glory or recompense.

• 8 •

There is American opera. There is also the Americanizing of opera.

Certain impurists always claim that if Bach had known our
piano he would have loved it; other impurists, myself among them,
love Bach's sound on the piano while allowing that *he* probably
wouldn't have. Sound, time, and space are no more transferable
than the meaning of experiences from century to century. Purists,
meanwhile, as I'm hardly the first to point out, can now cast a
searchlight into every cranny of the past and prove how who
played what; they can illuminate every facet of old music except
the crucial one—what it meant to those who heard it. We as nonbe-
lievers will hardly attend a Bach cantata as his listeners attended.
Likewise, if Mozart were alive today he would not stage his works
like Peter Sellars because he wouldn't have composed them. Mo-

zart and Bach are of their time, and they are dated. All art dates, from the moment it is created. It dates well or it dates ill, but date it does.

A generation ago Frank Corsaro's talent for turning stale chestnuts into *marrons glacés* made him the City Opera's chief caterer. Yet he was more brash than brave; he simply presented "other ways" for the tried-and-true. To give hypodermics to old warhorses is to take safe chances. True risks are in new works. Yet such was his reputation that, under Corsaro's direction, even world premieres seemed to be Alternate Versions. Today, now that anything can be said or seen, what do we say or see? The most radical stance will soon lie in being conservative.

Young artists will justify anything they make by stating that art must reflect the times. They don't yet realize that any work of art, good or bad, reflects the times simply by virtue of inhabiting the times; that all times are chaotic; and that art *is* the times, by definition, which is why art, no matter how political its intent, cannot change the times. And which is why modernizing the past is mere desperation: it can't win. As though Corsaro had never given Relevance a bad name, along comes Peter Sellars.

I admire Sellars's staging of *Nixon in China;* he and the composer breathe the same air. I sympathize, however, with those many who find his Mozart stagings *de trop.* What no one mentions in this dichotomy of motives is what most protrudes from the TV screen in *The Marriage of Figaro.* Mozart's plotting, with the set pieces and recitatives, runs according to leisurely and stylized 18th-century conventions—conventions which he himself established, moreover. Present-day comportment, on stage as in the street, moves faster and with less guile. To see well-off yuppies in the laundry of a skyscraper, forced by the music's pacing to stand still while intoning, in Italian, their formalized woes and joys, runs counter to both our and Mozart's metabolism. It's neither witty nor surrealist, it's dull, for we wish these modern characters to get on with it. Lyric actors, already inexpert in classical garb, are still more self-conscious in Manhattanese costumes as they voice their foreign text, feigning naturalistic gestures in tempo with artificial music. Even if they *could* act, their dress impedes: such dress demands speedy action, while the phrases force them to freeze. Even sillier are the supertitles in hip American. Does anyone really "get more out of it" now that "it" 's more timely? Why not commission a new opera about the Trump Tower *(Figaro)*, or that takes place in a Westchester diner *(Cosi)*, or in Spanish Harlem *(Don Giovanni)?*

Like his punk haircut and strained philosophy, Sellars's direction conspires to draw attention, not to the opera, but to himself. He can't realize that even the most conventional performance in the present of music of the past is already, despite authenticators, updated. We cannot *not* be timely. The most reactionary version of Mozart today is already, by its nature, *of* today—to a point where Mozart himself might not recognize it.

But wait. Are Sellars's tamperings a betrayal (if that's the word) of Mozart? Are they not rather a betrayal of Da Ponte? Close your eyes and the music remains intact. Thus, the oft-heard analogy that what modernizing directors visit on a Mozart opera equates what conductors might visit on a Mozart symphony via a Moog synthesizer is a false analogy. Symphonies, if you will, are legitimate, while operas—like songs—are bastards. I have never set a poem to music without feeling like an interloper: who am I (or who is Schumann or Ravel, for that matter?) to take this poem of Sappho, of Emily Dickinson, of Elizabeth Bishop—perfect artworks quite capable of standing alone—and presume to lend it some new and needed dimension? Yet I do it anyway. If the poet is alive, he/ she is usually both flattered and miffed by the resultant song which, no matter how workable from a singer's viewpoint (or earpoint), can never correspond to the poet's own inner music. A librettist, of course, unlike a poet, generally works in conjunction with a composer. Still, there are unlimited ways of staging a libretto while leaving the music intact. (So maybe we should ask Da Ponte how he feels.) But isn't there a point of no return, in staging, and hasn't Sellars—at least with classical operas—passed that point?

Recapitulatory Odds and Ends:
Tonal music works for both comedy and tragedy, atonal music works only for tragedy. The miasmal canvas upon which Schoenberg paints an unfocused soprano line in *Erwartung* is ideal for a melodrama of intensifying madness. When he chooses the same canvas for his Feydeau-like farce, *Von Heute auf Morgen*, he may well wonder why he gets no laughs. Comedy inherently requires resolution, while the twelve-tone system forbids resolution.

●

Do I set myself to music as do Menotti, Floyd, Sondheim, Tippett, and dozens of others? Yes, once in 1956 with a one-acter called *The Robbers* (after Chaucer). Marc Blitzstein, wincing at the self-conscious lingo, declared me lost in libretto-land, and proceeded to translate every phrase "from English into English" without altering a note.

Whatever my music may amount to, I flatter myself that of the two hundred authors I've set to music—some of them many times —none was less than important. If I as a prose-writer could produce something "important" enough to set to music, I wouldn't need to set it to music. My music and my prose answer to different drives.

A successful opera symbolizes for the song composer what hit plays do for poets: major acclaim by nonspecialized theatergoers. But a failed opera carries with it a more paralyzing aftereffect than a failed song cycle. If at first you don't succeed at opera don't try again: the world will not permit you to be burned twice.

Music by definition is larger than life: nobodies when singing become somebodies, villains when singing catch our sympathy. Since playwrights today are concerned with the humdrum, most composers fall back on the Orpheus legend in various guises.

Gunther Schuller in 1966 tried Kafka. But if despair in the abstract does not inspire credible song, at least Schuller had a voice. Among composers today are there voices anymore? Our opera composers are wildly eclectic, though are they as tough as, or even vaguely different from, their sires? Has Bolcom an identifiable voice? Has Ullyses Kay, in his deep-felt dramas on the lives of slaves? Has Paulus? Has Pasatieri? Like it or not, there is a Thomson sound, a Copland sound, and certainly a sound from Douglas Moore (his *Baby Doe* is part of our lingua franca), though these composers are scarcely radical harmonically. Is there also a Floyd sound, an Adams sound, an Argento sound? Barber, like Poulenc, had no really identifiable traits, yet he identifiably influenced Lee Hoiby; still, do you recognize Hoiby when you hear him?

What of the younger ones? Do Ellen Zwilich or Michael Torke —neither of whom shows any indication of ever writing for the opera stage—have a voice? There are more of them than ever, all technically slick, so God must want them. But as Lenny Bernstein said, He wants roaches too.

Which brings me back to the opening gambit of Virgil Thomson. Is there American opera? Yes, in the sense that any music written by Americans is American, whatever it sounds like. But no, in the sense that the bulk of American operas are founded on the Europe of the past.

I do not feel heartened. All the arts throughout the globe seem to be sagging (though fortunately one can never accurately judge one's own era). If there is a future for opera in English—by Americans as well as by anglophones everywhere, but not necessarily in other languages—this will surely be in an amalgamation of styles, the conservatism of unlimited borrowing. Like Corigliano's huge Beaumarchais machine, for example, or Glass's *Hydrogen Jukebox* on Allen Ginsberg poems, or Robin Holloways' overwrought *Clarissa*, about which the composer says: "I don't think my composition is imitation or pastiche. It's like the excitement of stumbling upon an old Roman road, and realizing that this was the way across this landscape that used to be used, that everyone understood it, and everyone went that way. And now I can go this way too. It might be a bit overgrown but it's still the directest way between two points. It went this way because this was a very good way to go."

There is no pure music. All music is vocal, albeit sometimes with the words removed. As language evolves, so will go all lyric forms. Originality is not the goal (anyone can be original) so much as individuality. Are there any individuals today?

Considering Carmen

1978

• 1 •

Some of my best friends are Carmens—starting with my father. When I was old enough to get around the keyboard I used to accompany him in Bizet's airs, ideal for amateur baritones. And Father chaperoned my first cultural outing, the Chicago version of *Carmen* starring one Coe Glade, with whom I fell in love.

These homey facts, waxing into a taste for mezzos, would never have struck me had not Robert Jacobson, over a soufflé at Café des Artistes, recently suggested I "do something on *Carmen*." Why me? "To avoid typecasting." Indeed, I have never in print examined a premodern composer, one not somehow concerned with being new, with changing things through innovation more than through mere excellence. Now, since being new is strictly a hang-up of twentieth-century artists, and since I too inhabit the century, my easy task had always been to show that nothing's new. But what do I know of Bizet?

Well, I have known his opera all my life. Still that knowledge is involuntary: it's the one opera everyone knows. *Carmen,* the most popular serious piece (or the most serious popular piece) ever penned, has entered the collective unconscious. As it happens, my young education converged perversely—and I believe correctly— around what used to be termed Modern Music. By the onset of puberty I had memorized *Petruschka, Pierrot* and *Daphnis,* not to mention Carpenter's *Skyscrapers* and Schelling's *Victory Ball,* yet I wouldn't have recognized a Brahms quartet, nor even a Bach gavotte. Contempt may breed contempt, but familiarity breeds only familiarity. Except for *Carmen*, I had to get used to "classics" as others get used to "moderns."

The past is a problem still, for I never turned into an opera buff. Nor do I enjoy pure song for itself rather than for how its composer manipulates the text. Also, like most composers, I'm more involved with my own music than with other people's. (But yes, I would rather hear that music sung by dumb singers with golden echoes than by smart singers with leaden echoes.) So finally I have a narrower knowledge of opera than many an amateur. Yet what I know is my own. As for what I know about *Carmen*, no sooner had Robert Jacobson bid good-bye than associations began streaming.

Northwestern, 1940. Despite Father and Coe Glade, it was less a love of voice than of verse which fired my first songs. I made a dozen settings of e. e. cummings before comprehending that these might actually be interpreted. Then one morning, overhearing *Carmen* practiced in the next studio, I decided to ask the young mezzo to read through my efforts. That she happened to *be* a mezzo was fortuitous; although my music thus far had been intuitively concocted around my own deepish hummings—vile to some, sweet to me (inside every composer lurks a diva longing to get out)—it was a decade until I learned there were strata to voices, hierarchies and lowerarchies of vocal literature, and that all singers, like it or not, are consigned to tessiturial castes.

The reactions to hearing those early songs emoted by Frances Maralda (where is she today?) set the stage for all my future music.

Philadelphia, 1943. Muriel Smith—she of the burning eye, blue burnished hair and butterscotch skin—now brought life to my sonic skeletons, then became the first of our Curtis group to defect to bigtime Manhattan as Carmen Jones. (Like Dietrich's Lola, Muriel's Carmen was more sisterly than sinister, and, singing in English, lent a likeability to the role new to Americans.) She was the first ever publicly to sing my tunes, among them a Cocteau quatrain named *"De Don Juan."*

Were the French deranged by Spain before Bizet? If the Gallic Iberia is forever as quixotic, at least to Spaniards, as Kafka's Amerika is to us, the teenaged Poulenc with Cocteau in 1919 gave that quixoticism the coup-de-grâce in their "Chanson Hispano-Italienne" titled *Toréador,* a crazy waltz which depicts a Venetian corrida:

> *Belle Espagnole*
> *Dans ta gondole*
> *Tu caracoles*
> *Carmencita . . .*

Jennie Tourel, between rehearsals for *The Rake's Progress,* first sang me those lines at the very site of their inception, Piazza San Marco, the French notion of an elegant bullring.

TANGLEWOOD, 1946. Before the curtain rises on the U.S. premiere of Britten's opera (for which the composer is present), Koussevitzky mounts the stage and begins to speak. "There is *Carmen* . . . and there is *Peter Grimes.*" Carmen? Is she an absolute by which to judge Peter? True, Britten may be a finer artist than Bizet, but more than one Brittenism was previewed in Carmen's cards.

New York, 1948. So far as my own music went, Nell Tangeman's wise, lush contralto became the defining instrument. During her brief peak, from 1948 to 1954, hers was the one "real" voice doing new repertory. All I wrote then was for her, and by extension all I write now comes from what I learned with her. I think mezzo. Nell and her friend Martha Lipton were learning *Carmen* simultaneously. Martha, who focused on—and speaks still today of—the gypsy's "broad scope of honesty, playfulness and courage," went on to sing the role throughout the land. Nell, who preferred the role's violence and bitchery, never sang it publicly, although at the end of her life she was studying it in German on the off-chance of an audition in Düsseldorf. *Frei sei was geboren, und frei will sei sterben!*

Free she was not. Unlike Carmen, Nell practiced the privileges of fame without the responsibilities; overcelebrating at parties in her honor, she would skip rehearsals next day. During her heyday she presented all my vocal music as well as premieres by Copland, Ives, Messiaen, Bernstein and Chanler. She was the first American to sing Jocasta's big aria under Stravinsky's direction. That's as close as she ever got to the Habañera, but it's close. Yet at the time of her suicide in 1965 no obituary appeared.

Paris, 1950. Samuel Barber arrives with violinist Charles Turner. They are preparing Barber's concerto for recording. Who is the rehearsal pianist? Why, Pierre Boulez. Barber kids the stoical Frenchman about the twelve-tone system. "Is the Habañera a row?" he asks. (How he loathes the imputations of the serial elite. He persists in addressing the perplexed René Liebowitz as Mr. Ztiwobeil. "Well, if a composer can't recognize his own name in retrograde, how can his listeners be expected . . . ," etc.)

Hyères, 1951. Robert Veyron Lacroix permits me to play "primo" in *Jeux d'enfants,* while there by the window, his pate turning the shade of a Café des Artistes soufflé in the Provençal sunset, Boris Kochno loudly recalls staging these goodies for Diaghilev. Boris claims to have heard Mary Garden as Carmen and found her wonderful.

Felix Borowski at Northwestern had taught us that Garden, after felling not only Mélisande, but Judith and Salomé and Thaïs and Louise, met her own downfall by tackling Carmen, defeater of all her sisters. Virgil Thomson saw her too, and found her "red-haired, small, psychiatric, intelligent, basing her action on Mérimée."

Sopranos who turn mezzo, like Callas or Price, fare better at Carmen than mezzos who turn soprano, like Verrett or Horne.

Hyères, 1954. A road company, replete with Bizet's bizarre orchestra and featuring the sadly deaf Valentine Tessier in the short rich role of La Renaude, unfolds *L'Arlésienne* upon the town square. We all are dazzled, conditioned by knowing that Freud once decorticated this meridional drama to the annoyance of its author, Alphonse Daudet. Also in the cast: a donkey, rented from the Toulon slaughterhouse. After the show Marie-Laure asks the manager what will happen to the animal. *Il rentre à l'abbatoir.* So she buys the beast, which lives in her stable for the next six years, fitted with a collar of silver bells that awaken us daily as he trots forth to graze on the front lawn. He is christened Alphonse.

Besides owning a donkey named Alphonse, how does Marie-Laure de Noailles—my best friend in France, but scarcely a Carmen —fit into these notes? Her maternal grandmother, Comtesse Adhéaume de Chevigné, was one of two models upon whom Proust fashioned his Duchesse de Guermantes. The other was Madame Emile Straus, widow of Georges Bizet.

They say that a rapport at no more than three steps remove can be construed between any two persons on Earth. Our friend Nadia Boulanger—alive and well and living in Paris—is the daughter of composer Ernest Boulanger who was already twenty-three when Bizet was born in 1838.

The heirs of some who die comparatively poor and obscure grow quickly rich and chic by wearing just their names.

Other Carmens who have shaped my end? Regina Sarfaty, Elaine Bonazzi, Betty Allen, Beverly Wolff.

And now enough of shapeless revery. How is *Carmen* shaped by the eight operatic components: chords, line, beat, tune, color, vocality (both solo and ensemble), formality (both sectional and overall), and theatrical panache?

• 2 •

Wagner loved *Carmen*. Contrary to general thought composers are more leery than indulgent of music which resembles their own. That Bizet was once deemed a Wagnerite seems now merely funny: *Carmen* is as wholeheartedly diatonic as *Tristan* is not. The Habañera? It is chromatic only melodically. Harmonically, with those 120 measures of seesawing over a pedal-D, it is more doggedly tonal than a Clementi sonata.

Nor was the lead-motive a Bizetian need; his airs once sung stay sung. True, strands dangling from certain early statements—Micaela's mainly—are sometimes tucked back into the formal fabric. But only the Death Tune, announced in the prelude, recurs and recurs and recurs, with that Cui-like augmented second which Frenchmen up to and through Ravel identify with sex, sex being always blamed on other countries and this interval deriving from Russia which used it to denote the wayward East.

Harmonically Bizet was not, as we say today, inventive: his chords are triadic, especially in set numbers, while diminished sevenths he employs forebodingly, according to the cliché of his day, to advance the plot. Chordal sequences, when at all tonally evasive, are so nearly always anchored to a drone that the device becomes a signature. Exceptional are the Séquedilla's precipitous modulations to the Neapolitan seventh, cribbed sixty years later by Prokofiev. And if the rare presence of secondary sevenths seems as pungent as, for example, the very cassia bloom José describes, the opening chords of the flower song could be by Fauré thirty years later, while the closing chords (as well as tune) were filched intact only fifteen years later for Tchaikovsky's *Pathétique*. So Bizet did shape the future somewhat, but through his harmonic quality, not originality.

His counterpoint was negligeable like that of all French com—posers. God knows their schooling italicizes polyphony as much as solfège, and Bizet's fugal improvisations in the parlor were as glittering as Liszt's. But the only considerable canonic forays found in written French music are chez Franck, who was Belgian. Oh, in *Carmen* there is a pseudo-fugato to close Act I; there are many little stretti-at-the-octave descents to close smaller scenes (hear the ends of the Street Boys' first chorus, of Carmen's first exit, of the first Entr'acte, of Escamillo's first exit); there is so-called part-writing, like the heavenly choir of Cigarette Girls (seemingly voices in imitation, actually just voices in harmony). But there is no Germanic concern for independent inner lines nor Italianate concern for two or more viewpoints expressed at once. Bizet flirts with neither undifferentiated nor differentiated counterpoint (to steal Thomson's terms), the one being the same material echoing itself, as in a fugue, the other being unrelated materials simultaneously executed, as in *Lucia*'s sextet.

(A sly pedant might propose that the opening chorus, "Sur la place," was built on an inversion of the Habañera—the inversion of Stravinsky's Jocasta.)

Like a vat of sangria being brought to boil, the Gypsy Dance of Act II is as physical as the rumble from *West Side Story*. Rhythm alone explains the mounting wallop. Not rhythmic interest, however, but rhythmic *lack* of interest: hypnosis rather than psychedelia, monotony in place of variety. Bizet does step up the tempo thrice, building from a metronome 100 to 138; but the chief tactic, as with *Boléro*, lies in piling on of dynamics and weight rather than, as with *Sacre*, an increasing of metric intricacy. In song as in dance *Carmen* is straightforward; meters are never more eccentric than a square three or four, nor within the bar do there occur rhythmic enigmas, Chopinesque juxtapositions.

A steady beat makes the dance tick, but what makes it "good" is the strong line traced over the tambourines (though this line too is unchangingly reiterated). Indeed, melody, which makes all good opera good, is what makes *Carmen Carmen*. *Carmen* seethes with tune, apposite and first-rate, some of it stolen. If Prokofiev's Neapolitan mannerism stems from the Séquedilla, the Séquedilla itself stems from the orchestra of Mozart's Commendatore, while the Habañera grew from a nightclub song. (Bizet may well have made thirteen revisions for Galli-Marié, but the final version of the Habañera remains so close to the original that Sebastián Yradier must live in history as its only begetter.) And as in the orchestra of Mozart's Commendatore, certain of *Carmen*'s most ravishing curves unfurl without the distraction of a human voice: for instance, the thirty-eight measures of the second Entr'acte wherein single winds weave a nearly three-octave gamut like a silver snake through gold harp strings.

To object that his tunes aren't always his, is to object to Shakespeare's or Beethoven's sources. It's an ungracious quip, the one about sexual prowess, "It's not what you've got but what you do with it"; yet we are now distanced enough from Bizet to hear him, not as his contemporaries heard him, for the plagiarist that he was, but for how personally he used his robbed goods.

His arias are true arias, not ditties with instruments. The difference? No aria can work on a song program (tell that to your stars) because by definition an aria leads from past to future, advancing the soloist in time and space, while a song is self-contained, sans plot, leaving the soloist where he began. Of Bizet's forty actual songs only one, "*Adieux de l'hôtesse arabe*," has much profile, and many of the others seem to be extracted from unfinished stage works and garnished with fresh words after the composer's death. If Bizet did not possess the gift of song (contrary to, say, Fauré, who lacked a sense of drama), his arias are nonetheless song*like* in that they will repeat themselves literally and with identical accompaniment.

•

Notoriously, *Carmen*'s Paris flop killed its composer although post-humously the piece became quickly a hit from Munich to Moscow. Can one sense the causes in another time and place? "It is lovable," Nietzsche felt, because "it does not sweat . . . Through it one almost becomes a masterpiece one's self . . . Farewell to the damp north." And farewell to Lohengrin, he might have added, for Nietzsche loathed the Wagner he loved, and betrayed him with a Parisian. But how exact was his French?

Insofar as a person not born to a language can presume to assess a native's accent, let me state that Bizet is often prosodically illogical. French being the sole European tongue without a tonic stress (no syllable having more value than another), any sung lay-out of verse can be argued as correct. Yet throughout *Carmen* one senses that words have been forced onto preexisting tunes, espe-cially the tunes of Don José; not only at the start of the flower song, with *la* strong and *fleur* weak, but in more tactile talky moments where declamation should be dictated by nature. Why, for example, with the phrase "Laisse-moi Te sauver" in the final dispute does José hit *Te* rather than *sau* on the highest note and strongest beat?

Something's amiss with Don José. By current American stan-dards he's a mama's boy (*un fils à papa* in French): his need to cast out both fiancée and career while reeling between mistress and mother strikes us as Freudian, while for the 19th century the predic-ament would seem more Roman than Romany (unless it were Jew-ish, since Halévy and not Mérimée contrived the situation). Were the tenor's lyric inspiration less grand, Americans would hear merely the bathos of this Spaniard behaving like an Italian singing in French for the sole delight of Germans.

Bizet is less expert at *le mot juste* than at *la phrase juste*. Winton Dean calls him a "master of the paragraph," meaning that "the rise and fall of the melody produced whole numbers that seem to spring forth complete from the first bar to the last." But if Bizet did com-pose paragraphs, they were stanzaic, for he was no prosifier; and though music can't rhyme it can certainly echo. Perhaps he was more a master of the sentence, or rather, of the verse. Such verse swells not through development but through repetition.

Yet through all *Carmen* flows the technical inevitability one

finds in a disco palace, a linking, an overlapping of numbers grant-
ing them both independence and interdependence, and sending
them all finally to flight like some doomed Greek family, heroes
and jesters alike, toward a horridly needed apotheosis.

Formally the opera bites off more than it can chew, then
chews it.

She's a liberated woman, she makes the rules, and like great ac-
tresses she speaks of herself in the third person, especially as she
nears the end. She's a merry and obsessive lover, but a sad and
gluttonous one too, and death more than lust seems her dish. At
the hour of her suicide—what else can you call it?—Carmen seems
fed up. Why? Music explicates where psychoanalysis fumbles. But
if Mérimée's tale continually instructs us (his limning of Spanish
Romany is no less morosely veridical than his Corsican mafia in
the masterpiece *Matteo Falcone*), who can deny that some pages of
the opera sound silly? The males of the chorus, extrovert Latins
though they be, are kidding when they ask Carmen when she'll
love them (love them collectively?), whereas José, in taking her
literally, shows himself crazy and provides his own doom. But Bizet
was not kidding (and surely he, not his librettists, was responsible
for the stretchings and ricochetings which veer toward farce) when
he invites our sympathy during the G & S exchange between Micaela and the Garde Montante. Operetta conventions of yesterday
are today unwilling suspensions of disbelief, and not only poor
Micaela suffers in our eyes as she giddily parrots her would-be
lover's remarks (*Sa mère, il la revoit* . . . etc.); Escamillo and Carmen
too, glamorous public figures, go around saying they're in love—
to just anyone.

There is little indication that Bizet and friends like Massenet or
Saint-Saëns, at least in their musical speech, were out for a revolution. If things were different after *Carmen*, the difference lay in a (to
us) minor French definition of what constitutes grand opera. So far
as the ear is concerned, *Carmen*, while becoming the indisputably
best lyric drama of its age in France, remains strictly in the tradition
of *opéra comique*, unaltered by Delibes or Hahn, by Poulenc or Sauguet, or by Rosenthal or Damase a century later.

Half the opera is choral.

Do the choruses, in their inevitability at scene setting, their directness of melody, their lean virile languor and bull's-eye femininity, provide the most gorgeously inspired minutes?

Before deciding, listen again to *"La cloche a sonné"* as the unison tenors for only twelve bars intone a series of tetrachordal arches more perfectly symmetrical than those of the Pont du Gard (no, architecture is not frozen music), and which, though they speak but once, satisfy our memory over the context of the next two hours. How almost immoral that so telling a fragment be followed by another more elegant still: unison baritones, against sixteen measures of fluxing hues among undulating cellos and near-motionless reeds, chant but two notes, over and over, only sinking ecstatically to a third as they give way to the long-awaited girls. Hear these girls now, this time in pairs, curling their vowels around each other like the very smoke they evoke, and growing, growing ever higher in the air. Oh, one could go on. Yes, the choruses do form the most beautiful moments.

Paradoxically, it is possible to conceive a *Carmen* (as opposed to a *Meistersinger* or a *Dialogues des Carmélites*) without chorus. The drama is between the few, not the many, and requires no kibitzing. Carmen's choruses are marvelous clothes on a marvelous body.

Had I never heard the orchestration but only seen it, I'd say it couldn't work. I would be wrong. The chances we are taught to avoid when scoring for voice with instruments seem not to be chances to Bizet. Balances or areas that on the page look top-heavy or empty are to the ear always right: the scoring is unstintingly crystalline.

But the scoring is not unusual. Beyond a predilection for low flutes, for solo bassoon, and for crossed strings (listen to the sudden soft parentheses between which, after fifteen minutes of rattling fanfare, Escamillo emerges in the final act and, with string quartet, speaks his piece, ominously intimate and self-contained as a black opal centered in a crown of a thousand diamonds), Bizet doesn't really run risks. The major difference between Germans and French is that in their orchestration the ones use doubling while the others do not. Of course, not to double (i.e., to reinforce, for example, the strings, with one or more winds at the unison or octave) is probably in itself a risk, like any vulnerable exposure, but it does make for an air-filled luminosity in which the vocalist is not forced to scream for his life, whereas the Germans had to breed a new race of singer to withstand their triple-thick orchestration.

• 3 •

While in Paris in 1947, enjoying some adventures in the line of duty entertainingly recounted in her current *Other People's Letters,* the Proustophilic historian, Mina Curtiss, coincidentally and almost by accident gained legal access to a cache of memorabilia which opened as unexpected a window onto cultural France as Watergate did onto political America. The cache was in the hands of one Magda Sibilat, the likeable but unstable and none-too-well-informed widow of the nephew of Emile Straus, himself heir to his second wife, née Geneviève Halévy, daughter of *La Juive*'s composer and, by a first marriage, spouse of Georges Bizet. The memorabilia were an acre of letters—letters from Bizet to all his family, letters from Gounod and rival geniuses to Bizet, letters to Fromental Halévy from Rossini, Verdi and Berlioz, letters which had never before been seen by anyone but the correspondents themselves. In Bizet's day letters were so frequent as to seem no more historically useful than our telephone. Yet surely no such thorough documentation has come down to us from any other artist of the epoch. In her pursuit of what she calls the truth about Bizet, Curtiss spent the next decade immersed in an accurate vision of the past, and by 1958 had published what is maybe the grandest profile ever composed on a composer, *Bizet and His World.*

Consider how many volumes appear every month, how much hidden data may still be around on the Second Empire, and how famous are such men as Duparc or Chausson, Gounod or Fauré. Then realize that no books are readily available on these men, nor are there decent biographies of even Debussy or Ravel. And the past fades with each passing day. Bizet's each passing day is meanwhile revived, as through a tea-drenched madeleine, and with it a new sense of the man's musical importance, thanks to the Curtiss book. Or is it not Bizet's book? since a good fifty percent is "in his own voice," drawing verbatim from letters judiciously woven into context.

Now, this new sense of Bizet's musical importance—is it a

matter of luck, of historic availability? Supposing the author had stumbled upon a store of, say, Meyerbeeriana, with Gounod in a walk-on role (as he has in the present book) and Bizet a mere cameo? Would the status of these figures be rearranged in our consciousness? Or is importance irrelevant to worth? (In a sense, because of his defining influence on Wagner, Spohr is more important than Wagner, as Rebikov is more important than Debussy.) Durability in music probably does not rely upon what is written about the music—or its composer—since the musical and the literary publics do not overlap. Mina Curtiss herself is a musician only secondhand (Marc Blitzstein's aid in this case was invaluable), though she is a born snoop. Thus her useful book appears built less on a devotion to music than to research. My copy's margins are sprinkled with notes.

Bizet made a living out of dying, at least for his closest relatives all of whom survived to enjoy his fame.

Marie Reiter, the family maid, at the end of her life in 1912 informed her grown son Jean that he was the offspring, not as was always supposed of Bizet *père*, but of Georges himself. She doubtless lied.

In musical accoutrements—sight-reading, singing, getting the point—Bizet was wildly talented. He could "do" anything. But so could many a prize Conservatoire graduate. Though his professional reputation was solid, his whole bourgeois life was passed as an overworked teacher and copyist with both social connections (all artists had those) and money problems. The woes and joys were those of today's composers: unrehearsed premieres, but premieres all the same; mixed reviews; jealousies. He retained boundless fidelity to those he admired, Gounod especially, and developed what looked like an American equation of failure with death.

If flop after flop is patiently chalked up by Curtiss (as by Winton Dean in his less factually documented but more musically canny biography), she is understandably defensive about her subject. The fact remains that Bizet's output was mostly mediocre. Even his best works—the young Symphony, *Jeux d'enfants*, parts of *The Pearl Fishers*—are in the salonistic genre of his period. There

were no first-class gods in France then, as he semiconsciously realized; those he invoked were ever foreigners (Shakespeare, Homer,
Michelangelo)—except for Meyerbeer, whom he classed with Beethoven.

There are no flukes in art. Yet *Carmen* is a fluke. Its high quality,
if not its style, is incongruous in Bizet's catalogue.

Curtiss hints that when it comes time to court Geneviève Halévy
there will be Jewish problems. There are not brought up again, nor
is it clear on which side of the fence such problems may foment.
For all her reference to the Halévy clan she never charts relationships. Here they are: Fromental Halévy (né Levy in 1799) composed
La Juive and ran the Paris Conservatoire. His younger brother Léon
wrote librettos for him. Léon's son Ludovic was co-librettist with
Meilhac of *Carmen*. Daniel Halévy, Proust's schoolfriend, must have
been the son of Ludovic (it isn't explained). But Geneviève, his
aunt, was the daughter of Fromental. She did marry Georges Bizet,
and they were not the ideal couple despite attempts at appearances
even reinforced by Gounod in his eulogy at Georges's grave. She
outlived her mate by over half a century of neurasthenic splendor.

Once I stated (and was roundly scolded) that Jews, being by
origin epic improvisers, mainly in stringed instruments, can't play
French music, French music being by nature concisely lyric with
built-in rubatos unneedful of "interpretation." How did Jews play
French music when they themselves began composing it? (Bizet
would have known, for in a sense, by osmosis, he composed it
himself.) What was musical life like among Jews in 19th-century
France? The Dreyfus affair may well have brought to the surface
an anti-Semitism in the upper classes (though as Proust himself
demonstrates, to be a rich Jew in France is to be just rich. Viz
the Rothschilds), but was any kind of Semitism visible in artistic
classes?

Bizet is said to have said, "If they want trash I'll give them trash,"
and wrote the toreador song. Just who are "they," snug in their
opera loges, crying "We want trash"? And just how is this song
more trashy than another?

The world knows Faust through Gounod (not Goethe) and

taureaumachie through Bizet (not Goya). Does the world know wrong? Toreador is a nonword, like glissando, good as any. We know love through Wagner.

Curtiss uses the witty locution "libretto-land," a locale dreamed up by Scribe, which Marc used to accuse me of inhabiting. But Bizet, composer of the exotic *Djamileh* (V. S. Pritchett recently wrote, apropos of Georges Sand, "A scene of Oriental luxury was indispensable to the Romantics: the looting of Egypt was Napoleon's great gift to literature"), kept his feet in patriotic gore and, unlike myself, was no pacifist. (Were there pacifists, *proprement dits*, in France before World War I?) Yet he reminds me, in his rapports with Gounod, of myself with Virgil, from whom I learned everything, but perhaps not without taints of rivalry.

The prose and principles of all this clique—Halévy, Gounod, Massenet and Saint-Saëns—were high-flown and golden and real, yet their art somehow lacked danger and kept to a lower plane than that of their non-French predecessors—Chopin, Schumann, Wagner and Verdi. Despite salty credos their sound was saccharine, none of it so purposefully tight as Poulenc's, their logical culminator. (How do Franck and d'Indy fit in?)

In 474 pages are but two sentences of bodily portraiture, these uttered by the young librettist, Louis Gallet: "[Bizet] had a very gentle, but very acute expression behind his indispensable eyeglasses; his lips were almost continually arched in a mocking smile. He spoke quietly, in a slightly hissing voice, with that air of detachment I always noticed in him." (For the record, in his preface to *Thaïs* Gallet comes up with a snappy definition: "A lyrical poem is a work in verse handed over to a musician to convert into prose.")

The rare success of Bizet's collaboration with Daudet, claims Curtiss, was due to "the capacity both men had of translating into living theatrical expression an intuitive psychological grasp of certain facets of human passion and behavior. This gift neither artist appears to have recognized in himself."

Do artists ever seek to "recognize" such gifts within themselves? Is not theirs but to do or die, saving reason to apply toward others?

What do I myself think about Bizet and his Carmen? Except that the requirements of this article have lately kept them uppermost in mind, I rarely think about them. Henceforth I shall readily admit that Carmen deserves her continuing glory: her musical worth is almost on a par with Pelléas, her narrative worth almost on a par with Aschenbach, her vocal know-how on a par with Norina.

Is *Carmen*, rather than *Fidelio* or *Lulu*, the perfect opera? Yes, because all the elements (beginning with the libretto—an improvement, at least in stageworthiness, on Mérimée's tale-*cum*-document) are first-rate: the traditional symmetries are perfect, the literal repeats are perfect, the exquisite banality is perfect. But perfection does not a chef d'oeuvre make. Many a masterpiece is flawed, for beauty limps, and grandeur, though spectacular, can turn top-heavy.

Then is *Carmen* a chef d'oeuvre? Yes, because the perfect elements all catch fire and gleam with life—they are, as we say, inspired, and together they jell: they have hardened into immortality.

Yet *Carmen* does not make my mouth water. (No offense, neither does Schubert.) I like everything about it except *it*. I do not object that in the final analysis the opera is really so corny and predictable, but my taste buds crave a Frenchness that did not yet exist, a longing for the almost edible sadness that resides in the sharp seventh recipes of Debussy and Ravel.

Perfection is a realistic goal, greatness is not. Greatness is an endowment—a postpartum present, if you wish—never consciously, nor even necessarily, bestowed by the maker. One can admit to the fact of, and even cheer, certain universal marvels without needing them, while in the private heart one elevates to Paradise lesser works which merely (merely?) satisfy.

To conclude these scattered notes I must choose between two lines:

Carmen is the most perfect opera ever composed, but it is far from great.

Carmen is great, but Bizet is not.

Bluebeard and Erwartung: A Notebook

1988

HISTORY. Every age—indeed, every hour—is without precedent and unduplicatable, but the uniqueness is clear only in retrospect; a chunk of time (today, for instance) remains a "period of transition" until withdrawn enough to be perceived, with the wisdom of hindsight, in relation to the minutes or months or milleniums that came before and after. Take 1910: We now see events and trends, juxtapositions and simultaneities, that could not have been imagined then, and which years hence will have continued to veer in and out of focus, perhaps to the vanishing point. This afternoon my perspective is on a year of European glamour: George V succeeded to the throne of England and remained till 1936 when I was twelve—why, I could have known him! Tolstoy died, *Firebird* was premiered, Halley's comet reappeared, Forster published *Howard's End*, and the first British exhibit of Postimpressionist art was held at the Grafton Gallery. (If American high art was not yet—perhaps still isn't—of import abroad, while the continent's world-weariness had not yet seeped into our land, we did boast a certain culture: Taft was president, T. S. Eliot penned *Prufrock*, Mark Twain passed away and Samuel Barber was born, Ives's *Unanswered Question* was four years old, Myrna Loy was five and Mae West eighteen.) Most importantly for the purposes of this paper, in Austria Schoenberg, age thirty-five, had just finished a "monodrama" *Erwartung*, while in Hungary Bartók, age twenty-nine, was completing what would be his only opera, the two-character *Duke Bluebeard's Castle*.

To say that a work of art "dates" is not to belittle it, since all art dates from the moment its maker declares it done, but some art dates well and some badly. *Bluebeard's Castle* and *Erwartung* are each locatable as products of their years. *Bluebeard* is less about medieval mores as glimpsed through the eye of Perrault's 18th-century Mother Goose as about the dawn of Freudianism in Hungary as seen through certain musical explorations of the time. Nor could *Erwartung* have sounded quite the same if conceived (but *could* it have been conceived?) ten years earlier or later. These operas, fruits of one zeitgeist and gloomy to the hilt, are nonetheless as different as their authors' fingerprints. Not as different, perhaps, as *Oedipus Rex* from Sheridan's *The Critic,* a double bill in which Laurence Olivier once dazzled us; but as a tandem tour de force being produced by the Met for a single diva it is surely more challenging. The contrast in mood being far subtler than between tragedy and farce, Jessye Norman must find not only a philosophical shift between the *kinds* of morbidity offered by the Austrian and the Hungarian, but a laryngeal shift from one role designed for a plangent mezzo and another designed for a clattering spinto.

Can music be described in words to a reader who has not heard that music? No, not insofar as the music, once the reader does hear it, will jibe in any real sense with the description. But a composer's intentions can be set forth in words by an outsider. Music on paper—rhythms, chords, counterpoint, tune, form, scoring, word-setting—is pure in itself (without the composer's apologies or essays), and speaks for itself. But the speech can sometimes be translated. A translation is what I shall now briefly try here, in the shape of random jottings from a highly personal notebook.

STORY. Béla Bartók was pathologically private, even to keeping his marriage a secret. Nevertheless, although he declined an introduction to Saint-Saëns while in Paris in 1909, young Bartók yearned to meet Debussy. "But Debussy is crude and surly," he was told. "Do you want to be insulted by Debussy?" "Yes," he replied. These two facts—Bartók's conjugal circumspection, and his adoration of the French composer—provide as cogent a key (dare I say skeleton key?) as any with which to enter and catch a first look at Duke Bluebeard's ghastly and wondrous castle.

Like Anatole France's *Thaïs,* like Somerset Maugham's *Rain,* like Tennessee Williams's *Summer and Smoke,* each of which is a confrontation between saviour and sinner in which sinner is saved and saviour sins, *Bluebeard*'s tale is palindromic, shaped liked an *X,* and so by extension is the music, more or less. About Béla Balázs, the librettist, there is scant information beyond the fact of his communism, which caused his exile for awhile from Hungary. The libretto seems to have been first meant for Kodály, with Bartók as second choice, but the two Bélas became friends and collaborated later on a ballet. The book owes a lot to Maeterlinck's *Ariane et Barbe-Bleue,* and a little to Maeterlinck's *Pelléas et Mélisande,* used by Debussy. (Schoenberg too composed a *Pelleas und Melisande,* an orchestral suite in 1902, although he was presumably unaware of Debussy's version, premiered the same year.)

After an irrelevant and usually omitted Brechtian prologue spoken by the Bard ("This story, ladies and gentlemen, is about *you . . .*"), the curtain rises on a vast circular Gothic hall, the Bard drifts into the wings, and a sharp light finds Duke Bluebeard standing in an open doorway with his bride Judith. (Why Judith? This woman is the reverse of the biblical heroine who decapitated Holofernes; neither is she saved at the last minute by her brothers; nor does she flee, deranged, into the forests of Alemonde and take the name Mélisande who, as Mary Garden contended, was the wife that got away. She is passive, albeit willful, and in love. This Bluebeard, meanwhile, is remote from the first model, Gilles de Retz who, when jilted by Joan of Arc for God and country, became a child murderer. Rather he seems a nice old absolute monarch attempting one last May-December marriage.) He descends the stairs, asking: "Judith, do you follow? Do you miss your family? Why have you paused?" "It's just that my dress was caught on a nail." She proceeds, although he tells her there's still time to turn back. But with the ardor of a woman in love she longs for the secrets of her husband's past, hopes to discover them by opening the seven doors visible in the castle walls, and thus bring light into his dark heart and home. Reluctantly he cedes the keys to her. The first door swings open in a river of scarlet flashes to reveal a torture chamber. The second door conceals an armory with blood-stained weapons. The third shows a huge treasury whose every gorgeous ruby drips with blood. Judith grows increasingly nervous. She opens the fourth door to the aqua glare of a magic garden and cries out at the splendor, but here also she sees that the roses bleed. "Who watered this garden?" she asks, but Bluebeard now urges her toward the fifth portal. She discovers the duke's endless domain all bathed in shimmering sunlight warming green velvet orchards. "Ah!" gasps the mezzo on her unique high C. (In *Erwartung*, a part conceived for soprano, the highest and longest note is a mere B, uttered midway through the drama on the word *Hilfe!*—"Help! For God's sake, quickly, can nobody hear me?"—the protagonist's only scream from her interior nightmare to the outside world.) Now Judith perceives the very clouds seeping blood. Bluebeard implores her vainly to refrain from the remaining doors, but she will go on. Behind the sixth is an infinitely mournful opalescent lake. What is its source? "Könnyek, Judit, Könnyek"—Tears, Judith, tears—and the Magyar syllables resound, clipped yet sustained, with a sadness that English can only hint at. Hesitant, but knowing he cannot refuse permission to open the final door, he reassures her with a sense of destiny: "Open, look, there are my former wives. The first came at morning. The second at midday. The third at evening." Out step three beautiful ashen women. Judith breaks down, knowing she is doomed to their fate. Bluebeard throws a mantle over her, crowns her with gold, they gaze long into each other's eyes, she pleads to be spared, he declares, "Lovely vision, Beauty tends you," she staggers beneath the weight of her robes and her knowledge and her grief, heads slowly toward the seventh door through which the other wives have disappeared, then she herself disappears and the door swings shut. "Night," sings Duke Bluebeard. "Nothing but darkness is here, eternal darkness . . . ," *ejjel . . . ejjel,* like Mahler's *Ewig . . . ewig,* and blackness floods the stage, engulfing Bluebeard in the unresolved second inversion of the F-sharp minor tonality with which the tragedy began an hour earlier.

Moral: Curiosity killed the cat.

Duke Bluebeard's Castle is a parable on what today would be termed an antifeminist stance in marriage. Neither Bartók nor Balász took a stand, allowing however that the inevitable is glum. This is a man's opera. The tragedy is Bluebeard's, not Judith's; she is the messenger who brought him the necessary night.

The palindrome is clear in the gradual switch between characters. Judith, at first passionate and protective, aches to free her husband from his past. Bluebeard, at first reticent and rational, nonetheless confides certain secrets, except for the last one, which would mean sacrificing his bride. But as the plot advances he grows increasingly dictatorial while she dwindles until she dissolves. The music mirrors this philosophical change—not perhaps as literally as Hindemith's *Hin and Zurück* which is symmetrical as a butterfly, yet enough for any music lover to perceive. During the first half Judith is in the foreground with her continually enthusiastic cantilena queries, while Bluebeard replies in fits and starts, monosyllabically; as their relationship crisscrosses, his voice grows longer and louder, hers more sporadic and ever fainter.

THE ACID TEST. Our judgment of a piece is always partly determined by the circumstances of our initial exposure to that piece. I first heard *Duke Bluebeard's Castle*, or some of it, on an autumn evening in the Poconos in 1958 (ten years before the dropping of acid, e.g., the use of LSD, was de rigueur for flower children) during a carefully supervised bout with mescaline, the hallucinogenic which supposedly opens the doors of perception onto our world as it really is, not as milleniums of human conditioning would have it be. Indeed, one does effortlessly see the universe in a grain of sand while being caressed by a snowy mass of clouds. But as the hours advanced I had a bad trip, the poplars seemed a fatal threat and bleeding veins streaked the sky. I didn't know it then, but my visions were similar to Judith's. At the height of the experiment my companion in crime, fellow composer Paul Bowles, knowing that under the drug "truth" speaks through art and that even a tone-deaf oaf can distinguish good music from bad, played a tape of the "Lake of Tears" from *Bluebeard*. I had never heard anything remotely like its melodic melancholy, its motionlessness (sound seemed suspended in time as well as space), and above all, its color. The highest compliment one composer can pay another is, "I don't know how you got that effect," and Bartók here had contrived an orchestration which it would take me thirty years to analyze; even today, with the full score on my knees, I'm not certain how the magic enters those twenty-nine swirls of demisemiquavers that surge, over and over, like blurred parentheses around the ceaseless plaint:

Waters, gray unmoving, mournful
Waters, mournful silent waters,
Waters still and dead: what brought them?
Weeping brought them, Judith, weeping.

Yes, I see on the staves that one flute and one clarinet repeatedly rise and fall at great speed in close harmony backed by three other flutes fluttertonguing, while one harp glissandos and another arpeggiates in close harmony with a celesta backed by muted strings divided into a thick A-minor triad—all of this pianississimo. But could I have guessed that the simultaneous hollow soughing stems from the sustained intoning of two low horns a fifth apart, doubled by a kettledrum chord and a large gong? Fifty separate human players produce this pale whisper. What if Haydn, not Bartók, had been played on that crucial night? Would I have been haunted with the same impression of breakthrough? In any case it is sonority chez Bartók—the hue of instrumentation in and for itself—that plays as strong a role in his opera as the two protagonists, and stronger than other of music's key components: melody, rhythm, harmony, counterpoint. The composer's orchestration is comparable to the scenery in an Antonioni movie; it determines the behavior and motives of the paltry mortals snared in its sonorous décor.

"Red streaks the storm clouds and glows through the secret garden," declared the critic of the *Dallas Morning News* after the American premiere in 1949. "Bartók has found orchestral red as others have found silver, and the white moonlight." What others? It would be nice to prove that Bartók *wrote red* as Debussy and Ravel wrote azure and ocher, or as Scriabin and Messiaen purported to depict every nuance of the rainbow. But that's metaphor. The fact is, at any mention of blood Bartók arranges for a minor second to emerge and throb among the instruments. So deft and persistent is the use of this interval that it has come to *mean* blood, the way harps and whole-tone scales mean water, or a single violin means amorousness. (Incidentally, in *Erwartung*—that "advanced" work which is really less advanced than simply more-of-same *in extremis,* or Wagner italicized—often from amid the psychotic fray a solo fiddle arises like an old friend and sighs "Love.") But these meanings are associative, not integral. Perhaps my bewitchment by this scene is also associative. This isn't the place to dispute the pros and cons of mescaline (which Henri Michaux called "the miserable miracle"), but to state that whenever I hear "The Lake of Tears" in whatever context I am drawn back into that drugged revelation of long ago. Similarly, Benny Goodman's "Goodbye" conjures up the smell of bread my sister was baking when the disk first turned; Bizet's Symphony evokes for me, and thousands of others, not a teenaged composer in France's Second Empire but a Balanchine ballet for which it was never intended; and "Willow Weep for Me" brings back the high school prom where I first fell in love.

STRAVINSKY, AND INFLUENCES. Biographies of Bartók teem with references to peers he claimed to be indebted to; but books about these peers, except for his national colleagues Kodály and Dohnanyi, grant short shrift to the Hungarian. For example, in Robert Craft's half-dozen volumes dealing with Bartók's most spectacular contemporary, Igor Stravinsky (Bartók's junior by fifteen months), the rare mentions are noncommittal, with three notable exceptions:

In 1959 Stravinsky is quoted: "I could never share [Bartók's] lifelong gusto for his native folklore . . . (and) couldn't help regretting it in a great musician. His death in circumstances of actual need has always impressed me as one of the tragedies of our society." But Stravinsky too incorporated with gusto *his* folklore into all of his most famous works, he simply didn't credit his sources as Bartók did. As for the latter's death "in circumstances of actual need," Stravinsky could have consulted his own publisher's (and Bartók's), Boosey & Hawkes, to learn that both they and ASCAP provided for the Hungarian's comforts until the last, and that even in the year of his death, 1945, he actually returned money, as Satie used to do, when he felt he had been overpaid. It is time that the story of Bartók's miserable end be laid to rest: it encourages the damaging notion that hungry artists are pure artists.

When Stravinsky himself died, in 1971, he was tended by a Dr. Lax who had in turn treated Bartók twenty-six years earlier. Craft quotes Lax quoting Bartók: "One of the most important things I learned from Stravinsky is daring." But Stravinsky's only response on the day of Bartók's death was: "I never liked his music anyway," to which Robert Craft (the Russian's amanuensis and chief keeper of the flame) adds: "A remark that, regrettably, rings true." Stravinsky would doubtless have remarked similarly on Schoenberg were it not for the brainwashing by Craft which led to Stravinsky's smarmy endorsement of the Austrian in his final years—that, regrettably, rings false—even to adopting the twelve-tone system and spawning pieces which hang from him like hobble skirts. And if he "never liked" Bartók's music, he nonetheless borrowed from it liberally. Whole pages from his *Symphony in Three Movements* (1943), for instance, are plagiarisms of Bartók's *Music for Strings, Percussion and Celesta* (1936), while the central section of Jocasta's air from *Oedipus Rex* (1928) is a rewrite of a central section of the last movement of Bartók's first String Quartet (1908). Meanwhile one seeks in vain for any influence of Stravinsky—other than maybe his "daring"—in the scores of Bartók. Which is not to say that Bartók is the more important artist (originality, in itself, is irrelevant to genius and not necessarily a virtue); indeed, Stravinsky at his best overwhelms the heart, is witty, even uplifting, and may ultimately rate higher than Bartók, who, with all his scarifying panache, is not high on humor. But Stravinsky wasn't a very generous person (he never acknowledged Bartók's offer in 1925 to play one of the pianos in *Les Noces*), nor had he a trustworthy ear (he found atonal Debussy's diatonic and mostly D-major final movement of *En Blanc et noir*, which is dedicated to him).

Though Bartók and Stravinsky each rose out of Debussy, the two are as dissimilar as an Airedale and a leopard (Bartók being the Airedale) which both diverged a billion years ago from the same maternal amphibian. Still, they are the French musician's principal heirs.

Specifically in *Bluebeard's Castle* Debussy's influence is pronounced, but more in morosely echoing empty halls of mood (in *Pelléas* as in *Bluebeard* the castle symbolizes the soul of its owner) than in harmony, more in oral device than in sonority. Debussy in his one opera is credited with creating the modern French recitative style, just as Bartók formed the Hungarian parlando-recitativo in *his* one opera. For me, *Pelléas et Mélisande* contains no recitative; rather, it posits a series of arias in miniature, or virtuoso turns in microcosm—to use the term Bartók made famous. The Pelleasian world contains countless examples of two-measure, three-measure, seven-measure sequences, restrained verbal outbursts complete in themselves yet part of the flow, and surely more tunefully infectious than Mozart recitatives. These outbursts, like tiny explosions in deep space, are patterns sewn on a huge instrumental fabric which is the core of the dramatic structure, which sometimes dominates with massive interludes, and which in the case of both composers claims the nonverbal last word. Bartók was proud of the affinity, emphasizing that his vocal style was in the "sharpest possible contrast to the Schoenbergian treatment of vocal parts." His melodies are more elastic than Debussy's, however, and stem tangibly from Hungarian peasant tunes. It's amusing that, as with Mussorgsky (another of his influences—and Debussy's too), peasant tunes dictate the swerves and curves when even the grandest of nobility is at song. As with *Pelléas, Bluebeard* has no ensemble singing, although the pair of voices eventually overlap a bit. But unlike *Pelléas,* which is sumptuously Spartan in that it boasts not one golden note too many and retains a dynamic level of mezzo-piano ninety percent of the time, *Bluebeard* is hyperthyroid, overly literal lest we miss the point, irritatingly climactic with lots of hysterical filler—what the French call *remplissage.*

Unqualified to judge the Hungarian word-setting, I know the text solely through Chester Kallman's dogged translation in trochaic tetrameter. But we are what we speak: even the nonvocal music from any nation resembles in stress and implicit prosody the language of that nation. Thus Bartók and Debussy, over and beyond their individual personalities, are as separate as the French and Hungarian tongues, the one arrhythmic, the other ripe with tonic accent. And thus, even Bartók's six "abstract" quartets are "in Hungarian." Since World War I most major gestures from the so-called serious music world, and all of them from the pop world, have involved the human voice. Bartók, in having devoted less than five percent of his total oeuvre to sung music, stands alone against the trend; yet in being influenced by his famous folksong research, his every instrumental measure reflects the intoned speech of his country.

Other influences? I hear *La Mer* at rehearsal number 105 when the minor-second blood motif begins to expand. I hear Ravel's *Asie* throughout the work, notably in the figure of one descending major third followed, a whole tone lower, by another—a figure echoed forty-five years later by the "Malo, malo" sequence of evil in Britten's *Turn of the Screw.* As with *Turn of the Screw* the influences from now on emanate from, not into, Béla Bartók. Would the slow-trilling woodwinds in *The Rite of Spring* resound quite that way without the slow-trilling woodwinds when Judith dips her hand into the bleeding crimson light at number 36? At number 50 could not Kurt Weill have penned those harp licks accompanying Blue-beard's jazzy little tune, "Trembling seizes all the castle, Joy that is alive invades it"? Even the ballet music from Bernstein's *On the Town*, the part which is a variation on the introduction to "We'll Catch Up Some Other Time," seems in turn to be a variation of the motive at number 81, and *that* in turn is a variation on Bartók's own two solo violins in unison, eerily iterating their descending triplets, at 54, over three icy transparent trumpets in a sustained triad. The deafening entrance of the organ, just before 75, represent-ing the blinding light of the wide countryside, has been imitated in all its modal splendor by every British composer since Vaughan Williams. (And the spooky recapitulation of the organ softly at the end, as Judith walks along the beam of moonlight through the seventh door, is a stroke of apt excruciation.) The clogged and stifling duet between the clarinet and horn at 60 in the clotted garden brings Richard Strauss to mind, in that, like Till Eulenspie-gel, it seeks, frustratedly, to climb, contradicting the overall im-pulses of the piece. For most of the melodic inclination in *Duke Bluebeard's Castle* is downward. Themes sag, fall, roll gradually lower and lower, like blood and tears that never cease to drip.

• 2 •

HISTORY. My first awareness of Schoenberg came from a limerick penned by my father after attending a lecture by the master, in the mid-1930s, at Chicago University's Mandel Hall:

> Here's to our German cousin
> Who handles his notes by the dozen.
>> Some of us slept
>> And some of us wept
> But none of us understood nozzen.

I soon grew to know *Pierrot lunaire* through the incomparable re-cording of Erika Stiedry-Wagner, and was bewitched by the expressionist illness of it all, but not beguiled as I was by French impressionism. I didn't *need* these songs, much less the later serial works which seemed to contain just too much information per square inch to qualify as . . . well, as *art*. Familiarity, crucial to comprehension and usually breeding simply more familiarity, in this case bred contempt. I listened to Schoenberg for decades yet never *heard* him. Did anyone so love and require him that they would rush home after work to bask, again and yet again, in the newest release of his Piano Concerto or Wind Quintet or String Trio? I learned to avoid Schoenberg's work because it pained me. Though I cannot prove it, I don't believe anyone likes—*enjoys*—it. Yet in 1947 no less a figure than Thomas Mann based his novel *Doctor Faustus* on a Schoenberg-type innovator. (Not being credited, Schoenberg sued, and later editions contained the following apology by Mann, albeit hidden at the end: "It does not seem supererogatory to inform the reader that the form of musical composition delineated in Chapter XXII, known as the twelve-tone or row system, is in truth the intellectual property of a contemporary composer and theoretician, Arnold Schönberg. I have transferred this technique in a certain ideational context to the fictitious figure of a musician, the tragic hero of my novel. In fact, the passages of this book that deal with musical theory are indebted in numerous details to Schönberg's *Harmonielehre*.")

Is Arnold Schoenberg a genius without talent? By genius I mean one over whom the creator spirit hovers like an electric halo igniting the gray matter, which reacts continually and in spite of itself, producing vital ideas, mostly noble but occasionally evil, which are then succinctly displayed to us outsiders so that we too are illuminated by what we did not know we knew. The term applies to saints, statesmen, and scientists, but if applied to musicians, only composers qualify, and not performing re-creators. A genius is by nature an innovator, yet whose notions are sometimes fully realized only by protégés with more talent. By talent I mean the knack for projecting *with charm* a unique gift, however small. Charm is indispensable. The word is disdained by many—including Kurt Weill who was laden with it—although no great music is without it, even Beethoven's. (Insofar as, say, Bruckner, who wrote in the swollen Beethovenian idiom, lacked charm, he lacked greatness.) Yes, Arnold Schoenberg is a genius without talent. His process though honest and sprung from a deep need—a need not to rescue tonality from Wagnerian chromaticism but to push it forward into an oxymoronic chaos made from order—proved to be a blind alley. The process was genial, however, inasmuch as it deluded for half a century a sophisticated public, gullible critics, and shrewd but minor composers with nothing to impart but rhetoric (all of which, if not quite evil—art has nothing to do with morality —is certainly sterile), with one exception, Alban Berg, a charming genius who could not have existed but for his teacher.

That said, *Erwartung* is not easily laughed off. Whatever the forever wandering atonal system cannot manage (and it cannot manage comedy, lightheartedness, camp, terse intrigue, which depend for their *charm* on resolution), it can serve as a base for unrelenting horror.

STORY. Like Bartók's collaborator, Béla Balász, *Erwartung*'s origin is something of a mystery. Nowhere in the forty-page booklet with CBS's recording is there mention of the circumstances of *Erwartung*'s libretto, not even the author's name, although the text is reprinted in three languages and subjected to a thorough psychoanlysis. Nor does Grove name the librettist (although it does state rather piously that "traditional tonal order could scarcely have met the demands of such a subject." Why not? Is *Lucia*'s diatonicism so much less psychotic?) The text, it turns out, is by Marie Pappenheim, a young medical student who also wrote poems, whom Schoenberg met through his brother-in-law Zemlinsky, and whom Berg had already approached for a libretto. What she came up with was a stream-of-consciousness soliloquy, *Expectation*, set down without revision, which Schoenberg, without further consultation, musicalized in a mere seventeen days of violent inspiration (although, as with *Bluebeard*, a production was not forthcoming for many years).

There are four scenes, of which the fourth is thrice the length of the other three together.

Scene I: A lost and nameless woman comes upon a moonlit path at the edge of a forest. In fits and starts and never-finished phrases she names the elements around her, as though to gain hold on her memories of "our garden," the crickets, the withered flowers. But the silence threatens, darkness stifles, and she gathers courage to enter the woods. "I'll sing, then he will hear me."

Scene II: Total blackness, tall trees close together. "Am I still on the path? . . . What's that? . . . Something crawled . . . Who's touching me?" Her terror mounts, she invokes her lover, "But you did not come . . . Who is that crying?," is scared by a screech owl, stumbles on something, "What's that? A body . . . No, just a tree trunk."

Scene III: Still a dark path, but the moon lights a clearing which the woman approaches. "Are you calling? And it won't be evening for ages . . . I'm so frightened . . . My darling, help me."

Scene IV: Brief orchestral interlude, like a *marche macabre,* leads to the path toward a house. She enters, dress ripped, hair askew, hands bleeding. "He's not here either . . . The unknown woman will drive me away . . . A bench. I must rest." She touches something with her foot—her lover's body, wet and red. Is he alive? She tries to drag him into the moonlight. "That terrible head . . . The moon is deceitful . . . because it is bloodless . . . Say something, look at me." Then the terrible scream for help, to a world outside of her nightmare. "Please don't be dead . . . Are you going to spend the day with me?" But as she gradually realizes that he *is* dead, she pleads, then scolds him for his infidelity. "Where did she run to when you were lying in your own blood? I'll drag her here by her white arms." But did the woman herself kill him, forget, then return to the scene? "Are you squirming for shame?" She kicks him. "How dearly I loved you, living far from everything, a stranger to everyone . . . Did you love her very much? . . . Don't say yes . . . Day is breaking for others . . . What am I to do here all alone, in this darkness? . . . Another interminable day of waiting . . . but you won't wake up. Where are you?"

Her darkness, like Judith's, is now limitless. "My lips burn and gleam . . . Oh, you are here . . . I was looking . . ."

And she will never, never stop looking.

TALKING WITH FRIENDS. Can one live with such a role? Some knowing friends replied:

"I learned it at the same time as Birtwistle's gory *Punch and Judy* and Tavener's gloomy *In Alium,* and became depressed," says Phyllis Bryn-Julson with a healthy grin. Is a singer what she sings?

"Well, at least she knows this piece will end, as distinct from the woman in *Erwartung* who cannot distinguish reality." Can you smile when you take a bow, as I once saw Nancy Shade do like a preening soubrette? "No, no. At least not until after the fourth or fifth bow. But the text and the music are perhaps not always equal to each other, and that fact lends a certain equilibriating objectivity to the performer."

"Look at the dynamics if you want to understand *Erwartung*," says Bethany Beardslee. "There are hundreds and hundreds of them, and their extreme variety is as vital to the interpretation as the hundreds and hundreds of disjunct notes. It's so syllabic. And for a mezzo's tessitura, so I, a soprano, must *think dark*." (She might have added that in the monolgue's 427 measures of music there are 111 metronome markings to be dealt with.) Is it real? "Oh no, it's unreal, like *The Turn of The Screw*. Yet Schoenberg is literal with the text, unlike Debussy who understates." Do you speak German? "No, but I speak some French. And no, I don't have perfect pitch. But perfect pitch can be a hindrance, especially in highly chromatic music. It's dangerous—not to say unmusical—to 'think pitches,' that is, to think from note to note rather than melodically, theatrically." Do you become depressed? "When I am singing I become the composer more than the woman. So in a sense I am standing apart from her, while being her, and am not depressed."

"It's all real: the forest is real, the night is real," says Susan Davenny Wyner. "The irony is that this real woman is trapped in time, as I was after my bicycle accident, when I lay in bed and felt my extraordinarily accurate ear become shakier. I still retain my perfect pitch, and that was helpful for the spikey thematic lines of *Erwartung*, but I no longer sing professionally." How *did* you sing it?—because when all is hysterical, nothing's hysterical: on the page there's little contrast and no relief. "It should be understated. And yes, I know German quite well."

Now I recall Debussy's understated setting of Verlaine's *"Colloque sentimentale"*: *Dans le vieux parc solitaire et glacé / Deux formes ont tout à l'heure passé*. How close are these "two forms" whose "eyes are dead and whose lips are soft and whose words we scarcely hear," to those in *Erwartung*? Music is not a universal language, taste does not cross frontiers. Yet it's always tempting to balance artworks against each other. The French parallel to *Erwar-*

tung is Poulenc's *La Voix humaine,* based word for word on Jean Cocteau's solo harangue for female voice. Both women are nameless, both for thirty minutes berate invisible lovers (one dead, one at the end of the telephone wire and who can't get a word in edgewise) with accusation and remembrance of things past, and both end up literally beside themselves. It might be amusing to concoct a double bill from the men's viewpoint.

• 3 •

ODDS AND ENDINGS. The casts of both operas are minimal, but the orchestras are massive in the prewar Diaghilev tradition. The gnarled contrapuntal forest into which Schoenberg's Woman staggers contains seventeen woodwinds, twelve brass, harp, celesta, glockenspiel, xylophone, six percussion, and sixty-four strings. (The Bartók forces are similar but with two harps and organ.) Yet we find page after page with very few instruments; like Stravinsky's *Rite of Spring* (1913), *Erwartung* is chamber music on a grand scale. And like *The Rite of Spring* it opens with a solo bassoon in its high register (can this be said of any other orchestra or operatic work in history?), even as it closes on those fluted bubbles of horror vanishing into thin air which, fifteen years later, Berg appropriated for "the Wozzeck sound." Nevertheless, if *Bluebeard* is heavy with *remplissage, Erwartung* is nothing *but remplissage:* it has more sting chords than a vampire movie, nothing is understated, every word is illustrated, Mickey-moused, italicized. The plot may deal in interior monologue, but the music is hardly introspective.

Diaghilev tradition. The ballet impresario was interested in neither composer. Odd—and they so theatrical! (When choreographer Pina Bausch turned to Bartók it was not to his dance scores but to a tape of *Bluebeard's Castle,* played onstage, and subjected to jolting stops and screeching starts.)

Their tendency to morbid texts and small casts is all Bartók and Schoenberg had in common. Their compositional languages resemble each other not at all. Every important twentieth-century piece contains a contagious ingredient—a salubrious virus—by which we grasp and retain it always. The ingredient is drawn from one (or a combination) of music's basic components mentioned earlier. *Bluebeard*'s gift to the ear is sumptuous harmony, clean tune, and enigmatic scoring ("Why I make so little use of counterpoint," said the composer, "is that in my youth my idol was not Bach but Beethoven"), and in this it resembles many another work of its time, from *Pelléas* to *Tosca*. *Erwartung* is unique in that we—or at least I—retain not tune or even color so much as texture: the wild yet logical intertwinings that represent the paths, lost and found, of the protagonist. If Schoenberg is not recalled specifically for his rhythm, that's because his mode, serial or not, is linear and cannot depend on the "barbaric" repetitions of a Stravinsky or the dance-like cross-meters of a Bartók.

In 1941 at Northwestern I heard Bartók and his wife Dita give a two-piano recital that included *En Blanc et noir*. Thomas Mann was on the same series. Four winters later Bartók died in New York. Unlike, say, Gide or Hindemith or Thomas Mann himself, or indeed many glorious creators whose fame and influence abates with their death, Bartók became world-famous overnight, and has remained so. Only Poulenc among composers has had the same fortune in our midcentury. *Bluebeard,* at sixty minutes, is double the length of *Erwartung.* The two musicians did not know each other. This paragraph blends afterthoughts on facts previously mentioned.

Some music needs no interpretation (just play what you see, please), like that of most French composers. Other music breathes by being given "meaning," warmth, and understanding, like that of most German composers. Imagine Fauré or Milhaud with emotive rubatos, imagine Bruckner or Mahler without them, and enter a nightmare of vulgar frustration. Schoenberg, even at his most "mathematical" can, without damage, bear a good deal of bending. I respect his music, marvel at it, am even stunned by it. But I cannot live with it: it lacks the prerequisite charm—the Terrible Charm of Goya or Rimbaud—and is overrich. Bartók is French in that he cannot bear much interpretation, the nuances are written into the note-lengths. This comparatively austere esthetic is one I can live with more easily, although with all his bedazzling scope Bartók never breaks my heart, as does his progenitor, Debussy.

If I were able to describe, accurately and convincingly and thoroughly, the music of another composer, there would be no need for that music, for I would have appropriated the composer's soul.

Therein lies the dilemma of the critic—that sometimes powerful but vaguely superfluous citizen. He can never put his finger on what finally counts most, since what finally counts most issues from within the music. Thus your surprise, when you listen for the first time to a piece you've seen described enthusiastically by a good critic, and are miffed: what he described was his enthusiasm, not the music itself.

In approaching these two short operas I have described not them but my relation to them. But just as only words can depict another person's novel, so only music can depict another person's music. Still, it is not for me to say, in words, how my own music might have sounded had Bartók and Schoenberg never existed.

PART FOUR

Epitaphs

Lenny Is Dead

October 1990

During the terrible hours following Lenny's death last Sunday the phone rang incessantly. Friend after friend called to commiserate, and also the press, with a flood of irrelevant questions: How well did you know him? What made him so American? Did he smoke himself to death? Wasn't he too young to die? What was he really like? None of this seemed to matter since the world had suddenly grown empty—the most crucial musician of our time had vanished. But next morning it seemed clear that there are no irrelevant questions, and these were as good as any to set off a brief remembrance.

I was nineteen in early 1943 when we met in his West 52nd Street flat. Despite his showbiz personality he had, and forever retained, a biblical look, handsome and nervy as the shepherd David who would soon be king and psalmodize throughout his days. To me, a Midwest Quaker, his aura was Jewish and quite glamorous, while to him I remained always something of a reticent Wasp who never quite got the point. How well did I know him? To "know well" has to do with intensity more than with habit. Everyone in Lenny's vast entourage felt themselves to be, at one time or another, the sole love of his life, and I was no exception. The fact that he not only championed my music, but conducted it in a manner coinciding with my very heartbeat, was naturally not unrelated to love. Years could pass without our meeting, then for weeks we'd be inseparable. During these periods he would play as hard as he worked, with a power of concentration as acute for orgies as for oratorios. In Milan, in 1954, when he was preparing *La Sonnambula* for La Scala, I asked him how Callas was to deal with. "Well, she knows what she wants and gets it, but since she's always right, this wastes no time. She's never temperamental or unkind during rehearsal—she saves that for parties." Lenny was the same: socially exasperating, even cruel with his manipulative narcissism (but only with peers, not with unprotected underlings), generous to a fault with his professional sanctioning of what he believed in.

Was he indeed so American? He was the sum of his contradictions. His most significant identity was that of jack-of-all-trades (which the French aptly call *l'homme orchestre*), surely a European trait, while Americans have always been specialists. If he did want desperately to create a self-perpetuating American art, his own music, even the Broadway scores, was a grab bag of every imaginable foreign influence. Night after smoke-filled night we could sit up arguing the point, for Lenny ached to be taken seriously as a sage. Nothing was ever resolved, of course, not so much because musical philosophy is an impotent pursuit as because he was less a thinker than a doer. Yes, he was frustrated at forever being "accused" of spreading himself thin, but this very spreading, like the frustration itself, defined his theatrical nature. Had he concentrated on but one of his gifts, that gift would have shriveled.

I last saw Lenny in May when, with two other people, we went to a dance program, afterward to a restaurant. His role, as always, was to be the life of the party, but repartee fell flat, the concerned pronouncements were incomplete, his breath distressingly short, and he disappeared like a ghost in the midst of the meal. A month later we spoke on the phone, not about health or music, but about the plight of our mutual protégé, a young Romanian student without a passport. Lenny could simultaneously focus on his navel and on the universe, even in his agony.

Was he too young to die? What is too young? Lenny led four lives in one, so he was not 72 years old but 288. Was he, as so many have meanly claimed, paying for the rough life he led? As he lived many lives, so he died many deaths. Smoking may have been one cause, but so was overwork, and especially sorrow at a world he so longed to change but which remained as philistine and foolish as before. Which may ultimately be the brokenhearted reason any artist dies. Or any person.

So what was he really like? Lenny was like everyone else, only more so. But nobody else was like him.

Epitaph for Aaron

December 1990

Aaron Copland's most beautiful song, at least for me, opens with these words by Emily Dickinson:

> *The world seems dusty when we stop to die —*
> *We want the dew then, honors seem dry.*

What dew can be brought to my vanished friend, so honored elsewhere today by the dusty world?

Well, that world, he might like to know, weighs far less than before. When Bernstein died, seven Sundays to the hour ahead of Copland, our American orchestras seemed suddenly unimportant as they returned to the yoke of foreign leaders with their "dusty" programs, as though Lenny had never paved the way for a timely repertory. Similarly, with Aaron gone, whose upcoming works can we now look forward to with the throbbing joy of our youth? Where anymore is expertise combined with nostalgia, simplicity combined with power?

These maybe unfair words are penned in the heat of mourning, and echo the sentiments of one milieu and generation. I'm forgetting Aaron's own forgetfulness which for a decade precluded all creativity. But I do not forget the traits that everyone cites: his open laughter at terrible jokes, or his time-consuming interest in other composers' work (not necessarily a frequent virtue). Nor do I forget traits that many overlook: his repressed tears at a sorry love affair, his exasperation at mediocre hangers-on.

Like all artists he was a child, but where some play at being grown-up, Aaron's childishness had a frank visibility that I've never seen elsewhere, except perhaps in Ravel, of all people. Someday I must expand a theory about their resemblance—in their target if not in their arrows. For although Ravel was lush where Copland was plain, both stressed the craft of *dépouillement*, of stripping bare. And has it ever occurred to you that in their "representational" music they seldom portrayed an adult world? Ravel with his toys, his Daphnis, his affinity for animals, was *L'Enfant et les sortilèges* incarnate. Copland's Common Man was an abstracted man, like his ballet personages who were eternal adolescents in the wide open spaces. He was forever drawn to the pubescent realm of *The Tender Land* and *The Second Hurricane.* Both were urbane (they knew "everybody") but dwelt far from the madding crowd, Copland in sophisticated innocence, Ravel in naive sophistication.

But all that's for tomorrow. Today I merely hope that Aaron Copland is as close as possible to the great Frenchman. That hope is my dew.

Virgil Thomson

1989

When I first beheld Virgil Thomson, nearly fifty years ago, he was on a stage for one of those benighted roundtables about Meaning in Music. His fellow panelists, straining for a definition of the art, were about to settle for the Bard's "concord of sweet sounds" when Thomson yelled: "Boy, was he wrong! You might as well call poetry a succession of lovely words, or painting a juxtaposition of pretty colors. Music's definition is: That which musicians do." Which settled the matter. If Shakespeare erred, albeit divinely, Congreve did too, with his "charms to soothe a savage breast." Thomson, like all composers, disdained metaphoric ascriptions to music as mere cushion for the emotions. His businesslike summation was the first professional remark I'd ever heard from a so-called creative artist, and I was soon to hear more, from the horse's mouth, when I quit school at age nineteen to work with the master.

I already knew of course that he was born in 1896 in Kansas City, excelled at Harvard, then moved to France in 1920. And that in the next two decades he sent back to America not only trunkloads of sonatas and songs, but quartets and symphonies, a ballet called *Filling Station,* scores for movies of Pare Lorentz, a best-selling book called *The State of Music,* and, above all, a collaboration with Gertrude Stein, *Four Saints in Three Acts,* which was then and perhaps remains the most viable opera by any American. American he utterly was despite, or maybe because of, the removal from his homeland which gave him a new slant on his roots. For it was he who first legitimized the use of home-grown fodder for urbane palates. He confected his own folksong by filtering the hymns of his youth through a chic Gallic prism. This was the "American Sound" of wide-open prairies and Appalachian springs, soon borrowed and popularized by others.

At the start of World War Two, Virgil Thomson returned from Paris to begin his fourteen-year stint as critic for the *New York Herald Tribune*. And the rest, as they say, is . . . well, it's geography. Thomson single-handedly changed, for a time, the tone of serious American composition from the thickish Teutonic stance which had dominated since before MacDowell to the transparent Frenchness of those in the Boulanger school.

He was at his peak when we met in 1943. As his in-house copyist, for which I received twenty dollars and two orchestration lessons a week, my daily chores were done on the parlor table within earshot of the next room where—propped in bed, a pad on his lap, an ear to the phone—Virgil ran the world of music. During those first months, by being accountable for his every note, by heeding his ever lucid but never repeated dicta on instrumentation, and by eavesdropping on his talk with, say, Leopold Stokowski or Oscar Levant or colleagues at the paper, I gleaned as much, esthetically and practically, about the terrifyingly golden milieu of my future vocation as in all the previous years.

Virgil the author, as his ten books attest, was the world's most informative and unsentimental witness to other people's music. These qualities were enhanced by his addressing the subject from inside out—from the standpoint of the maker—and by his readability which owed so much to Paris where, in art as in life, brevity is next to godliness. Beside him, other critics were superfluous. They may have shared his perception, even exceeded his scope, but none boasted his knack for cracking square center with that perfect little Fabergé hammer.

Virgil the musician, over and beyond his affable innovation (based not on new complication but, ironically, on age-old simplicity), was our sole composer as convincing in song as in opera. His music cannot be assessed on the same expressive basis as any other music, even Satie's, since his more than any other depends on words. If Virgil never received a bad review (or, except for the Stein operas, a really good review), it's less because reviewers were intimidated by Papa than because they didn't know what to say about this seeming inanity. In fact, the inanity was sophistication at its most poignant. His every phrase is aria-in-a-microscope, built from but two or three intervals. The result differs from folksong only in the ambiguous accompaniment and eccentric literariness. The songs are rarely sung right, but despite their sparseness they do need to be heard to be believed. They are not *Augenmusik*, yet the critic's ear is not often given to listening to them, even in imagination. Thomson's unique urge was to codify simplicity, the way others have been urged to codify complexity.

Virgil the man had concerns, but not anxieties like we morbid others; he didn't agonize about the daily news—which may account for his longevity. Emerging from anesthetic after an operation three years ago, he asked: "Will I live?" When the doctor said yes, Virgil replied, "In that case I'll need my glasses."

His music resembles himself, is impatiently terse, free of padding, sensuous without self-indulgence, not especially warm but often quite dear. It is also very, very witty—if that adjective makes sense when applied also to non-vocal works. His art is generous by its very frugality—we recall it accurately forever.

If in texture Virgil Thomson was American as apple pie, in "message" he was French as *tarte Tatin*, because he was not a specialist. During the decades of our friendship (sometimes warm, sometimes cool) I never thought of him as less than this century's most articulate musicologist and most persuasive opera-maker. Like all artists he was able to do what cannot be done. Through his prose he convincingly evoked the sound of new musical pieces, and through his musical pieces he continues to evoke the visual spectacle of all our pasts.

When I last beheld Virgil Thomson two weeks before he died, he was esconced as usual in that armchair near the piano, gazing at paintings by dear friends—Stettheimer, Arp, Grosser, Bérard— that had for so long hung on his east wall at the Chelsea. In the dreamy murmur that was now his sole voice (contrasting with the glib staccato that once so intimidated most of us), he announced: "Just sitting here, day after day after day, I realize how beautiful my pictures are." That is how I like to remember him—a general practitioner, in taste as in talent, never blasé, dying as he had lived, among an array of old acquaintances.

NED ROREM

Robert Phelps
1989

When Becki, knowing I couldn't be present for her husband's memorial, asked me to invent a "Ned-like" statement that could be read aloud, my sole impulse was to pull out a file of some seventy-five Phelps letters, beginning in 1959 when we first met at Yaddo, and ending only a few months before Robert died. Here I was confronted with sheafs of rainbow paper covered with typscript and garnished with upside-down longhand postscripts, homemade valentines, and Scotch-taped news items. I hadn't looked these over since they were first received, but what I feared would be a mournful half-hour turned into a whole afternoon of nostalgic jollity.

If the knack of writing letters began to gasp with the rise of the telephone, for me it was kept breathing uniquely by Robert Phelps. Incapable of cliché, his missives are him to the bone: witty, lewd, sage, generous, gossipy, aggressively self-effacing, monstrously opinionated without bitchery, engrossed by the literary life in general while being always directed to a unique recipient, and generally weaving something extraordinary out of something ordinary. Listen to this random phrase from February of 1966:

> On the other hand, I had a lovely time with Marianne Moore one evening. At eleven P.M. I carried her across a snow drift—she weighs about as much as a largish robin's egg. Then she introduced me to her doorman (she lives here in the village now) and took me for an hour's tour of her new apartment, complete with footnotes, just like one of her poems.

280

Or this a week later:

> What a delicious pedant you are. I am a pedant, too, but always ashamed to appear so. I incline to affect inadvertance, a tireless and *airless* little sin.

Or this in April:

> Do you know the paranoid Marguerite Young, or her fogbound novel about Miss MacIntosh? She cornered me at a party last week, and has phoned four times since— urging me to write an article about her, and even offering her own dotty ideas as to what I should say. Her impossible book has sold 40,000 copies and she is still complaining. Authors are worse than composers (but not as bad as death and taxes).

Taxes were a constant preoccupation in his letters (he and Becki were forever being audited and otherwise dunned), and so was death. Here he is in May of 1966, on learning that my sister's husband had been killed in an auto wreck in Uganda:

> I tried to reach your parents on the phone the other night, but no one answered. I'll try again. What a radical change the death of your brother-in-law will make in their lives—though perhaps for their own good. Certainly your mother won't ever feel unneeded again, with six fledglings to help. But what a shattering thing the death of a young father is! It's against nature. It fits into no pattern we can have for understanding or visualizing ourselves. It's just a fluke, a hole in the parachute; unforeseeable, unlikely.

Memorial propriety prevents my quoting from gamier entries, though Robert would not concur, and would be vaguely disappointed to hear me allow this. His notion of me had much to do with a conjectural fantasy, a fantasy I tried to live up to, partly because I adored Robert and partly because it seemed useful. Eulogists customarily declare how much the deceased has changed their life, but such declarations are generally metaphoric. My life, however, would have been crucially different were it not for Robert

Phelps. His image of me came through my diaries more than through the actual and soberer fact of me. Or at least that's what *my* image of *him* always suggested. Robert being a frantic Francophile and my early diaries being all about France, Robert took it upon himself to arrange for their publication. I didn't paper my room with rejection slips like many beginners; the first publisher to see *The Paris Diary* took it, hired Peter Deane as copy editor, Robert himself as prefacer, promoted it with a vengeance, and followed it up with four more books. Thus for the past quarter century I've led two parallel but unrelated careers in a sort of delicious schizophrenia for which Robert must take sole credit.

"It's not enough that I succeed, my friends must fail," said Somerset Maugham in a quip all artists can savor. Robert could announce, "It's not enough that I fail, unless my friends succeed," though in fact he was the least failed person I've ever known, insofar as he pursued his unique vocation with an uncompromising expertise. Where most artists steal from their predecessors without giving credit, Robert gave credit but did not steal. He elucidated. The elucidation was creation. Years spent in support of Colette, then of Cocteau and of Jouhandeau, were not years of reflected glory, but years of tailoring adoration into something self-perpetuating. Vicariousness as high art.

When I strolled through the streets of Paris with Robert during his first trip there, he was forty-two but behaved like an adolescent in Paradise: every ash can was a holy grail. Pausing at a below-average fruit stand to buy a kilo of strawberries (*kilo* was a Colette word so it must be the proper amount), he was, of course, burdened with more than he bargained for. Yet in writing of Paris he was as far from naive as his idol, Janet Flanner, and equally trenchant. Here he is on the French, using Jules Renard's *Poil de Carotte* as springboard:

> If you have ever lived in France, you will find some of this view, this inveterate aplomb, this stoic assumptiveness, in the concierge of your hotel, in the lady who collects your ticket at the Métro, in the young apprentice in a blue *salopette* who bicycles to his job very early in the morning. It is not the view of the French which has been sold to tourists all these years: haute cuisine, cancan

girls, ciel-de-Paris, castles-on-the-Loire. It is closer to the view Frenchman have of themselves: undeluded, self-sufficing, able to live on very little, unsentimentally efficient about gustatory and sexual satisfaction, firm about property values, keen at survival, and taking profound pride in this.

Yet when I asked him once to supply a text for a choral piece I was planning, he turned not to his own prose but to that of Janet Flanner, excising from her work nine unrelated paragraphs which, in their redigestion and juxtaposition through Robert's viewpoint, became a brand-new form of literature and utterly singable.

While rereading his letters I cannot believe him dead; his words, indeed his very being, jump from the page today with the same vitality I so envied three decades ago. If, over the past two or three years, his forces were noticeably waning, transferring themselves, or so it seemed, to Becki and to Roger, Robert's writing retained a vitality that will long outlast the century.

Fred Plaut's Pictures

1988

The future will judge our century as it judges all centuries, not by the political turmoil but by the art. Producers of art are a family, a mere few thousand at any given time compared to the billions who surge and vanish with the tides. Though some family members spat, they offer a united front to the Philistine world. They are at once solid and fragile: the best of what they create will by its nature outlive the Philistines, while the carnal fact of them will mostly fade forever. Still, traces of that carnal fact can now sometimes be preserved through photography, just as what they create is preserved by concert, gallery, and printing press.

Fred Plaut, an artist himself, was privileged to know hundreds of his siblings—know them in a manner unique to our century, by ensnaring their song on disk, and by stilling their persona on film.

Narrowly escaping deportation from France to Hitler's eastern camps, through the frantic interventions of his fiancée, American soprano Rose Dercourt, Fred managed to emigrate to America. Destitute at first, he gradually became the most valued recording expert in the land. Partly through his prestige as chief recording engineer for Columbia Records, partly through the entrée of his cosmopolitan spouse, he met the glamorous subjects for his second profession, photography. These were mainly musicians—some performers, mostly composers. Now, it is no secret that while Fred until his death remained the doting, gruff, virile and very Teutonic mate of his precious Rose, Rose was conducting an esthetic liaison with the doting, suave, garrulous and very Gallic Francis Poulenc.

This was no infidelity, since Fred was included in the platonic *ménage à trois* as, among other things, court photographer.

His studies of Poulenc, with and without Rose over the years, form a diary of growth: witness the musician's jollity superceded by—or even superimposed upon—the feigned arrogance, the sophisticated lewdness, the vulnerable self-assurance, and finally the near-suicidal *tristesse*. The Frenchman's life is caught by the lens with accuracy and artistry: All this, mind you, in black-and-white, medium of the great photo-portraitists, from Nadar to Horst, and including Fred Plaut.

The family was not exclusively musical. Look there at Marlene Dietrich, posing yet not posing as she listens to a playback during a recording session. Nothing of her face is visible—it is lowered into the crook of her arm over which hangs a sheath of blond silk —but she is instantly recognizable by that gorgeous body's violent concentration, those knees and high heels, the cool heat that quivers on the page. Look at Noel Coward, debonair and brusque as the public knew him, never at a loss, cigarette holder serving as an épée, enigmatic smile. Yet beneath the veneer gleams the generosity which his friends all knew, the willingness to listen which the famous, when they are sure of themselves (so rare), are able to afford. Or look at Edith Sitwell, snatched from reality for a split second and frozen forever like a medieval moth. But was it reality, or rather the gaudy supercilious trappings she donned to disguise her ugliness and to persuade the world, with some success, that she was the Empress of English Eccentrics? Well, it's her reality. And Fred Plaut's. And now ours, too.

My own reality, when I see today how Fred saw me decades ago, is less shaken than enhanced, as though filtered through a new dimension. I can revive to the very odor the tone of his studio those lost mornings; I can recall what I had for breakfast. Yet is that me staring up from the creamy cardboard? It's as much me as my music heard on a phonograph: a me who no longer exists, but who will paradoxically outlast me.

Fred too has outlasted himself, and that is the charm of his art and all art. A moment, an hour, a day, will repeat and repeat and repeat itself eternally through the work he has bequeathed.

Recalling Elizabeth

1992

When she died at ninety-two, Elizabeth Ames's entire adult life had been spent as director of Yaddo, which she co-founded a half-century earlier and which functioned solely according to the tone she set. True, she had had to step down eight years earlier: her freely roaming mind, the cancer of her eye, the near-total deafness, precluded much give-and-take except with those few who were still on her wavelength. In fact, current guests never saw her; all too quickly her name entered legend as that eccentric dowager of yore. Yet she remained in her perfect little house right there on campus, Pine Garde, imagining, as she spoke audibly to her invisible mother and sister, both long gone, that she was still in charge. For she was still surrounded by the paintings of dozens of friends —Hyde Solomon, Rosemarie Beck, Nell Blaine—and of signed first editions of seemingly every 20th-century author. These were her abiding friends. (What makes a house a home? Books that one still reads, and pictures that one continues to see, that become part of, or that absorb, one's personality.)

I like to feel that I was on her wavelength. At her death I was more bereft than with the passing of certain younger souls, maybe because there had been more years in which to grow accustomed to her. Or maybe because I felt guilty: "We never looked our last upon each other."

Were I to list the few "older" women besides my mother who have most affected me, they would surely include Elizabeth Ames, along with Nadia Boulanger and Martha Graham. Each was one of a kind and knew her worth. Each, though employed in a pursuit which by its nature shunned biases and encouraged the all-purpose sensuality of Art with a capital A, inclined nonetheless to give benefit of doubt to males before females. Each, by virtue of her fanatic allegiance to a Sacred Call, died a nonagenarian. And each, despite other people's endless speculations about her Spartan love life, was a creature of temperament and carnally fulfilled. Indeed, Elizabeth (Mrs. Ames to most guests), although her groom died on their honeymoon during the 1918 influenza pandemic, was later to fall in love with writer Leonard Ehrlich (who died young too), whose niece, Marianne, became thereafter the apple of Elizabeth's eye.

Less than an hour into our initial meeting, in the spring of 1959 during the first of my twenty-some visits to Yaddo, Elizabeth and I learned we were, in certain ways, chipped off the same block. The most crucial chip was our mutual adherence to organized pacifism, she as convert to the Society of Friends with the zeal of all converts, I as so-called birthright Quaker with a more relaxed approach to the religious, if not to the philosophical, angles of the True Way. We took to attending Sunday Meetings together. How can I forget our first such attendance in the very old Meeting House, a landmark of nearby Corinth. Into this same building two centuries ago, said Elizabeth, some Mohawk Indians noisily entered, brandishing tomahawks. When they beheld the worshippers, heads bowed in silent oblivion, they set aside their weapons and bowed their heads too.

As the years passed, especially in the winter months, we took to having our silent meetings à deux, before lunch, next to Elizabeth's fireplace, over which hung a small Robert Henri of a countryscape with yellow silos. These meetings, often as not, were less silent than chatty, since we both spoke "as the spirit moved us." Then, during our lunchboxed meal, the spirit moved us to gossip, mostly about other inmates. For example, when Alison Lurie's *Real People*—a transparently fictional portrait of Yaddo, in part necessarily mean and raw—came out, I wondered what Elizabeth thought. "Well," said she, "Alison will not be invited back." That's as near as I ever heard to a negative opinion from Elizabeth about a guest, though were the guest a man she might have paused. Still, Lurie's novel for its very truth had impact, and was better than other pictures I know, despite a sarcastic portrayal of Marianne Erhlich.

Marianne was the only outsider who, during her occasional stays with Elizabeth, was allowed to join the regulars in the dining room. She had a modest soprano voice upon which Elizabeth doted no less than did Citizen Kane on the voice of his second wife. Because I was poor, Elizabeth sent me sixty-five dollars a month for a year—the interest from a mortgage—which she hoped would permit the leisure for me to compose something for Marianne. I did, in fact, in 1964, write a cycle of ten songs called *King Midas,* on poems of Howard Moss, and dedicated the cycle to Elizabeth Ames.

Elizabeth was present for every evening meal, always at the central table. Guests sought out or avoided that table according to how they felt about her, or how they wished her to feel about them. Her conversation, glittering and intelligent, dominated the meal. She spoke in well-rehearsed sentences of the old days. Days when Yaddo boasted not only the copious vegetable garden it still retains, but its own dairy and livestock. (She recalled tearfully how, when the three Jersey cows were driven off to the slaughterhouse, they gazed at her sadly from the back of the truck.) Days of feuding, carousing, and slander, when "Carson wouldn't speak to Katherine Anne," or when David Diamond and John Cheever reeled home from a night at the races, or when she—Elizabeth—was forced to ask Robert Lowell to leave after his accusations that "Yaddo was communist supported." Days when the colony sponsored concerts produced by Copland, open to the public. (The first program featured Marc Blitzstein's new string quartet whose three movements were marked Largo, Largo, and Largo.) Days when Yaddo was a trysting place, fomenting marriages tragic and fruitful. (By my time Yaddo provided no more scandals, no wild parties, no sex, at least not for me—well, yes, twice maybe—and no apparent laziness, just occasional record playing or moviegoing and regular diligence all around.)

But with all her supple evocations, Elizabeth was not easy. Persons shunning that central table felt freer by the window; Elizabeth's deafness precluded general exchange, nor could she adjust to those unable to pitch their voices just so. And she had her proper side, was even imperious, a touch Victorian, stern about the dinner dress-code (skirts for women, jackets for men), leaving handwritten advice thumbtacked on the mail table. Virgil Thomson, who didn't take to her (the feeling was mutual), likened her to a hostess at Schraffts. Norman Podhoretz, who was tickled by her, compared her to a schoolmarm handing out demerits. Cheever, who adored her, called her a BMOC, as he called all professional women.

Meanwhile, her compassion. On Labor Day 1963, riding one of the colony bikes, I whizzed out of control down the lake-road hill, flew through the air, crashed on my left foot. For a month I was on crutches. During that month Elizabeth, each evening promptly at 6:15, called for me at West House (I never inhabited other than the Pink Room there, that sumptuous loft drenched in private green sunshine), had me lean heavily on her shoulders as we crept down the stairway, and thence escorted me to the Mansion. She was almost eighty.

Her eye condition stemmed from a beautician's accident forty years earlier. A white-hot curling iron glanced the cornea, permanently damaging the oil glands. In her eighties the condition aggravated, causing her huge physical stress even as her mind gave way.

Here on the desk is a manila folder containing fifty-one letters from Elizabeth Ames. (It is kept in a cabinet with other such missives, more and more of them from friends who will never write again.)

13 July 1959

Dear Ned,

I'm awfully sorry you won't be coming back for September, but I'm glad you've made the decision that seems best; and of course your doing that, taking the job, won't affect the commission, so go on with it when you can. If two prose selections seem equally good to you, will you let me choose between them? And will you keep it so that Marianne, going on with her training, might sometime aspire to performing it?

27 August 1963

How fine that such beautiful words will find, for themselves, music which you will write. To think about this fills me with joy, and that you will put my name with it seems a rather solid matter, especially since I am sure you know that I do not ask for such a lovely honor . . . and one more detail: this new [financial] arrangement will continue for about a year, or a little longer.

14 March 1964

Hearing your songs did not leave me where they found me. Art is for life when it rises to such beauty, such perfection as I found in them.

May 1964

This check has been delayed since my financial agent has been finding out how much longer the payments on the mortgage I told you of would continue. Now he tells me this is my last payment to you. Sometime I would like to contribute further to your using to the utmost your fine talents. For me they are not surpassed in your generation . . . I'm glad you are happy at the prospect of having your parents in New York. When family relations are valued, nothing at all can take the place of them.

20 August 1967

I should not have suggested that you play for Marianne in the public way I did. Don't feel bound to play anything with her unless you really care to. I hope you are well. Perhaps you'll join us at dinner tonight? Love.

21 June 1968

Thanks for sending me the copy of Pound's *Antheil* with your introduction. I haven't read it yet and may not very soon, due to the trouble I've been having with my eyes for so many months now. And because the situation has cost so much money, I'm not contributing anything just now to the arts.

8 June 1971

I have to be at the hospital late this morning for some tests . . . Sorry to put off seeing you.

22 February 1974

> It is written in my book that you will dine with me next Wednesday, and do, please.
>
> Elizabeth

Can I deny that, despite our nearly forty-year age difference, despite Elizabeth's old-fashioned discretion and dowdy demeanor, despite my frequent impatience with her high-mindedness, and despite my own libidinous bent, there was a trace of eroticism between us, as there is perhaps between virtually any two persons who meet, if only for a millisecond? Yet if we never spoke of sex, much less of homosexuality, we did speak of the "exceptionality" (her word) of the Creator Spirit, and of the need for money. Elizabeth was not herself a Creator Spirit like Boulanger and Graham (she didn't produce anything); and, as her letters indicate, she too had need of money. In a sense she was a philanthropist without funds. Her role at Yaddo, unlike directors of other artists' retreats, was of Mother Hen, and her flair was one of high exceptionality.

The one-phrase note of 22 February, scrawled in blue pencil, was the last I heard from her. (In the summer of 1974 I bought a house in Nantucket, my own private Yaddo.) Her handwriting wavered on the page like her memory until all rational contact was short-circuited. Which could be why she never wrote her oft-promised autobiography; more likely she felt that if she could pen the Jamesian tales of Yaddo that came so richly in speech, the tales would no longer belong to her. And Yaddo was her single and desperate possession.

In 1970, when Curtis Harnack took over the directorship from a resistant Mrs. Ames, Polly Hanson—an underappreciated poet and Mrs. Ames's whipping-boy for years—stayed on to bridge the gap. The gap was soon filled with more relaxed air and more public image. Harnack was good at raising money during his seventeen years at the helm, and a thrillingly rare example of a practicing artist running a successful business while becoming not only more prolific as an author but more communicatively expert. He had been there already for seven years when on 28 March 1977 Elizabeth Ames died in the Saratoga Springs Hospital.

I have no memory of my side of the correspondence with Elizabeth. But I did keep a copy of the letter I wrote to Harnack that week.

Very dear Curtis—

I don't know what to say, or quite what one is supposed to do now. Sometimes an "expected" death is the saddest. Elizabeth's life seems to have been very short. And we never said good-bye . . . Well, anyway, you surely know how I feel. And there are so many questions I'll want to ask when next we meet. Meanwhile, please, please include me in any formal memorial you may be planning eventually. Elizabeth was major in my life.

Recalling Freda

1994

All history is Rashomon. Even an experience shared only last evening becomes an idyll or a nightmare this morning according to who's remembering. Thus my recall of Freda Pastor fifty-two years ago will differ from yours, or theirs, or even from my own of twenty or ten or two years ago. But though facts swerve with time, affection remains stationary.

When I arrived at Curtis, age nineteen, in 1943, for what would become a year's stay, I knew only the mores of the Middle West. Here suddenly was a rarefied academy of intense juvenile virtuosos with competitive Russian parents. The halls quivered with the high-powered purposefulness of Serkin, Piatigorsky, Bonelli, and with the formidable female presences of Madame Vengerova, Madame Gregory, Madame Schumann. Even the composition class, although all Wasp and retaining a reserve which to me was more comfortable if less dramatic than the extrovert performers, was dominated by our ancient Maestro Scalero and his near-incomprehensible latinized speech. Only my piano teacher, Miss Pastor, seemed normal, with her straightforward American stance and Philadelphia accent.

I see her now as natty, stylish, with a pillbox hat over her ash-blond hair, well-clad in tweedy suits with blouses of tan and cream silk. Was she a trifle patronizing? Her other pupils—"piano minors" they were called—were younger and less proficient, while I had already dallied in detail with the complete contemporary keyboard repertory. Like any self-respecting composer I was immersed in the music of my time at the expense of music of the past, but felt a need to, so to speak, expand backward. If Scalero was disapproving of my previous education, Miss Pastor was impressed. She and I agreed that during the coming seasons I would study all of the so-called thirty-two and forty-eight (school parlance for the Beethoven sonatas and the *Well-tempered Clavier*), as well as all Chopin and Schumann and Brahms. This I did with the goal of gaining broad acquaintance rather than mastery: mere mastery was for the piano majors, poor dears. Thus I owe my basic repertorial knowledge of classical piano literature to Freda Pastor.

When I left Curtis after twelve months, I did not come back for thirty years. It was then like reentering the immutable past—nothing had changed. The first human to greet me was Freda (we were now on a first-name basis), unchanged except that her hair had turned to the gold of autumn leaves. We quickly renewed acquaintance. When in 1973 with two singers I gave a concert at the Walnut Theater, Freda gave a party of such friendly luxury that it remains in the memory more warmly than the music. And when in 1980 I joined the faculty we became colleagues—though one never quite outgrows the student-teacher relation.

As much as anyone, Freda Pastor *was* Curtis. Like her husband Ralph Berkowitz, who lent luster to the hitherto pallid noun "accompanist," Freda—the fact of her—extended to the last recesses of the Institute.

With anxiety one saw her weaken and fade, yet clinging always to the image of Locust Street where she lived and learned and loved. When she left us finally last December, it was not so much life itself that she resisted abandoning, as the school. But then, for Freda, the two were one.

Tomorrow the perspective may shift. But for today, this is how I picture the Freda of yesterday: with a wisp of wistful love, and a lot of nostalgic admiration.

PART FIVE

Remnants

Lenny on My Music

1992

During the decades that I observed him working with other people's music, Leonard Bernstein was always The Composer personified, never the distanced performer. Whether interpreting his dear friends Copland and Schuman, or his dear friends Haydn and Mahler, he was inside looking out—the creator of his re-creations. (This obtains also to L.B. as interpreter of L.B. the writer.) Such acquisitive subjectivity allowed him to sculpt each phrase in music's history as though he'd authored it, allowed him—in our age of "fidelity" to the past—to be wildly supple not just with color and speed but with cuts and additions, altering the very guts of a work. For example:

The first of my three big pieces which Lenny conducted was the Third Symphony. When he saw the manuscript in 1958 he promised to premier it the next spring, on one condition: that I reorchestrate the Largo for just strings. Okay, I said. But didn't. He forgot the condition (I think) and played the Symphony anyway.

The second piece, an eight-part suite named *Sunday Morning*, he introduced to New York in 1980. It had already been heard with other orchestras elsewhere and was, so far as I was concerned, a fait accompli. Yet L.B. sought to switch the order of movements, an order nonetheless preordained by the Wallace Stevens poem on which the suite was modeled. I vetoed the switch. No hard feelings.

Last and most intriguing was Lenny's approach to the Violin Concerto. Although he was to conduct it with the auspicious Philharmonic, Lenny did recognize the six-movement Concerto for the chamber music it was. (Only five winds, one trumpet, timpani and strings.) Still, he felt the quiet close was a letdown. "At the very finish, how about letting Gidon hold that high D," suggested Lenny, "then segue into a repeat of the last twenty-four measures of the fifth movement, crescendoing to a bang-up ending." I acquiesced. But the resulting effect wasn't Me; the notes were mine but the device was Lenny's. After the second of the four scheduled performances, soloist Gidon Kremer suggested we revert to Rorem's original version—the version, thank God, which is here recorded.

Lenny deeply needed to be The Onlie Begetter of all art, a need which on the face of it seems conceited, but which in truth was flattering, caring, even humble. In regard to my own music he was, in fact, a begetter more than he knew. The jazzy movement of the Symphony, like hundreds of my vocal archings, owes everything to the flow of the L.B. precedent through the collective unconscious.

Yet our metabolisms ticked at different tempos. Lenny, the flamboyant Jewish extrovert, always inclined toward stretching my slow tunes into a Romantic taffy as though they were German; I, the reticent Wasp, have always felt those tunes should be outlined rigidly, French-style, even a twinge faster than marked, lest listeners yawn.

How do I feel about the present recording? The Concerto was originally cast for Jaime Laredo who performed it often during the mid-1980s. Jaime's tone, like a graceful Latin storm, is endearing to my Gallic ears. Gidon's attitude, at once more intellectual and more Slavic, seemed at first jarring. But Bernstein and Kremer are delicious foils for each other, and combine to make a legitimate version of this pliable piece. The recording itself? I have never heard my music so expensively glamorized. I'm dazzled by the intimately sumptuous engineering, the virtuosic stance, the dangerous tempos which show a side of myself I never knew existed.

On Childhood Reading
1985

We are what we read, and for better or worse we choose our own menu despite the will of parents. Thus I quickly took shelter against *The Wind in the Willows* (whose all-male anthropomorphism slights not only females, but the dignity of the wilds), while venturing into the more abrasive gales of Wilde, Louÿs, and Cocteau.

Oscar Wilde's *Fairy Tales* still seem today, of all "children's literature," the most touching, well-crafted, gorgeous, and imaginative. Pierre Louÿs's *Aphrodite* (which I had memorized before puberty), in depicting the world's most seductive courtesan who kills and then is killed for the one she adores, reflects any young person's notion of the propriety of love-as-excess. And Jean Cocteau's *Les Enfants terribles*, by portraying a pair of well-off adolescent bohemian siblings who come to what grown-ups call "a bad end," swayed a generation of Parisian youth, and by extension, me.

With all my current musical discipline and patient prosifying, I remain—and am thrilled to remain—the condemned nightingale, the fatal vamp, and the self-destructive child.

Sarah Orne Jewett

1985

To me, Sarah Orne Jewett was merely an "authoress" whose middle name turned up in crosswords, until my sister Rosemary gave me *The Country of the Pointed Firs* thinking I might make an opera out of it. What an antidote to the lubricious navel-gazing in so much of today's writing, including my own!

"If I were asked," wrote Willa Cather in 1925, "to name three American books which have the possibility of a long, long life, I would say at once, *The Scarlet Letter, Huckleberry Finn,* and *The Country of the Pointed Firs.*" Indeed, what Cather later did for Nebraska, Jewett had by 1896 done for Maine—lent to one state of the union a graspable color, a humanized identity, a very smell and taste by which all ensuing descriptions must be judged. Knut Hamsun did it for rural Norway in the early years of the century, as did Louis Hémon for northern Canada, and Jean Giono for meridional France. By "it" I mean the glorification—or codification, if you will—of the strange laws of nature, of the rational magic which, although surrounding us daily, we are, because of urban pressures, no longer trained to perceive, much less to need. Jewett captured the uncapturable by putting into literature that which is nonliterate, is speechless. Our concept of geography is always forever changed by art, and Jewett made a real place into a fictional extension of herself. As Debussy's *La Mer* never reminds me of the sea (although the sea reminds me of Debussy), so the forlorn coast of Maine no longer belongs to itself but oozes Jewett as I drive through.

Born in that state in 1849, she lived her whole life there, commemorating patiently and securely what she knew best: the Protestant peasant perception of a flora and fauna that are no more. "In the life of each of us," she said, "there is a place remote and is-landed, and given to endless regret or secret happiness; we are each the uncompanioned hermit and recluse of an hour or a day; we understand our fellows of the cell to whatever age of history they may belong."

If I were sentimental, I would recommend this book as others recommend *Walden*, hoping it might urge us toward a better world. But of course, there is no better world.

Myrna's Memoir

1987

The Movie Star is a quintessential American breed which could only have been spawned in a Protestant republic without saints or royalty. For those of us who grew up between the World Wars, movie stars were better than nobility—being always beautiful and responding to a wilder fancy, and more mysterious than stage stars; being so gigantic on screen and so remote in their West Coast Valhalla. Yet despite their unapproachability ("they" did not exist, only their aura), they represented a tangible goal: if every guy in our democracy could become president, every gal could become a film actress. My caring parents exposed me to the best in classical music and legitimate theater, but the very oxygen of my youth was simultaneously drenched in popular song and motion pictures which were no less crucial to my future as a composer. Still, if it never occurred to me as a boy that I might actually know a star, time does march on, arts do interlap, and by the 1950s I often wrote music for the New York stage, and in Paris worked with movie people. Somehow that didn't count: theater folk were too accessible, while movie folk—at least in France—weren't quite the "real" thing, being more involved with high art than with narcissism. Not until the 1970s, long after the grandeur of Hollywood had sagged into the banality of television, did I find myself occasionally squiring one of the greats—Myrna Loy.

In public she still stopped traffic. If I took her to a concert featuring my music, nobody paid me heed. People stared, whispered, sometimes even dared speak to this oddly familiar creature

(Myrna Loy is the only big name to appear in movies each decade since the twenties), while she smiled magnanimously and tilted her famous nose. In private she adopted candor, talked to you about you, or about some pertinent concern like liberal politics or housing for the homeless. It was precisely her need to contemplate other than her ego that allowed her sanely to survive the weird pressures of the Studio System and its ensuing collapse, when many another idol faded into Sunset Boulevard. Myrna Loy was involved, always, with the present, not easily suffering the nostalgia buffs. Still, here before me was a woman who on film had emerged from giddy vamp, sadistic Asian, and German spy into slick comedienne and Perfect Wife (four times divorced in reality), dramatic lover, and Perfect Mother (childless in reality), and then moved on to character roles, and finally stage and TV. She was Roosevelt's favorite actress, had been leading lady to Barrymore, Gable, Grant, Powell, Tracy, Power, and was, in 1937, voted Queen of the Movies in the most comprehensive national poll ever held. But although surely privy to every backstage skeleton in the closets of yore, Myrna Loy was not prone to gossip.

As she talked importantly of our malfunctioning government I used to gaze at her without hearing, seeking instead the source of her utterly economical style: did that cool, all-knowing look of affectionate irony stem from turning her eyes but not her head, or from turning her head but not her eyes? And I would say to myself: Beneath that satiny sherry-hued coiffure, and behind that wisely mischievous glance, ah, what she knows!

What she knows is now revealed in a thorough memoir whose worst feature is the title, *Being and Becoming* (meaningless because reversible, and because, as my English teacher used to say, it lacks the memorability of an *R* and a *T*), and whose best feature is the adroit support of the cocredited author, one James Kotsilibas-Davis, who has not so much written as assembled the book. The bulk is literally in Myrna's voice—the sentences *sound* with her husky and quizzical twang, and with backtrackings and repetitions larded with many an "Oh, brother" or "Ye gods." Into the chapters are spliced statements from old friends, lending a fresh tone, and telling us what Myrna cannot—about her beauty, magnanimity, intelligence, patience, talent, and intermittent aloofness.

Etcetera . . .

Carnegie Hall

1990

I lost my virginity in Carnegie Hall. Many times. And found it too.

Put another way: The process of simultaneously losing one's innocence through a revelation while retaining that innocence through the same revelation presents a paradox unique to artist and art lover. In Carnegie Hall I first learned (without immediately realizing it) that childhood fancies can be forever preserved through music.

Beethoven's complete piano works were unfolded to me in Carnegie Hall by Schnabel in 1943. So, in succeeding months, were the sonatas and songs and suites of Barber and Ravel and Copland by Horowitz and Tourel and Koussevitzky. Did it occur to me then that the glow of legend might soon be met by the fact of myself in the story?

The first hearing of my own music in that hallowed hall came in 1949 when Mishel Piastro led the Philharmonic in an Overture in C which had won the Gershwin Memorial Award. (I deserved the prize, but the piece did not.) Since then, about half of my orchestral works have received either their world or local premieres in Carnegie: First Symphony (Antonini conducting in 1956); Third Symphony (Bernstein, 1959); *Lions* (Ehrling, 1965); *Air Music* (Schippers, 1975); *Assembly and Fall* (Gosling, 1976); Third Piano Concerto (Atzmon, 1983); and String Symphony (Shaw, 1986).

Today, five thousand concerts later, in auditoriums that have mushroomed throughout Manhattan, where one risks growing jaded, I return as often as possible to 57th and Seventh, to be rekindled by the ghost of my youth when all music was a surprise, and where the best of it remains always new.

Jane Bowles

1993

If, like most first-rate artists, Jane Bowles was madly exasperating, she was quickly forgivable too. Her disorganization, her self-pity, her defensively anti-intellectual stance, her irksome dread of any imminent decision, be it whether to go to Sweden tomorrow or what to choose from the menu tonight, were balanced by a magical gift for making you feel you were the sole creature in her universe. Jane was a child with a bad limp, who longed to be a grown-up and didn't know how, so she drank, one-upping your litanies of victimization as you drank with her. When Gordon Sager once complained: "The odds are against me: I'm Jewish, homosexual, alcoholic, and a communist," Jane retorted: "I'm Jewish, homosexual, alcoholic, a communist—and *I'm* a *cripple!*"

None of which would be interesting if overnight she had not become a grown-up author of singular organization, writing of disorganized little girls who long to grow up but don't know how. The unique manner of her unique matter makes of Jane Bowles a major minor-writer. Her entire oeuvre fits between two covers; yet each of the nine works is so unlike the others that, in variety if not in girth, she almost resembles—may I say it?—Henry James himself. Jane is the master of the lunatic fringe, and that's good enough for me.

Ravel and Debussy

1995

Ravel and Debussy, the mother and father of modern French music, were so alike in esthetic and vocabulary that it's become fashionable to claim how different they were. In fact, the differences are superficial: like Comedy and Tragedy they are two sides of the Impressionist mask. Good musicians of the same generation often come in pairs wherein both speak one language, but with divergent accents—of optimism and pessimism, for instance, or of concert hall versus opera stage. Witness Mozart and Haydn, Mahler and Strauss, Copland and Thomson, Britten and Tippett, Poulenc and Honegger.

In formal matters everyone agrees that Ravel was a classicist, Debussy a free versifier. Yet the orchestral masterpiece of each one proves the reverse. Ravel's *Daphnis* is a loose rhapsody, Debussy's *La Mer* a tight symphony. Melodically Debussy was short of breath, like Beethoven, while Ravel spun out tunes that were minutes long, like Puccini. Contrapuntally they were, like all the French, unconcerned. Rhythmically they were, like all the French (because of the unstressed national speech from which their music springs), generally amorphous. Harmonically they dealt in the same material of secondary sevenths, except for the whole-tone scale, which Ravel avoided. And coloristically they both excelled, making rainbows from a lean palette. Their game could be called Sound, sound taking precedence over shape, over language.

Socially they were strained allies. The younger Ravel paid homage to his semi-rival by orchestrating certain of Debussy's works. The older Debussy paid homage to Ravel by appropriating the device of his *Habañera,* and of certain piano figurations. But Ravel in private felt that Debussy was a thief, while Debussy called Ravel a trickster—and a trick, he said, can astonish only once. They both had strong personalities and so were inimitable; but they were contemporaries, after all, bearing the same chronological relationship as Liszt to Franck, or as Copland to Barber. (Satie, whom we think of as Papa, actually lay between them, like Lucky Pierre.)

As for their songs, of which we are about to perform five, neither was prolific compared to their German cousins, Debussy having composed ninety, Ravel a mere thirty. Their taste in texts was similar—Mallarmé, for example, among their peers, and a predilection for medieval lyricists.

The Marot *Epigrammes* are early Ravel, dating from 1897 when the composer was twenty-two. The Villon *Ballades* are late Debussy, dating from 1910 when the composer was forty-eight. The poets are both 15th-century, Villon being fifty-five years older than Marot, even as Debussy was thirteen years older than Ravel.

Who Is Sylvia?

1990

Sylvia Goldstein *is* Boosey & Hawkes, and my dependence is so egomaniacal that even tonight I'd be capable of saying, "Congratulations, my dear. By the way, I really liked your revision of clause four in that recent contract."

Such reliance after thirty-eight years is total. When she visits Nantucket my questions are not about business but about the way to make sun-tea, when to plant daffodils, where is the North Star, what was the trip to China like, how is the U.S. Senate formed. She answers sagely, patiently, while knitting little wool ear-warmers for us all. What she doesn't know isn't worth knowing—about copyright, permissions, recalcitrant poets, recipes, gardening, travel, sewing, politics, the care and feeding of cats and dogs, and especially of composers.

If she took the time she could write a definitive history of American composers, for there are none she hasn't known, from Argento to Zwilich. Still, discretion is her forte. If I've never heard her complain, despite real and terrible tribulations, neither have I ever heard her speak ill of living musicians. (Well, hardly ever.) Instead, she offers a shoulder to cry on, and seldom sleeps—except, of course, at certain concerts, and on the Long Island Express.

Without her wisdom I'd be half as smart. Without her professional intervention I'd be only half a composer. And without her friendship I'd have only half a life.

Being Sixty-five
1988

The sole category of human endeavor that cannot be cornered by flat rules is the so-called Creative Act. About butchers and bakers, lovers and Latvians, actors and oboists, even men and women, certain irrefutable generalities can be laid down. But no sooner do you posit a fact about the anatomy of, say, painters and playwrights, than along comes a playwright or painter to refute the fact by example. The product of the creative artist, even a third-rate one, is unique because (unlike children, who are also a unique product) the artwork cannot reproduce. Whether the artwork springs (as children do) from the passing union of separate entities is mere metaphoric speculation. Artists don't agree amongst themselves, and don't much care, as long as their inspiration holds out. Ives's *Unanswered Question* is really an answered question by dint of being art—complete in itself.

Still, there are four simple-sounding questions often asked of composers and that I find tough to answer. Usually I change the subject. Composers seem more enigmatic to laymen than do sculptors or poets because in kindergarten we all learn to build mud pies and to rhyme cat with rat, whereas the rudiments of musical composition are withheld. Now, instead of changing the subject, let me in this brief space take a stab at some replies.

When do you work?

People long to hear that a composer composes when the magic strikes—in gardens, at funerals—or at least that he follows a rigid plan starting daily at 5:00 A.M. Well, I'm not quite sure when I compose. I do get up late, and then try anything—washing dishes, phone calls, crosswords in *TV Guide*—to postpone that first (what to call it?) responsible crash of concentration that gets juices flowing.

Yet by the end of any year I manage to squeeze out an hour's worth of music (not to mention little essays like this one, reviews, even whole books, plus a schedule of teaching, rehearsing, concertizing, socializing, and reading three hours a night). Of course, all is relative. Just as there is a difference in kind between an hour on the subway and an hour making love, so there is a massive disproportion between the time spent scoring an hour-long oratorio with orchestra and an hour-long solo for flute.

But such paperwork is the tip of the iceberg. Notation, that visible final process, is a small percentage of actual composition, proportionate to the moment of parturition after months of pregnancy. The notation can be feverish, yes, although for me these days it lacks the lurid intensity of my adolescence. Intensity does increase as deadlines loom (I've had many deadlines, and have never, knock wood, missed a one), during which, if I can't actually write notes for more than sixty minutes a day, I can orchestrate for six hours at a stretch.

Thus my life turns around being a composer: on a train, in a bakery, at the dentist's, there's always a sonic problem nagging the brain, and my every waking gesture relates to the métier. This admission is horrendously self-centered, though one might argue that artists, finally, are the least egotistical of creatures since their work outlasts them and becomes the world's.

For whom do you compose?

For myself, no doubt. If I cannot beguile myself, how beguile others? (The best music intends to beguile, and that goes for even Beethoven and Schoenberg at their most "serious"; don't let any academic tell you otherwise. Insofar as music lacks charm it lacks greatness.) Whatever my music may be worth, it contains a grain that cannot be found in anyone else, even Orpheus. That grain nourishes me.

Naturally I compose for others too—at least for one mystical other who cares and who is maybe a person from the past, or myself in the future. But "the audience" is crucial. Practicality is

professionalism. Nothing is more demented than to write for posterity. So I declare without facetiousness that I write for one who
pays: The solidest prod for activating ideas is a commission that
keeps a roof over my head and spells out who's to play my piece
when.

What does your music mean?

I've been writing music since ten, and writing about it since
thirty, but I still don't know what music means, even my own. Nor
can I, as a sometime author, begin to say on the typewriter what I
elsewhere "say" on the staff. (Mendelssohn: "It's not that music is
too vague for words—it's too precise for words.") The arts are not
comparable; if they were comparable we'd need only one. Nevertheless the other arts—literature, dance, painting—each has immutable implications, whereas music (at least nonvocal music) can
never be proved to make programatic sense. Melville's and Turner's verbal and pictorial versions of the sea mean sea to everyone
instantly, but Debussy's *La mer* means sea only if the listener has
been alerted, in words, beforehand. Music cannot be divided, as
literature can, by terms like prose and poetry, or as painting can, by
terms like concrete and abstract. If journalism or diaries represent
on-the-spot reaction while novels or plays represent reflection, can
music be similarly pigeonholed? Not by me. Sometimes I'll give an
instrumental piece an imagistic title *(Lovers, Winter Pages, Lions)*,
but the title is tacked on after the fact.

Like most listeners I can distinguish between sad and happy
music, but the distinction rises from conditioning, from convention,
unlike other arts wherein sadness is universally recognized. Does
art stem from its maker's experience? Probably, although too much
experience leaves little time for art. When I compose "sad" music,
do I compose it while sad? Or from what I once learned of sadness?
Or from what I feel sadness is supposed to sound like? Music's
power lies in its indefinability. Perhaps it can "mean" sad or happy,
but nothing more specific: It can't mean green, or married, or cauli-
flower, or even quizzical or caustic.

How do you fit in?

I feel daily grateful, even blessed, that, unlike ninety-nine percent of Americans who are miserably geared toward moneymaking

in any form, I have always known what I wanted to do, known how to do it, been encouraged to do it (beginning with my precious parents), and am appreciated for doing it, even though "it" in the ken of the general public—which scarcely admits the existence of what's sometimes called Serious Music—is an eccentric and non-moneymaking pursuit.

PART SIX

Out of Nantucket
1984

I have a house in Nantucket at the foot of Sunset Hill. Isak Dinesen herself could not have been more attached to hers than I to mine, although hers, at an altitude of over six thousand feet, was surrounded by a vast pottery-colored farmland and was shared with various wild creatures plus an array of "native" servants, while mine, at sea level, is the core of one emerald acre of bismuth-colored roses and is shared with three cats—Sam, Princess, and the venerable Wallace—plus the musician James Holmes, my wisest friend on this planet.

Classically named the Gray Lady of the Sea, Nantucket Island —actually a twelve-by-four-mile spit—floats due south of the thrice-larger Martha's Vineyard fifty kilometers into the Atlantic off Cape Cod, and is the last stop on the way to Lisbon as the gull flies. That gull, which in this region looms thicker and whiter than its red-billed mainland cousin, gazing straight down from its heights will espy in the shallow depths not a Gray Lady but a stationary whale spouting a filament of land called Great Point toward the north, and, toward the west, swirling its tail into a pair of minuscule islets, Muskeget and Tuckernuck, both inhabited. You will not be astride a gull but in a twelve-seat plane, stable as a kettledrum, as you near the Earth whose mammalian identity graduates quickly into an undifferentiated bristle of impenetrable jungles a mere yard high which in winter are a uniform brown and in summer—the present season—grow green as Eire. Other visitors approach by water: regular ferries from Woods Hole and Hyannis disgorge frantic tribes with, alas, ever more automobiles, the last daily delivery arriving like a ballet at midnight on the ancient, glimmering Uncantena.

At the airport a taxi chauffeured by Mrs. Peterson, or perhaps by Bertha O'Neill, will take you, via Macy's Lane (yes, Manhattan's store was founded by Nantucket Quakers) to Old South Road, one of the half dozen arteries that traverse the island. Heading toward town—gravel pits on either side, then blighted evergreen forests softened by, in April, the broadest array of jonquils to be found in New England (some ninety varieties dot the roadside with the random largesse of a benign Midas) or by, from June through October, the lavender sage that coats the hillocks with a scent as melancholy as your grandmother's cedar chest—you arrive at the rotary where the *Inquirer & Mirror* offices, flanked by a short-order kiosk, represent your first glimpse of local human fauna. Veering left past the Finast (fresh produce a specialty: ruby lettuce, plum-sized blackberries, fragrant snowy Portuguese bread), past the high school lodged between a manicured cemetery and a bright yellow sports field, and past the Cottage Hospital (cheery and small yet equipped for most eventualities including death and dentistry), you mount a hill topped by the famous windmill where Mrs. Peterson (unless it's Bertha) will shift gears. If this is your first visit you may wonder how you, who have lived and loved in the isles of Greece, will accommodate yourself to such puritan landscapes; then again, perhaps the sea air here *is* purer than any in the world, and perhaps one *can* already sense as tough a solidarity as when, a century and a half ago, Ishmael noted "there was a fine boisterous something about everything connected with that old island." Indeed, Nantucket has more than once verged on legal secession from the state of Massachusetts.

The car starts up, descends into Prospect Lane where on the right the bourgeois saltboxes become more and more elegant, their tidy window boxes sparkling with early pansies like elfin blue-plate specials of poached hummingbird eggs, while on the left an expanse of two more cemeteries, the Catholic Saint Mary's and the Protestant Prospect Hill, separates tactfully for the start of Hummock Pond Road. And soon there's yet another cemetery. Hear Robert Lowell:

> *. . . this old Quaker graveyard where the bones*
> *Cry out in the long night for the hurt beast*
> *Bobbing by Ahab's in the East.*

Why so few tombstones? Tombstones are vanity. So cross to the bottom of Main Street, but don't turn right (we'll do that tomorrow) —although the route seems tempting as it skirts the small observatory where 137 years ago Maria Mitchell discovered a major comet, then curves past those rich clapboard mansions, past the so-called Three Bricks erected by Joseph Starbuck in the late 17th century for his three sons, past the twin Greek Revivals built by William Hadwen in 1845 for his two nieces, toward the quaint business center all shaded by massive sycamores and elms imported from the mainland long ago, and dominated by the cutely exasperating cobblestones which lead a hundred yards beyond to the renovated docks with their boutiques of scrimshaw and peanut butter fudge, bookstores stocked with not only apposite lore but the complete poems of John Ashbery, and galleries with high-priced portraits of seagulls in aprons. Turn instead into New Lane, keep straight for a quarter of a mile, make a sharp right at West Chester Street, cross North Liberty (avoiding Sunset Hill, because this afternoon we'll go up there to see the "Oldest House"), continue alongside four or five homes—including Jessica Woodle's, which is almost hidden by fourteen-foot privet sculpted into stately waves—turn right again at Wesco Place (titled for Nantucket's original Indian name, Wesko, after a certain white rock at the foot of what is now Straight Wharf), and park across from the Nortons', our nearest neighbors. (He is a mason, she tends the Hub.) Get out, pay the fare—six dollars—and turn around.

You'll see a roomy acre enclosed front and side by a white picket fence in good condition, and in back by split rails merging into a wild privet wall shared, as a dividing nicety, with Mrs. Woodle. You are looking at the back of my house, once a functional structure built around 1918 by a Macy, today an ivy-covered pleasure made into a humble silk purse by JH, three stories high with a pinewood deck and a trellised patio. The house slumps (the southwest corner sinks two feet lower than the northeast; you can slide through the rooms), but this defect, like much else in Nantucket,

NED ROREM

can be written off as quaint. Come into the kitchen, open the fridge, help yourself to that frosty pitcher of cranberry juice (from our celebrated bogs) and perhaps a brownie or two. Avoid for the moment the parlor, which needs dusting, and where the piano is strewn with the organized mess of four simultaneously ongoing manuscripts, and climb the fourteen stairs—recently carpeted in mauve plush—to the top-floor landing. Directly before you is the little bathroom, and to the right, two doors. Enter the second of these and there you will see me at my mother's old polished desk, about to place a period at the end of this sentence.

I have no feeling for Nantucket as for Chicago or Paris. Childhood and adolescence in Chicago represent the discovery, violent as Vesuvius, of art and sex. Postadolescence and early adulthood in France represent the confirmation, disconcerting as Molière, of love's fragility and the meanness of death. These representations, like everything that is past, have dissolved into gold. Nantucket is the present and the future.

Nantucket's as varied as Texas or Provence, but in miniature. Grand open fields, rampaging bulls, wrens and falcons, fruitful ponds and towering oaks, English mews and Yankee prairies, all as though viewed through glass at the Museum of Natural History. There is even a disease, sometimes fatal, unique to the island, babesiosis, transferred through a tick.

Nantucket and Martha's Vineyard are not rivals any more than Los Angeles and San Francisco; they just don't think about each other, the inhabitants of one never having, for the most part, set foot upon the other. Architecture is different, the Vineyard's tending to the lime-and-peppermint gingerbread of New Bedford, Nantucket to the sober gray-shingled saltbox which is indigenous. Intellectually too, at least in summer, they diverge. Nantucket seems to lure rightwing Wasps, vaguely indolent except for their support of a first-rate concert series of standard 19th-century repertory. Martha's Vineyard harbors Democrat Jews and creative artists of mainly literary bent. Nantucket hosts fine writers too (Frank Conroy, Russell Baker, David Halberstam), but neither island has yet spawned spokesmen as Nebraska and Iowa and Maine spawned their Cather and Harnack and Jewett. And neither island is musical (as opposed to painterly or literary or theatrical). Perhaps no American small town is.

Is Nantucket claustrophobic? Eden becomes hell when you can't leave, and leaving is hard when you're hemmed by a moat, although the Gulf Stream does keep the thankful area cool in summer and warm in winter. Are there rich folks? Some. But if they wanted a ready-made house for more than a million they'd be hard put to find one, despite real estate's being higher here than anywhere except Caracas.

Although every beach has public access, you'll always find one on which to be almost alone. "There is more sand there than you would use in twenty years as a substitute for blotting paper," wrote Melville. "What wonder then that these Nantucketers, born on a beach, should take to the sea for livelihood! They first caught crabs and quahogs in the sands; grown bolder, they waded out with nets for mackerel . . ." Etcetera. Yet the whaling Melville finally sang of was pretty much a lost profession by the time of his *Moby-Dick*. Mystique and recipes remain.

(Bluefish Chowder: In a quart of salt water cook a large bluefish, flaked and boned. Add a dozen diced potatoes, 2 pork-fried onions, salt and pepper and parsley and dill. Cook some more. Stop heat and add a quart of heavy cream with a tablespoon of sherry. Thicken with flour.)

On which to be almost alone—did I say? The enroachment of the quadrimillion-dollar rock racket permits not only enclaves of cultured adults to avoid conversation, but arranges that even youthful loners on the fawn-hued shores bring transistors to blot out the glamorous roar of the eons-old waves. My musically insomniac ears, which agonize at a faucet dripping blocks away, are forever on the *qui vive* for that telltale throb, near or far, which spells the blight of rock.

One day is much like another. Differences are signaled not by variety of invitations (I scarcely know anyone here and no one knows me; after ten years I have yet to dine at the Opera House or in Sconset's Chanticleer) but by behavior of pets, or weather. Even the wet days are much like the dry so far as routine goes, except that when it rains we always receive a visit from a grand red-bibbed pheasant and his retinue of unmarried daughters.

Today is bright. Princess, so-named because she's a tomboy but still seems a naive kitten though she's now a plump grown-up, has slit with tooth and claw the cherubic belly of a baby rabbit so that the creature, bathed in the optimistic sun and frantic with shock, drags its own exposed innards across the lawn while the cat kibitzes alongside. I manage to get the rabbit into a cardboard box, my heart beating no less wildly than its, not sure what I'll do (submerge it? smash it? offer it to the vet?), when it leaps forth bloodily and vanishes beneath the mock orange bush, followed by Princess. Guiltily I retreat into the house. Evening. Father on the phone says that nature takes its course. Princess purrs at my feet as I type this.

I write almost never about Family—those nearest, like JH or Rosemary or parents. Are they taken for granted? Too close for focus? Aren't they the stuff of novels? Highs and lows in the day-to-day pattern emerge only through passing melodrama, so it's more difficult—less normal?—to write of Family than of transient episodes. If the fugitive Siennese piazza, the iceberg perceived from the submarine, the one-night stand's steamy afterglow, or the countess's frigid rebuff conspire to set the pen aflutter, Nantucket meanwhile has become Family, thus mute, meaning musical.

Here is where I realize my profession as composer, far from the madding phone. Now, my music is perhaps no less compromising than my prose. However, a diary differs from a musical composition—or a fictional narrative—in that it depicts the literal moment, the writer's present mood, which, were it inscribed an hour later, could emerge quite otherwise. A composer doesn't notate his mood, doesn't tell the music where to go—it leads him.

No, music doesn't have literary sense, but musicians sometimes pretend it does, and during stays in Nantucket I've written many a specifically programmatic piece inspired by the scenery. If *Views from the Oldest House,* a suite for solo organ, represents aspects of the town mainly because I claim (in words, not notes: notes can't make factual claims) that it does, another suite, *The Nantucket Songs,* for soprano and piano, being settings of other people's words about Nantucket, may be taken as an actual vision of the landscape. Among these "other people" is William Carlos Williams whose poem for one of the songs speaks of the removed and one-dimensional calm that so many find, without seeking, while on this island:

Flowers through the window
lavender and yellow

changed by white curtains—
Smell of cleanliness—

Sunshine of late afternoon—
On the glass tray

a glass pitcher, the tumbler
turned down, by which

a key is lying—And the
immaculate white bed.

Most of my life has been spent like a cuckoo in other people's nests. Not just those sad sublets and hostels that students and travelers all must occupy, but in the grand homes of friends (sometimes platonic) for years on end. With Guy Ferrand in Morocco where I composed my first everything. In Hyères and Paris with Marie-Laure de Noailles at whose table I encountered the crucial minds of Europe. In America at the colonies, mainly Yaddo which for fifteen years was a second home. The primary home was forever at the heart of big cities, paying and paying and paying rent. I was forty-three when JH appeared, the one with whom I would pass the rest of my years. Since then I have had none of the liquor that menaced my life, so the texture of that life swerved radically. Of the three goals to which all aspire—success in love, in society, and in profession—only two are plausible simultaneously: you can't have a smooth love life, a rich social life, and still get your work done. Opting for work and love (already a handful), summers were now spent in coastal resorts, again paying rent, until 1974 when, never having owned property, I decided to buy a house.

Why Nantucket? We had been here a year or two earlier as a second choice (the Frontenac in Quebec was booked solid) and, fog-bound for a week, found it clammy and overblond and perhaps too doggedly heterosexual. But we gave it another try, renting Melva Chesrown's "cottage" (as fine houses here are called) as a kind of perverse change from the hitherto unproductive scenario, and every day was coppery and odiferous. I wrote *Air Music*, made pies, felt no competition, was content. But why buy? Well, partly for what was lacking: the artistic and sexual tension-and-release of Fire Island and the Hamptons, the mosquitoes and cars and pollution of even the Cape, and the urgently convoluted converse of educated Europeans. Partly, too, because of age: twenty years earlier could such an urbanite have been happy to play the summertime shepherdess in this humble *hameau*?

But among the rare positive attributes of aging is the involuntary urge to find patterns: if I had not exactly forgotten that I too was reared a Quaker, I had suppressed it; suddenly this Quaker island spoke—as we Quakers say—to my condition, and the condition was not godly but juvenile, free of lust and longing, like a child alone in the giant potential of his nursery. Anyone can waste himself but only I can pen my tunes, and the time had come.

That smug observation keeps me pushing. Now for company I enjoy scouring our birdbaths while goldfinches wait in a row, as once I enjoyed cruising the alleys of Tangier—though the secret gardens and byways through the hills of Nantucket-Town evoke, more than you'd think, the medinas of North Africa. (The urge to find patterns.) If I'm now as skilled as any at making small talk at the Hub, or at not seeing this or that acquaintance at the A & P, I can embrace the total solitude of week after winter week with nothing but work, or fling myself in springtime with an ecstasy as unembarrassed as Edna Millay's upon the foliage at Altar Rock, Nantucket's highest point (I think), from which uncurl five footpaths wending seemingly toward five magical townships with smoking chimneys and yellow lanterns, and which reminded JH during his nervous breakdown of *Pride and Prejudice,* and helped to cure him.

How trying must I be to cope with, ceaselessly bewailing doubts about health and talent! How benevolent JH's tolerance and tact, with unbounded gifts for building a home with both hands and heart.

Reason, a human concept, evolved along with human life. But humans have yet to posit a reason for life. The human flaw—unlike the animal perfection—is knowledge of life, i.e., of death, of scope, of form. But form too is a human concept which evolved, etcetera.

For an hour or so, around three o'clock, I went down to the back lawn and lay in the lowered plastic yellow deck chair trying to read (Prokosch), drowsed, gave up. It's rare on Nantucket that heat grows so thick. Procrastination's par for the course. With Sam on my lap, Princess preening nearby, and Wallace wheezing over there in JH's basement hideaway, I simply watched through heavy eyes the motion of buzzing clover, the bumblebees, the perspective of cats, the burning sky where fat pink clouds reflected the peonies' perfume which just managed not to be sickening, and thought of Latouche's "Lazy Afternoon," and of the dead, and of Mother and Father at their retirement home in Cadbury—or yesterday in South Dakota fifty years ago. An exquisitely satisfactory moment. To note it here is, in a way, to defile it.

Index